Disability in Japan

Disability and chronic illness represents a special kind of cultural diversity, the 'other' to 'normal' able-bodiedness. Most studies of disability consider disability in North American or European contexts; and studies of diversity in Japan consider ethnic and cultural diversity, but not the differences arising from disability. This book therefore breaks new ground, both for scholars of disability studies and for Japanese studies scholars. It charts the history and nature of disability in Japan, discusses policy and law relating to disability, examines caregiving and accessibility, and explores how disability is viewed in Japan. Throughout, the book highlights the tension between individual responsibility and state intervention, the issues concerning how care for disability is paid for, and the special problem of how Japan is providing care for its large and increasing population of elderly people.

Carolyn S. Stevens is Professor of Japanese Studies and Director of the Japanese Studies Centre at Monash University, Australia.

Japan Anthropology Workshop Series

Series editor:
Joy Hendry, *Oxford Brookes University*

Editorial Board:
Pamela Asquith, *University of Alberta*
Eyal Ben Ari, *Hebrew University of Jerusalem*
Hirochika Nakamaki, *National Museum of Ethnology, Osaka*
Kirsten Refsing, *University of Copenhagen*
Wendy Smith, *Monash University*

Founder Member of the Editorial Board:
Jan van Bremen, *University of Leiden*

A Japanese View of Nature
The World of Living Things by Kinji Imanishi
Translated by Pamela J. Asquith, Heita Kawakatsu, Shusuke Yagi and Hiroyuki Takasaki
Edited and introduced by Pamela J. Asquith

Japan's Changing Generations
Are young people creating a new society?
Edited by Gordon Mathews and Bruce White

The Care of the Elderly in Japan
Yongmei Wu

Community Volunteers in Japan
Everyday stories of social change
Lynne Y. Nakano

Nature, Ritual and Society in Japan's Ryukyu Islands
Arne Røkkum

Psychotherapy and Religion in Japan
The Japanese introspection practice of naikan
Chikako Ozawa-de Silva

Dismantling the East–West Dichotomy
Essays in honour of Jan van Bremen
Edited by Joy Hendry and Heung Wah Wong

Pilgrimages and Spiritual Quests in Japan
Edited by Maria Rodriguez del Alisal, Peter Ackermann and Dolores Martinez

The Culture of Copying in Japan
Critical and historical perspectives
Edited by Rupert Cox

Primary School in Japan
Self, individuality and learning in elementary education
Peter Cave

Globalisation and Japanese Organisational Culture
An ethnography of a Japanese corporation in France
Mitchell W. Sedgwick

Japanese Tourism and Travel Culture
Edited by Sylvie Guichard-Anguis and Okpyo Moon

Making Japanese Heritage
Edited by Christoph Brumann and Robert A. Cox

Japanese Women, Class and the Tea Ceremony
The voices of tea practitioners in northern Japan
Kaeko Chiba

Home and Family in Japan
Continuity and transformation
Edited by Richard Ronald and Allison Alexy

Abandoned Japanese in Postwar Manchuria
The lives of war orphans and wives in two countries
Yeeshan Chan

Tradition, Democracy and the Townscape of Kyoto
Claiming a right to the past
Christoph Brumann

Religion and Politics in Contemporary Japan
Soka Gakkai youth and Komeito
Anne Mette Fisker-Nielsen

Language, Education and Citizenship in Japan
Genaro Castro-Vázquez

Death and Dying in Contemporary Japan
Hikaru Suzuki

Disability in Japan
Carolyn S. Stevens

Disability in Japan

Carolyn S. Stevens

LONDON AND NEW YORK

First published 2013
by Routledge
2 Park Square, Milton Park, Abingdon, Oxfordshire OX14 4RN

Simultaneously published in the USA and Canada
by Routledge
711 Third Avenue, New York, NY 10017

First issued in paperback 2015

Routledge is an imprint of the Taylor & Francis Group, an informa business

© 2013 Carolyn S. Stevens

The right of Carolyn S. Stevens to be identified as the author of this work has been asserted by her in accordance with sections 77 and 78 of the Copyright, Designs and Patent Act 1988.

All rights reserved. No part of this book may be reprinted or reproduced or utilised in any form or by any electronic, mechanical, or other means, now known or hereafter invented, including photocopying and recording, or in any information storage or retrieval system, without permission in writing from the publishers.

Trademark notice: Product or corporate names may be trademarks or registered trademarks, and are used only for identification and explanation without intent to infringe.

British Library Cataloguing in Publication Data
A catalogue record for this book is available from the British Library

Library of Congress Cataloging in Publication Data
Stevens, Carolyn S., 1963-
 Disability in Japan/Carolyn S. Stevens.
  p. cm. – (Japan anthropology workshop series)
 Includes bibliographical references and index.
 1. People with disabilities–Japan. 2. People with disabilities–Services for–Japan. 3. People with disabilities–Government policy–Japan.
 I. Title.
 HV1559.J3S74 2013
 362.40952–dc23   2012035803

ISBN 13: 978-1-138-95055-9 (pbk)
ISBN 13: 978-0-415-51701-0 (hbk)

Typeset in Times New Roman
by Sunrise Setting Ltd, Paignton, UK

For Tomo, Sora and Zenry

Contents

List of figures	xi
List of tables	xii
Preface	xiii
Acknowledgements	xv
Note on transliterations and translations	xvi

1 **Introduction: thinking about anthropology, disability and Japan**   1
  Disability definitions 3
  Disability studies in English 6
  Disability studies in Japan 14
  Book outline 17
  Concessions 19

2 **Disability in the Japanese context**   23
  Ideologies of disability in Japan, past and present 23
  The contemporary demographics of disability in Japan 28
  Disability activism in Japan 33
  Conclusion 42

3 **Disability, language and meaning**   44
  Disability discourse in Japan 47
  Examples of discriminatory language in the public sphere 52
  Kotobagari *and freedom of expression 56*
  Conclusion 58

4 **Disability policy and law in modern Japan**   61
  Welfare policy for people with disabilities in the twentieth century 65
  The Japanese legal structure 67

x Contents

    *The Six Laws of Welfare (Fukushi Roppō) (1947–64)
and other related laws 69*
    *The Law for the Promotion of Employing People
with a Disability 78*
    *The Basic Act for Persons with Disabilities (1970)
and the Services and Supports for Persons with
Disabilities Act (2005) 82*
    Issues 88
    Normalization and neoliberalism 89
    Conclusion 92

5 **Disability and the lifecycle**   95
    Prenatality and infancy 96
    Childhood 104
    Young adults 111
    Older adults 116
    Conclusion 118

6 **Caregiving and the family**   121
    The Japanese family and caregiving 124
    The family as caregiver: the writings of Ōe Kenzaburō 128
    Changing care: long-term care insurance 131
    Conclusion 134

7 **Accessibility and the built environment in Japan**   138
    Japan as a barrier-free society 140
    Architectural and attitudinal impediments 142
    Accessibility theory versus reality: empirical examples 143
    Barrier-free features and their 'proper' use in public places 144
    Public and private space/public and private citizens 150

8 **Conclusion**   155

    Notes   163
    Bibliography   168
    Index   184

List of figures

4.1	A conceptual chart of Japanese laws related to disability	63
7.1	Shopping mall in Nippa, Yokohama	140
7.2	Notice on a lift in Yokohama Station	145
7.3	'Manner' notice at Yokohama Station (Tōyoko Line)	148
7.4	'Manner' notice in the car park of a shopping mall, northern Yokohama	148
7.5	'Manner' notice inside a train carriage on the Tōyoko Line	149

List of tables

1.1	Priestly's four approaches to disability theory, abridged (1998: 78–83)	11
2.1	A snapshot (by age and residence) of the Japanese population with a disability, 1999–2006	29
3.1	*Sabetsu yōgo* (discriminatory terms related to disability)	49
4.1	The relationship between the major laws concerning people with disabilities in Japan	87
5.1	Children with physical disabilities in Japan, 1965–2006	105
5.2	Age of diagnosis of intellectual disability, general age statistics and children's statistics	107
5.3	Place of diagnosis of intellectual disability, general age statistics and children's statistics	108
5.4	Severity of intellectual disability, general age statistics and children's statistics	109

Preface

The Japan Anthropology Workshop series moves into a new dimension in this volume, for it offers a whole range of angles to approach the subject matter in hand, and therefore, by a greater variety of means than usual, enables us to reach the deep understanding of Japan that our series has come to represent. While all our books are built on ethnographic data, and this one is no exception, a broad subject like disability requires more comprehensive work to pick through the euphemism and concealment that surrounds it in any society. Carolyn Stevens is extremely well placed to execute such a study for she is not only an excellent scholar of Japanese society, but has strong personal involvement through her husband, her in-laws, and most of all, her daughter, Sora, who has a disability that requires almost full-time care and attention.

The book is firmly located in general theories about disability, the difficulties of defining the term, and in speaking about its various manifestations in different societies and different welfare systems. Stevens thus draws on a wide range of comment and criticism from this somewhat marginalized field before focusing her main analysis on Japan. She draws on demographical statistics, legal documents and public discussion, but always in the context of a brilliant analysis of the way that language may obscure as much as it elucidates in the field of disability, handicap and any number of other, often rather euphemistic, words. Her anthropological approach takes nothing at face value, and a chapter which addresses the issue of accessibility is particularly astute as it picks through the facilities of the so-called 'barrier-free' society that Japan is supposed to have become.

Attention is paid throughout to the family and other carers as well as to the opinions and behaviour of members of the wider society. One chapter addresses the detail of various stages of the lifecycle, starting with tests that can be administered during pregnancy and the various decisions and responses that occur. The early part of life is given more space than the later part because Stevens feels that the disabilities associated with ageing have already been well covered in the literature. Another chapter examines the roles of the family in the caregiving process; here Stevens makes the very apt point that people who are apparently normal also need and give care to one another, because we all have needs, even in a society like the USA where emphasis is placed on the importance of independence and individuality.

Stevens draws on the work of the Nobel Prize-winning Japanese author, Ōe Kenzaburō, whose own disabled son inspired him to include a character with disabilities in almost all his works of fiction. One of his ideas is to emphasize the normality of caring for, and including, such characters in regular life, and Stevens also illustrates this point from her own experience. Sora means 'sky' in Japanese, and while Sora's intellectual limitations – such as a lack of speech – must have brought a great cloud into the life her parents expected for her, and for themselves, when they chose that name, this book makes clear the silver linings that living with disability also brings. The book also makes a carefully crafted and much-needed contribution to the anthropology of Japan.

Joy Hendry

Acknowledgements

This book is both a personal and a professional statement: in the first instance I must thank my family and friends, especially those who are also carers of children with disabilities. In my research and in my personal life, I have benefited from the very important work of UNIQUE, a rare chromosomal disorder support group, which has given very significant support to my family over the years as well as creating bridges between families who would otherwise feel isolated. I especially have been grateful for the support and friendship of the duplication 4p mothers that I met through UNIQUE, and in particular Sarah Brown Dodd, mother to Gabby, who has a very similar karyotype to that of my daughter. Working with Sarah to create a Duplication 4p Family and Friends Network has been enormously rewarding, and the discussions that arise from that group have had a great impact on the way I view disability and society both as a mother and as a scholar.

Professionally, I am indebted to Joy Hendry of the JAWS series and Peter Sowden at Routledge for their constant encouragement and support. Research assistance was first provided by Hideko Nakamura, and in later stages by Anika Ervin-Ward; David I. Kelly provided expert and patient bilingual copyediting services and general comments throughout. Other colleagues – in particular, Vera Mackie, Laura Miller, Karen Nakamura, Sonia Ryang, Jeremy Breaden, Hugh de Ferranti, Michelle Hall, Christine Yano and Mark McLelland – also generously offered their expertise and support throughout the writing of this book and their contributions were invaluable.

This book presented a new challenge for me with its focus on legal documents, and assisting me were many good colleagues in the Faculty of Law of Monash University. Stacey Steele of Melbourne Law School spent much of her valuable time discussing the Japanese legal system. Judge Gen Ueno, visiting scholar to the Melbourne Law School in 2010, and Professor Kazuhiro Nishida of Okayama University Law School were also extremely helpful in discussing disability policy and law in Japan, both past and present. Ikuko Nakane was very helpful with advice on difficult legal translations.

Previous versions of research presented in this book appeared in the following journal article: 'Living with Disability in Urban Japan' (2007), *Japanese Studies*, 27(3): 263–78. I am grateful to the editor, Associate Professor Judith Snodgrass for her permission and contribution to the development of this research project.

Note on transliterations and translations

In this text I have used the Hepburn system, except in cases where words have entered common use in English (Tokyo, for example). Japanese names are presented in the order of family name first, personal name second, as is Japanese linguistic custom. I have, however, followed individual preference for the transliteration of names of Japanese authors who have published in English. Translations, except where noted otherwise, are by the author.

Owing to constant changes in the overseas currency market, I have kept monetary figures in the text in yen; in July 2012 the Japanese yen was trading at 79.93 yen to the US dollar.

1 Introduction

Thinking about anthropology, disability and Japan

Anyone who knows me knows I have a daughter with a disability. This is not the same as having a disability myself, but I, like all parents who are also caregivers, 'live with a disability relationally through their children' (Panitch 2008: 17). Living disability 'relationally' means that my close relationship with a child with a disability gives me first-hand experience of both the challenges and achievements that come with living with a disability. It is because of this relational experience that I decided to write this book as an exploration of an/other social world in Japan, that of disability. This social world is often not visible – or audible, or tactile – to people who have no or little contact with disability in their daily lives. While there are very few who have no contact at all with people with a disability,[1] for those who do, often the contact is limited in time and in scope (e.g. the interaction with an elderly relative at the end of life, or a short visit to a special school).

While incorporating a mix of research methods, this project relies mainly on anthropological intellectual frameworks in its approach. This choice is deliberate, as anthropology aims in the first instance to understand, without prejudice, the meaning of human difference. Kasnitz and Shuttleworth, both anthropologists of disability, write that '[a]nthropologists seek the other to find themselves' (2001: 20). While some anthropologists look at geographically 'foreign' cultures to learn about 'universals' of human nature, the anthropology of disability looks at embodied *difference* as another important indicator of what it means to be human. Disability and chronic illness represent a state that is considered 'othered' relative to our expectations of what the 'able-bodied' are (in other words, healthy and productive members of society). As an anthropologist with a specialization in Japanese studies, early in my career I researched marginalized communities in urban Japan, including the elderly and the physically and intellectually impaired (Stevens 1997); I specifically chose to study the Japanese underclass because I saw that their social existence threw into relief challenges to values to which the mainstream social classes aspire. By working with the unemployed and the homeless, the elderly and people with intellectual disabilities, all of whom were grouped together both geographically and symbolically by the virtue of their marginal position in society, I learned new ways to conceptualize the meanings of terms such as 'home', 'family' and 'work' in contemporary urban Japan. And, as Kasnitz and Shuttleworth (2001) emphasize, learning about these concepts in contemporary urban Japan was instructive to my interpretation of similar, yet different, phenomena of homelessness, poverty and social isolation in places I called my own (New York City, where I attended graduate school, or Melbourne, where I have lived since 1994). My work in Japan was purely etic, where the anthropologist is an outsider to the culture being studied. Not only was I not Japanese, I was also not a homeless person and I was not a day labourer; in the activist as well as the academic discourse, I was not a *tōjisha*, or 'a person [directly] concerned' (McLelland 2009: 196). While this might have been seen as politically problematic, or at least an obstacle, I found that outsider status allowed me some objectivity in my analysis of the phenomena and, I hope, some flexibility of thought as I did not carry much of the cultural baggage that accompanies social marginalization in Japan.[2]

Similarly, any research I might conduct in disability studies, in Japan or elsewhere, would be considered 'etic'. Yet, after the birth of my daughter, who holds Japanese citizenship and has a severe intellectual disability, any further study of social marginality via disability in Japan was no longer about an exotic 'other', but firmly about 'us'. She was diagnosed at birth with a rare chromosomal disorder, classified as an unbalanced translocation by our geneticist. Her condition is rare enough that she has no named syndrome, only an individual karyotype. She shares that structural disorder with only one known living person: her father's cousin, who, at the time of writing, is living in a residential institution in Japan. Through my child's diagnosis, we learned of a secret family history, which spoke volumes not only of general social attitudes about disability but also of the quality of distinct personal relations within the Japanese extended family. Because of this close personal connection to myself and to disability in Japan, I was compelled to learn more, and discover just why the translocation had remained a secret for more than thirty years. But it would be an overstatement to say that my approach to the study of disability in Japan has shifted from etic to emic merely as a result of the existence of a family member with a disability. I am still not Japanese, and not a person with a diagnosed disability. I know, however, that sinking feeling when my daughter is being excluded from an activity, or when a specialist programme is structured in a way that sets her up for failure because of her particular disability. Furthermore, because she is non-verbal, this means she shares the problem facing many others with profound intellectual disabilities who find it difficult or impossible to express themselves as '*tōjisha*' (McLelland 2009: 189). I have tried to the best of my abilities in this research to act as my daughter's voice whenever and wherever I can.

Using my experience of relational disability as part of the research could be considered a kind of autoethnography; as defined by Duncan, it is different from ethnography because

> the researcher is not trying to become an insider in the research setting. He or she, in fact, is the insider. The context is his or her own. Through autoethnography those marginalized individuals who might typically have been the

exotic subject of more traditional ethnographies have the chance to tell their own stories.

(2004: 3)

It overlaps with, but can be distinguished from, reflexivity, which describes a consciousness of the researcher's 'presence, standpoint, or characteristics [which] might have influenced the outcome of the research process' (Wall 2006: 3). Duncan observes that autoethnography should always be 'triangulate[d]' with other scholarly sources for legitimising interpretations (2004: 5). Muncey writes that the method is one of the few where 'the author can say "I" with authority and can respond immediately to any questions that arise from the story' (2005: 10). Wall suggests that feminists who use autoethnography counter male bias in the existing male-dominated literature (2006: 2–3). Nevertheless, autoethnography has its critics: Coffey warns of the potential for autoethnography to result in 'self-indulgent writings published under the guise of social research' (1999: 155); Sparkes writes of an array of negative labels for the method, ranging from 'narcissistic' (2002: 212) to 'self-conscious navel-gazing' (215). These tendencies to view autoethnography as an illegitimate form of scholarship are in turn criticized as arising from our modernist privileging of the scientific 'objective' model as a way to understand all aspects of the world around us (Wall 2006: 2).

Still, I wanted to include some autoethnography because of the insights I think it affords. As Duncan writes,

> [i]n traditional ethnographic research, gaining permission to become a participant observer in the lifeworld of those being studied is often a challenge. However, for autoethnographers already fully immersed in the focus situation, issues of accessibility, permissibility, and unobtrusiveness do not present such obstacles.
>
> (Duncan 2004: 5)

My research for this book comprises primary and secondary sources 'triangulated' with autoethnographic vignettes. Through speaking to people in Japan, reading the material in Japanese and English, and spending time in Japan as a mother of a child with a disability, I have relied both on other people's accounts of disability in Japan and also on my own direct experience, resulting in a mixed approach with the benefit of insight as well as objectivity.

Disability definitions

Disability, as understood in a variety of contexts, can be defined in numerous ways: there is medical discourse, special educational discourse and even activist discourse. In this section, I will outline some of the more interesting definitions, first in the English language literature, and then in Japanese. In general, the authors who focus on social and cultural dimensions are of most interest. Of course, concrete definitions can be useful: for example, Rosemarie Garland

4   *Introduction*

Thomson defines disability as the 'theoretical opposite' of 'the concept of able-bodiedness', although we must include in that definition the concept of 'able-mindedness' as well (1997: 49). The United Nations' definition of disability breaks it down into three parts, separating disability, impairment and handicap:

(a) Impairment is 'any loss or abnormality of psychological, physiological, or anatomical structure or function'. Impairments are disturbances at the level of the organ which include defects in or loss of a limb, organ or other body structure, as well as defects in or loss of a mental function. Examples of impairments include blindness, deafness, loss of sight in an eye, paralysis of a limb, amputation of a limb, mental retardation, partial sight, loss of speech, mutism.
(b) Disability is a 'restriction or lack (resulting from an impairment) of ability to perform an activity in the manner or within the range considered normal for a human being'. It describes a functional limitation or activity restriction caused by an impairment. Disabilities are descriptions of disturbances in function at the level of the person. Examples of disabilities include difficulty seeing, speaking or hearing; difficulty moving or climbing stairs; difficulty grasping, reaching, bathing, eating, toileting.
(c) A handicap is a 'disadvantage for a given individual, resulting from an impairment or disability, that limits or prevents the fulfilment of a role that is normal (depending on age, sex and social and cultural factors) for that individual'. The term is also a classification of 'circumstances in which disabled people are likely to find themselves'. Handicap describes the social and economic roles of impaired or disabled persons that place them at a disadvantage compared to other persons. These disadvantages are brought about through the interaction of the person with specific environments and cultures. Examples of handicaps include being bedridden or confined to home; being unable to use public transport; being socially isolated.

(United Nations 2003–04)

In short, the UN's definition of disability is any physical, medical and/or intellectual impairment that impedes an individual's ability to take responsibility for his or her daily functions. The handicap that it results in is a restricted ability to participate in public life through social, political and economic interactions wider than the individual's immediate family members and carers. This restriction often results in social isolation and low levels of financial and educational achievement. Michael Oliver, a British sociologist and disability activist (and a person with a disability himself), takes the distinction between disability and impairment further and states that 'my definition of disabled people contains three elements; (i) the presence of an impairment; (ii) the experience of externally imposed restrictions; and (iii) self-identification as a disabled person' (Oliver 1996: 5). As for the relationship between disability, impairment and the body, Oliver writes that 'disablement has nothing to do with the body ... [but we do] not deny that impairment is closely related to the physical body. Impairment is, in fact, a physical description of the body' (1996: 35). Tom Shakespeare, another noted UK disability studies scholar, reminds us that the distinction between impairment (which is biological) and disability (which is social) is similar to the feminist distinction between sex and gender (2006: 29–30), suggesting that disability studies could emerge as a forceful intellectual movement similar to feminist and gender studies.

If 'impairment' is the physical (or, say, 'objective') attribute that sets the disability/disablement process in motion, a focus on social interaction helps us understand disability subjectively, in wider usage and across different cultures. Kasnitz and Shuttleworth describe disability as 'a socially and culturally constructed category [that] has important implications about how societies differentially distribute power'; they go on to say that

> [d]isability exists when people experience discrimination on the basis of perceived functional limitations. A disability may or may not be a handicap, or handicapping, dependent on management of societal discrimination and internalized oppression, particularly infantilization and paternalism, and on cultural and situational views of cause and cure and of fate and fault.
> (Kasnitz and Shuttleworth 2001: 20)

Disability disrupts social relations for a number of reasons, the first of which is segregation, resulting from stigma (see Goffman 1997). Thomson notes the term 'stigma' is handy, because it can be conjugated to express a variety of processes that surround social stigma: 'stigmatizer', 'stigmatizing' and 'stigmatized' all allow for a proper understanding of the relationship between subject and object; 'stigmatization is an interactive process in which particular human traits are deemed not only as different, but deviant' (Thomson 1997: 30–1). Furthermore, she points out that most members of society have some degree of stigmatized attribute, and the subset of 'perfect', unstigmatized, individuals consists of a very small number of people indeed (32). Another example of a source of stigmatization, as cited by Thomson, is the idea that people with disabilities are 'threatening', because they 'signif[y] what the rest of Americans fear they will become' (41) or, as Davis writes, '[a]lthough identity politics is popular these days, what people fear is that disability is the identity that one may become part of but didn't want' (2002: 4). The neoliberal ideal of personal independence, self-reliance and eventual material and psychological success is shattered by the notion of dependence. In his book *The Body Silent* (1987), anthropologist Robert Murphy revealed that one of the most upsetting results of his acquired disability was the uncomfortable reaction his disability prompted in others, which stemmed from the unpleasant foreshadowing his presence cast on able-bodied others, fearful of a similar fate. Disability causes 'social discomfort' in people without disabilities because during interactions they tend to focus disproportionally on the existence of the disability rather than on 'the presence of someone with a disability' (Jaeger and Bowman 2005: 21). Other social reactions include 'pity' and 'inspiration' (both

6 *Introduction*

of which can be condescending) and dismissing the existence of a disability (22–3). Because of this stigma and segregation associated with disability, scholars believe that disability status must be seen as equivalent to other critical attributes such as race (see Campbell 2008) and gender, with particular affinity with feminist studies (Thomson 1997: 19–30).[3] It is this dissatisfaction with attitudes that place people with disabilities in negative and/or inferior positions in relation to the rest of society that forms the foundation of critical disability studies.

Why are definitions so important? Whether in Japanese or in English, terminology and communication have a complex relationship to our understanding of reality, both arising from the context and moulding its perception. A case study from Japanese special education shows how powerful terminology can be. In Abe's synopsis of postwar special education reform, he notes that changes in the special education system to address more recently identified learning disabilities (such as dyslexia and ADHD) have been hampered by people who are unwilling to embrace the term 'LD' (pronounced *'eru dii'* in Japanese, an acronym borrowed from the English phrase 'learning disability') because Japanese knew what the 'D' stood for, and were put off by the equivalent term *'shōgai'* (disability) (1998: 94). The words used to describe disabilities in Japan carry heavy meanings – so burdensome is their use that they can impede progressive attempts to support children with learning disabilities. Abe concludes this is because parents of these children who had trouble in school were reluctant to align their own children with other *shōjigaiji*. Acknowledging the importance of this example to our understanding of disability in Japan, a detailed discussion of the cultural and linguistic meanings behind the word *shōgai* and other disability-related terms is included in Chapter 3.

Disability studies in English

Much of the conceptual framework underpinning the definitions given above arises from a body of interdisciplinary scholarship known as disability studies. Marks observes that '[i]t is a central concern of disability studies to demystify the conventions operating in the organization of knowledge about "impairment" and "disability"' (1999: 151). Yet, within this scholarship, the most developed of which is primarily in English, there are some competing views. Most commonly considered as the first paradigm to be widely used to understand the phenomenon of disability (and ability) is the medical model – sometimes also called the 'individual' model (Priestly 1998; Swain and French 2000: 570; Shakespeare 2006: 15) – which focuses on specific, medicalized conditions that create impairments, which in turn require treatment or, even more desirably, a 'cure'.[4] Quinn writes that the medical model arose from the 'illness model' in the 1950s, which posited a special status for sick individuals, who were 'excused from certain expectations based on [their] illness' (1998: xix). The medical model is also called the individual model because 'it locates the "problem" of disability within the individual' (Oliver 1996: 32). It rests on a 'traditional deficit approach' (Shakespeare 2006: 30), which takes the onus of responsibility for disablement

Introduction 7

away from society and focuses on the shortcomings of the individual. The United Nations' definition of disability leans towards this medical/individual model in the 'World Programme of Action Concerning Disabled Persons'. Its first two aspects contain medical terminology ('prevention' and 'rehabilitation') while the third is social ('equalization of opportunities') (United Nations 2003–4).

Disability studies scholars have found the medical/individual model problematic for a number of reasons. Oliver finds it unsatisfactory as it is 'underpinned by ... the personal tragedy theory of disability' (1996: 31). Unlike others, however, he does not conflate an individual model with the medical one:

> It is not *individual limitations*, of whatever kind, which are the cause of the problem but *society's failure* to provide appropriate services and adequately ensure the needs of disabled people are fully taken into account in its social organisation. Further, the consequences of this failure *do not simply and randomly fall on individuals but systematically upon disabled people* as a group who experience this failure as discrimination institutionalised throughout society.
>
> (Oliver 1990a: 33, emphasis added)

The medicalization of disability further clouds the issues by producing an overlap, as there are many individuals who have a variety of problems with physical or intellectual functioning and yet are not considered disabled (Oliver 1990a; Swain and French 2000: 570). Some chronic illnesses, for example, can be considered disabilities, while others are not. Multiple sclerosis, arthritis and epilepsy (depending on the severity, and whether or not the illness is 'under control') are illnesses or medical conditions that can be ambiguous in the context of defining disability (Thomson 1997: 13). Even when a medical or other physical condition does not cause significant problems with functioning, it can cause social impairment through its presentation to others: 'physical disability is a disruption in the sensory field of the observer' (Davis 2002: 50). Intellectual disability, if considered distinct from physical disability, has been further problematized by scholars such as Goodey (2003), who argues that the medical model may be misused across these disability borders:

> Of course, it must be and generally is acknowledged that the distinction between these categories [of physical and intellectual disabilities] is not as tidy as it appears to be. Nevertheless, the fact that both categories share the same noun encourages us to apply a medical or disease model in the same way to intellectual as to physical disability.
>
> (2003: 549)

The medical/individual model tends to separate people based on the 'medical definitions of impairments', rather than allowing people with disabilities to come together effectively in collective solidarity (Davis 2002: 11), and this further prevents them from participating fully in society. When oppressed people are

8 *Introduction*

isolated, their collective power to enact social change is weak. To address this, the 'social model' eschews medical diagnoses, and instead states that

> disability is defined as a social oppression experienced by people whose bodies and minds are labelled as different or impaired. Society disables people with impairments, through negative attitudes, environmental barriers and institutional discrimination. The result is that people with perceived impairments become disabled people, denied the opportunities and support to take up the rights and responsibilities of full citizenship ...
> (Stone 2001: 51)

Other scholars refer to it as the 'disability paradigm', which

> regards disability as a socially constructed phenomenon, and is based on the view of disabled people as a minority group, much like women or persons of color targeted with social discrimination and denied full access to the mainstream life of the community. According to this perspective, once the oppression is revealed, the assumptions of the medical view (the more impaired, the less quality of life) are exposed as false.
> (Paxton 2000: 150)

Another variation on this terminology is illustrated by Jaeger and Bowman's 'medical perspective' and 'social perspective' (2005: 14–15); their descriptions also include terms such as 'emphasis' and 'focus' to refer to the way the two models have differing priorities. They then go further to describe a 'materialist perspective' – which in fact refers to what Priestly calls the 'social materialist perspective' (see below), where the emphasis is on economic oppression of people with disabilities – then a 'postmodernist perspective', which is said by them to break down disability experience as splintered and complex, as in feminist, race and queer disability studies (16).

Davis further categorizes the social model as a 'British model', as many of its proponents are based at UK universities, and its main contribution is that it makes a clear 'distinction between impairment and disability'; disability is thus a 'social process that turns an impairment into a negative' (2002: 12). Two of the early British scholarly proponents of this model were Vic Finkelstein (a psychologist) and Michael Oliver (a sociologist). Shakespeare highlights that the 'benefits of the social model approach are that it shifts attention from individuals and their physical or mental deficits to the ways in which society includes or excludes them' (2006: 29). The ways in which people are excluded from society can range 'from individual prejudice to institutional discrimination, from inaccessible public buildings to unusable transport systems, from segregated education to excluding work arrangements' (Oliver 1996: 33). Supporters of the social model in the UK (and the USA) were influenced by disability activism and developed their theories in line with these political movements (Shakespeare 2006: 26).

The ways in which society excludes people with disabilities as listed above demonstrate the social model's ability to understand and analyse a broad range of discrimination. Because of its wide scope of concerns, Priestly says that the social model can be split into two parts, the first focusing on 'structural and material conditions' while the other aspect is 'more concerned with culture and representation', as set out in detail below (1998: 76). Despite its allure for activists, Shakespeare warns against relying too heavily on a social model, for the experience of living with disability should not be portrayed as having 'nothing whatsoever to do with individual bodies or brains' (2006: 31). Accordingly, we can say that disability causes individuals to experience social exclusion but the kinds of exclusion they experience are not all the same. The extent of a physical or intellectual disability (or its combination with a chronic illness or condition) can change the lived experience of oppression. People with different disabilities experience oppression differently. The social model should, therefore, not exclude the variety of experience people with different disabilities have.

While British scholars have been credited with the creation of the social model, North American scholars have also contributed to disability studies in English in distinctive ways. Lennard J. Davis, Professor of Disability Studies at the University of Illinois, summarizes the important volumes by American scholars in his book *Bending over Backwards: Disability, Dismodernism and Other Difficult Positions* (2002: 31–46). In my research, I have found insightful the work of Davis, as well as Rosemarie Garland Thomson, Devva Kasnitz, Tanya Titchkosky, Susan Wendell, Sharon L. Snyder and David T. Mitchell, and my colleague in Japan anthropology, Karen Nakamura. Davis' synopsis of this research notes a constant tension between US disability studies and research into race (2002: 36), and Thomson and Wendell have written strongly about the intersection of gender and disability in US society (Thomson 1997; Wendell 1997). Davis also notes the tension in disability studies both in the UK and in the USA that arose from the different priorities of scholars in the social sciences from those in the humanities (2002: 43), and many of the American disability studies scholars listed above (in particular, Thomson, Wendell, Snyder and Mitchell, and Davis) have excelled at integrating disability awareness in the study of literature and philosophy. As summarized by Marks, '[i]n the UK, the discipline has broadly focused on disabling social structure and policies ... whilst in the USA, the discipline has ... addressed the historical, cultural and socio-psychological conditions producing disability' (1999: 188). Shakespeare credits American disability scholars with integrating 'normalization theory' into the social model (2006: 22), especially with reference to people with intellectual disabilities. Shakespeare notes that the US tradition has focused on disability as a personal attribute constituting 'minority group' status, rather than focusing on 'social oppression' as in the British case, but both parties agree that the disability arises from failures in the built environment and social environment rather than maladjustments on the part of individuals (2006: 24).

Shakespeare also credits Scandinavian researchers for the 'Nordic relational model', which he attributes to these states' extensive welfare systems, and this strand of research has influenced disability studies in the United States more clearly than in England. In this model, the idea of 'normalization' is influential, and the distinction between disability and impairment is not so striking as it is in the UK; Shakespeare senses this is because of the differences in languages used to describe them (2006: 25). An important distinguishing characteristic of the relational model is its stress on the relative meaning of the word disability, that 'a disability is relative, a continuum rather than a dichotomy'; Shakespeare sees this as incompatible with the social model, whose adherents believe that because disability arises from oppression, and all social oppression is equivalent in its wrongness, there should be no distinguishing between individual situations. He also observes an absence of political activism in Nordic scholarship, perhaps because of the relatively greater support people with disabilities receive from their welfare states (2006: 26).

The social model also created differences in opinion about priorities, and we cannot consider it as a simple 'binary distinction' to the medical/individual model (Oliver 1996: 30; Shakespeare 2006: 10). Shakespeare writes that it would be 'dangerous to conclude that the distinction ... [between the approaches] is robust' and that we must 'rescue the important insights and findings of other scholars from the dustbin marked "medical model"' (2006: 18–19). In fact, Shakespeare goes as far as to say:

> Disability studies would be better off without the social model, which has become fatally undermined by its own contradictions and inadequacies. To reject the British social model does not mean returning to the bad old days of medicalisation and individualist approaches before the UPIAS [Union of the Physically Impaired against Segregation] revolution. There are many other, more robust, ways of conceptualising disability, which retain a commitment to equality and justice for disabled people, but do not base the analysis on a mistaken bracketing of bodily difference ...
>
> So from one extreme – the cultural assumption that disability is equated with dependency, invalidity and tragedy – the disability movement swung to another – the political demand that disability be defined entirely in terms of social oppression, social relations and social barriers.
>
> (Shakespeare 2006: 28, 31)

He calls for a 'relational approach to understanding disability', one that shows 'disability as a relationship between intrinsic factors (impairment, etc.) and extrinsic factors (environments, support systems, oppression, etc.)' (57). The importance of impairment is illustrated when one is confronted with the possibility that the 'creation [and the maintenance] of a disabled "ideal type" – either as a neutral or benign experience, or as a negative and tragic experience – does not do justice to the complexity and the variability of the experience of disability' (Shakespeare 2005: 224).

What to make of this argument about the social versus the medical model? Priestly's approach divides prevalent ways of thinking about disability into four different considerations, and is one method that demonstrates the alternative foci the social model can take, both in contrast and in interaction with the medical/individual model. (See Table 1.1.)

Table 1.1 Priestly's four approaches to disability theory, abridged (1998: 78–83)

	Materialist	*Idealist*
Individual	1 Disability is the physical product of biology acting upon the functioning of material individuals (bodies); the units of analysis are impaired bodies. Also known as the 'medical model': the product of biological determinism or personal tragedy manifested in the material condition of the individual. Research is concerned with physical rehabilitation, drug development and surgical intervention.	2 Disability is the product of voluntaristic individuals (disabled and non-disabled) engaged in the creation of identities and the negotiation of roles; the units of analysis are beliefs and identities. Prominent in the theoretical field, it focuses on cognitive interaction and affective experience. Disability is the product of personal experience and the negotiation of social roles between individuals. The units of analysis are identity and experience, focusing on the 'adjustment' to impairment and 'attitudes' towards people with impairments.
Social	3 Disability is the material product of socio-economic relations developing within a specific historical context; the units of analysis are disabling barriers and material relations of power. The commonly understood 'social model'; central to the mobilization of the disabled people's movement; predominantly British and male scholars.	4 Disability is the idealist product of societal development within a specific cultural context; the units of analysis are cultural values and representations. Disability is viewed as a social construct; similar to cultural relativism, it assumes that the construction of disability is a product of specific cultural conditions.

What divides the social model theories (positions 3 and 4) from the individual model theories (positions 1 and 2) is the assertion of the former that disability has some real collective existence in the social world beyond the existence or experience of individual disabled people. While individual experiences differ, there remains an essential level of commonality in the collective experience of discrimination and oppression. Social models run the risk of obscuring or excluding the experience of impairment.

While these categorical boundaries are certainly invented ones, and thus porous and not exclusive, I find Priestly's configuration helpful for its distillation of ideas about how discussions of disability can be framed and what the priorities of certain schools of thought are. It is also important to note that the individual/medical model and the social model were not created in an academic vacuum in the 1980s; Michael Oliver notes that these two positions rest on the familiar distinction between 'impairment' and 'disability', which he notes was made first by the Union of the Physically Impaired against Segregation in 1976; disability activists borrowed this explicitly (1990a).[5] Oliver calls for a kind of power sharing between these two mindsets: 'To put the matter unequivocably, the medicalisation of disability ha[s] given doctors power and left disabled people powerless. The social model is not an attempt to take power away from doctors and give it to disabled people, but a prescription for sharing power' (1990a: 6).

Another Canadian scholar, Tanya Titchkosky, describes the experience of living with a disability in a manner that integrates the individual and social models. She is dyslexic and writes frankly about her disability as well as the experience of her partner, who is blind (2003). Her approach to the individual experience of different disabilities and the socially constructed category that surrounds them is straightforward:

> Seeing Rod as blind is dependent upon somehow seeing Rod himself as a mistake; he *should* have been sighted but for some tragedy. Understanding my self as dyslexic means knowing that I did not make a mistake but, instead, there is something mistaken about the ways in which I make sense of driving and direction. I am mixed up – I did not merely get mixed up, or cause a mix-up. Something has gone wrong, and ordinary life is not being done in its ordinary fashion. But what is wrong is seen to belong to disabled people in a more intimate and personal way than it does to others.
>
> (Titchkosky 2003: 14)

What is interesting about this passage is the way in which Titchkosky concerns herself with the importance of both medical and social issues. Even if their disabilities are completely different, resulting in different attitudes towards the person (a 'tragedy' versus a 'mix-up'), the *socially* constructed 'wrongness' that results from the disability is inseparable from the *biological* person. Like race and gender, the biological-ness of disability, while socially and culturally constructed, should not be privileged, but nor can it be discarded.

Scholars who subscribe to the social model are aware that not all disadvantages are the same. Oliver writes that one of the drawbacks of the social model is 'the way it connects, or rather doesn't connect with the experience of impairment' (1996: 37). Impairments impose difficulties differently. Amundson and Tresky define these as

> Conditional disadvantages of impairment (CDIs): Disadvantages that are experienced by people with impairments, but which are produced by the social context in which those people live.
>
> Unconditional disadvantages of impairment (UDIs): Disadvantages that are experienced by people with impairments but which are produced irrespective of their social context.
>
> (cited in Ralston and Ho 2007: 620)

Disability movement activists have primarily focused on CDIs as they believe they are the most commonly experienced (621), and their resolution has the potential for transforming society, though one could argue that there is no disadvantage irrespective of social context, as all our experiences are determined cognitively and socially. UDIs are, in other words, an aspect of the medical model that cannot be overlooked.

It might be tempting to focus on the strength of the social model in cases where the disability does not have a medical cause, as noted by Goodey in his discussion of intellectual disability, which he sees as inherently different from physical disability:

> correspondingly disability activists apply their alternative 'social' model to the intellectual category as well as to the physical ... If there is any certain connection between the two disabilities, what unites them is merely current social practice, particularly exclusion and discrimination. These unifying social phenomena do not, however, prove the soundness of the social model, because it works differently in each of the categories. It is one thing to change the built environment but another to change a whole conception of what it is to be human, as defined in intellectual (dis)ability. While a social model of [intellectual disability] may hold good hypothetically, inasmuch as intelligence is relative and historical change will also be normative change, it is not much practical help for those people who find themselves marginalized by the way we live and think about ourselves here and now ... [because] those cultural norms [change only] slowly ...
>
> (Goodey 2003: 549–50)

Shakespeare, who has written extensively on the need to move beyond the social model, concurs with the point that 'the distinction between biological/individual impairment, and social/structural disability is conceptual and empirically very difficult to sustain ... There can be no impairment without society, nor disability without impairment' (2006: 34). This difficulty is echoed by Lennard J. Davis, who says that disability is an 'unstable category' (2002: 23) and 'porous category' (86); this instability means it is hard to define, but this 'allows disability to transcend the problems of identity politics' (23). Others have called the concept of disability 'revisable' (Edwards 2003: 526), considering its history from both the medical and cultural perspectives. Why is its meaning so variable? Davis points to the division between disability and impairment (noting that the former does not exist without the latter): impairment is also an unstable term, as new illnesses and medical conditions are discovered every day (2002: 23). His example of Samuel Johnson, the revered British essayist of the eighteenth century, illustrates this pointedly: Johnson's idiosyncratic behaviour and the scars of his past illnesses would today certainly result in his 'institutionalization', complete with shock therapy and antidepressants, rather than allowing him to function in his own way as one of the leading intellectual figures of his time (49). Davis thus asks us to consider that our definitions of disability have evolved based on our social understanding of the body and the mind according to the unfolding of medical knowledge over the years. Who can say how disability will be defined in another two hundred years? Medicalization continually destabilizes the category of disability as '[a]nyone can become disabled, and it is also possible for a person with disabilities to . . become "normal"' (Davis 2002: 80).[6]

Oliver concedes that the social model appears to have disconnected from the medical model in the former's 'assumed denial of the "pain of impairment", both physical and psychological', but responds that the social model has been a 'pragmatic attempt' to alleviate other kinds of pain (1996: 38). He concedes that, in the long run, the social model would not ignore the medical model; the ideal situation would be one where the social model informs the medical profession effectively so that the two work together fruitfully. A new social model would also be improved by taking some of the focus away from social oppression as a driver in its description of disability, for this creates a 'circularity' of argument.[7] A relational or interactive approach also allows for variability in the 'personal attitudes and motivation' of individuals (61). Personally, I have found the interactive model of disability as proposed by Shakespeare to be congruent with my understanding from the point of view of a mother of a child with a severe intellectual disability, whose life is a quite different experience from that of those who are impaired visually, or who are deaf, for example. In my experience, profound intellectual disability cuts across all human abilities, whether they are communicative, social or physical. People with disabilities all experience social oppression in some shape or form, but my daughter's experience of social oppression (in her eyes, she is oppressed because I won't let her eat dirt in the garden) is very different from that of a person with a psychiatric disability seeking employment.

As noted above, much of these academic developments in disability studies occurred in the English language literature, but Priestly notes that approximately 80 per cent of the world's population with a disability live in developing countries. Therefore, he critiques disability studies as a discipline because 'the academic literature of disability studies consistently privileges minority accounts (especially, those from Western Europe and North America)' (2001: 3). Certainly there is potential for further diversity in disability studies scholarship, which is still nascent. The next section examines how scholars and activists have viewed disability in Japan, how they have been influenced by the intellectual hegemony of British and American disability studies, and what specific contributions they make to this field.

Disability studies in Japan

While there is no doubt that my thinking about disability has been influenced by this very rich body of literature in English, it has also been complemented by Japanese scholarly and activist research. One of the major sites of disability research in Japan is the Research Institute of the Japanese National Centre for Rehabilitation. Founded in 1984, it proclaims that it promotes an interdisciplinary model of medical, engineering, sociological and psychological research (Kokuritsu Shōgaisha Rihabiritēshon Sentā n.d.). This centre's title reflects, however, a strong sense of the medical model, considering the prominence of the term 'rehabilitation'. Another large institution promoting disability studies research is the Nozominosono (translated as Garden of Hope), a residential facility, or '*koronii*' (colony) in Takasaki City, north-west of Tokyo. Established by the government in 1971, in 2003 it became an 'independent administrative corporation' (*dokuritsugyōseijin*) titled the National Centre for Persons with Severe Intellectual Disabilities Nozominosono. It now includes a research centre under the jurisdiction of the Ministry of Health, Labour and Welfare with more than four hundred residential clients from around the country. While providing similar services to those of other residential facilities, it also conducts surveys and research in intellectual disability.

The Shōgaigakkai (Japan Society for Disability Studies) was formally founded in 2003, following activities of informal groups and seminars in the 1990s (Nagase 2008; Tateiwa 2006) and its first convention was held in June 2004 (Ishikawa 2004). This follows other kinds of social activism in Japan: disability activist movements, inspired by other activist movements of ethnic minorities in Japan in the 1970s, were spurred into action in the 1980s (see Takagi 1999). Since 2005, the Shōgaigakkai has published an annual journal *Shōgaigaku Kenkyū* (*Disability Studies Research*). Suzuki (2008), in her introduction to a special issue on Japan in the highly regarded American journal *Disability Studies Quarterly*, summarizes the main contributions in the field of Japanese disability studies. She points first to the work of Tateiwa Shin'ya as one of the leading figures in this discipline. His co-authored book on independent living (Asaka *et al.* 1990, revised and expanded in 1995) is thought to be 'ground-breaking' in the field of Japanese disability studies (Nagase 2008) and set the stage for developments in the field in the early 1990s. Since then, he has also written on ethical issues regarding people with disabilities and terminal illnesses (Tateiwa 1997), ALS (amyotrophic lateral sclerosis, also known as Lou Gehrig's Disease) (Tateiwa 2004) and euthanasia and right-to-die issues (Tateiwa 2009), as well as recounting the history of the Japanese disability studies and feminist movements (Tateiwa 2010). Tateiwa's discussions of disability and disability studies (*shōgai/shōgaigaku*) reflect an influence of disability research in English. For example, his entry 'Disability/Disability Studies' in a dictionary of contemporary ethics starts with definitions from the 1980 World Health Organization's International Classification of Impairments, Disabilities and Handicaps and then proceeds to outline the '*kojin moderu*' and '*iryō moderu*' (individual and medical models, respectively), noting their deficiencies; the following section defines the '*shakai moderu*' (social model), quoting Michael Oliver, one of its self-proclaimed 'originators' (1990a). Tateiwa sees shifts in Japanese disability studies as related to and part of the wider disability studies movement:

> the idea [of the social model] can be found in disability movements around the world, including those in Japan, particularly since the 1970s. The individual model and the medical model focus primarily on the individual body and its defects, and ascribe the responsibility of solving its associated problems and issues to individuals, which in effect justifies control by the medical and welfare specialists through their treatment and training practices.

16 *Introduction*

> The social model, instead, argues that disability manifests as a disability within the mesh of social relations and [calls us] to pursue a solution to the problem through the transformation of the social system and social relations. The social model values the experiences of the people who live with disabilities themselves and emphasizes the importance of the participation and contribution of those with disabilities to bring about such social change.
>
> (Tateiwa 2006: n.p., translation by the author)

Additionally, Hoshika Ryōji's book *Shōgai to wa nani ka: disabiriti no shakai riron ni mukete* (*What is Disability? Toward a Social Theory of Disability*, 2007) is another example of the integration of the social model in Japanese disability studies. Another resource is the joint project between the Ministry of Education, Culture and Technology (MEXT) and Ritsumeikan University entitled 'arsvi', an abbreviation of the phrase *Ars Vivendi*, meaning 'the art of living' (arsvi.com 2010a). The arsvi website is linked to many academic and activist publications from the disability studies community in Japan. Its motto is *'ikite zonjiru o manabu'* ('we learn through living and being') (ibid).

Ishikawa Jun is another important figure. A sociologist who is also blind, Ishikawa co-edited the book *Shōgaigaku e no shōtai* (*An Invitation to Disability Studies*) with Nagase Osamu (Ishikawa and Nagase 1999) and chaired the inaugural meeting of the Japan Society for Disability Studies (Ishikawa 2004). Ishikawa has also written in English, asking philosophical questions about the realistic outcomes of disability studies. In one of his essays, he asks his audience to reflect on the word 'consideration'; one could argue that social consideration takes on a more significant meaning in the Japanese context because of the customary emphasis in personal relationships on thoughtfulness towards others, set in contrast against the *wagamama* (selfish) mindset. This makes his argument all the more powerful:

> There is a stubbornly fixed idea that 'there exists a majority of people who do not need consideration, and a minority of people who need special consideration'. However, the correct view is that 'there are people who have already been considered and people who have not yet been considered'. The consideration given to the majority is so much taken for granted that it is not even seen as consideration. In contrast, consideration for minorities becomes visible as something special.
>
> (Ishikawa 2004)

Yōda Hiroe is Professor of Human Development and Welfare at Osaka City University, and she has written in disability studies in both Japanese and English (Yōda 1999, 2002). Her critique of the Japanese social welfare system with regard to disability points to three major problems: a lack of 'vision', apart from rehabilitating those who are deemed to have the ability to contribute to society in some way (2002: 1–2); an over-reliance in understanding disability on the medical model (4–7), which tends to see disability as 'incurable' in contrast to diseases or medical conditions that are 'curable' (6); and lastly, that Japanese society relegates people with disabilities to 'dependence on their families' (7). She critiques Japanese society as a whole, saying that it tends to view people with disabilities (and their families) with sympathy, yet at the same time 'shows little concern about the quality of life these disabled persons are actually experiencing' (8).

The above sections outlining internationally accepted definitions of disability, handicap and impairment, and their problematization by scholars in the UK, USA and Japan, constitute a lengthy preamble to the study of disability in Japan, but are crucial to set the parameters of the ways in which we understand the empirical data. Despite the cultural differences between Japan (as the 'East') and the USA and the UK (as the 'West'), the English language literature contains useful tools for understanding disability, and the Japanese literature has been explicitly influenced by these ideas. At the same time, there will be occasions when we see difference rather than similarity between the USA, UK and Japan; rather than seeking to find 'faults' in these Anglophone models, however, I believe these differences will demonstrate the weight we must give Japanese language, history, culture and society in our investigations of the meaning of disability. It is through difference that we can recognize and understand context.

Book outline

This volume encompasses a variety of social issues that are touched by disability. Chapter 2 provides a contextual ethnographic background for the study of disability in Japan, including a brief history, demographic sketch and activist landscape. 'Nothing about us without us' is the rallying cry of the disability movement in the West (Charlton 1998), and this is also relevant to Japan. The connection between activism and the study of disability in Japan is an important one, as both serve to raise awareness about disability rights as well as call us to re-examine our ideas about disability privately and publically.

In the next chapter, I investigate language, as it is through words that we express our ideas and feelings about disability. The Japanese language, like other traditions, is a malleable and evolving one, and Chapter 3 outlines the developments in the recognition of disability through communication, and the disjunctures where historical terms and contemporary concerns clash, primarily in the context of legal terminology and mass media expressions. This clash not only identifies discriminatory practices, but also – and more importantly – throws into relief the tension between individual responsibility and state control, and censorship. Chapter 4 outlines the policies and laws that relate to people with disabilities. Like language, law also contributes to the definition of disability status, as without legal recognition, programmes to support people with disabilities cannot be implemented. In Japan, as in other societies, the Constitution makes provisions for services, both financial and other kinds of support, for people with disabilities that vary depending on the kind of disability experienced and its severity. One of the main issues addressed in this chapter is the impact of the Shōgaisha Jiritsu Shien Hō (Services and Supports for Persons with Disability

18 *Introduction*

Act), enacted in 2005. It was meant to streamline application processes and provide equity and transparency of decision-making, but it has also had an effect on the way we understand the position of the welfare recipient, in a transition from a fully subsidized client to a 'user pays' system. Understanding the social welfare laws, which encompass personal identity, medical care and employment/financial support, is crucial when piecing together the experience of living with disability in Japan, and how the state – and larger society as well – recognizes and supports people living with disability.

So often disability in Japan is conflated with ageing, and this is for a good reason: Japan is one of the fastest ageing societies on the planet. Combined with a low fertility rate – at the end of 2008, Japan's rate of 1.37 was slightly higher than that of Italy or South Korea but well below those of other developed countries (Statistics and Information Department – Minister's Secretariat 2009) – this means that Japanese society is quickly 'greying'. The most recent national census, conducted in 2005, states that Japan's current aged population is 1.5 times larger than the child population (Ministry of Internal Affairs and Communications 2005d).[8] This has important ramifications for the nation's future, because if a significant proportion of the population is non-productive (through ageing, and its associated medical conditions and/or disability), the productive proportion must work harder to support them (through national subsidized medical care and pension payments). As a comparison, the current proportion of children in the general population is 13.7 per cent, significantly lower than the level of 35 per cent in 1950 (Ministry of Internal Affairs and Communications 2005d: 16). With a falling fertility rate, the numbers of young (read: productive) people are set to dwindle further, shrinking the source of income tax that can support the burgeoning senior citizens' programme budget. While this is an important issue, I feel that ageing in Japan has overshadowed our understanding of disability in ways that displace the experience of younger people with disabilities. Chapter 5 is entitled 'Disability and the lifecycle' for that very reason: to give voice to the needs of other people with disabilities, and to show how disability plays out in different stages of life. While end-of-life care of the elderly has been well documented and discussed elsewhere,[9] this chapter focuses more closely on disability at different stages of life, and discussions of education and employment outcomes for people with disabilities are important here.

While disability policy described in Chapter 4 is implemented at state and/or local government levels, individuals most often first confront disability (in either their own lives or those of family members) at home, where the private sphere encompasses all kinds of care. Because of this close relationship between disability care and family responsibility, Chapter 6 focuses on disability from the caregiving perspective, and interrogates family structures and their traditional caring roles. One of the most revered intellectual figures in literature and social commentary, Nobel Laureate Ōe Kenzaburō, has a further distinctive contribution to make: he has written eloquently about disability in Japan from a father's viewpoint. He observes that the family of a child with a disability is important because it performs the social role of the state in microcosm (a 'family writ large', 1996: 96). Following the lifecycle model, caregiving is also a concern for end-of-life disability carers, as the numbers of elderly in Japan are predicted to increase to the extent that almost 32 per cent of the population will consist of people over the age of 65, a 12 per cent increase from 2005 (Statistics and Information Department – Minister's Secretariat 2009). The recently implemented Long-Term Care Insurance programme is a key development for both kinds of disability (lifelong as well as end-of-life) as it confronts the social ideology of how families view their caring roles. While changing expectations (some of which are unwieldy and unrealistic), it also commodifies caregiving, making it a part of the 'affect economy', where people are paid to care.

Accessibility, or the creation of a 'barrier-free society', originally caught my attention as the first and most immediate issue that arose when I travelled to Japan with my daughter. More than merely an inconvenience, I came to understand that barriers to mobility were symbolic of the larger ideology that surrounds attitudes towards people with disabilities and expectations of public participation. Although any change can be seen as a first step, in general I found as many negative as positive outcomes from the new barrier-free Japan. Pushing my little girl throughout metropolitan Tokyo, I found that her chair became a focal point of our experience there, and it was then that I understood why the wheelchair is a commonly used and recognized 'badge' of disability, as it became the 'elephant' in the train station day after day. Accessibility can have an enormous impact on public attitudes because it marks the shift from helping people with disability (in other words, 'normalizing') to focusing on change in mainstream society; the democratic tendencies of 'universal design' also reflect this desire to understand disability as a 'normal' part of daily life. The worldwide 'barrier-free' movement began in 1974, but it was not until 2001 that the term was adopted by the United Nations as part of its treaty on the rights for people with disabilities. The Fifth Standard Rule on the Equalization of Opportunities for Persons with Disabilities declares: 'States should recognize the overall *importance of accessibility in the process of equalization of opportunities* in all spheres of society' (cited in Iwarsson and Ståhl 2003: 58, emphasis added).

Concessions

This project is about 'body as text' (Titchkosky 2003: 114), but it is also about minds, ideas and beliefs. I have no medical training, aside from the experiences I have had at the children's hospital by my daughter's side, but at the same time I am an experienced user of medical services for people with disabilities. I am not a lawyer, but I have gained experience from living under legislation as a parent of a child with a disability; I have applied for benefits and been both successful and unsuccessful in these pursuits, learning much about how the system works and what it privileges.

This book is not based on lengthy participant–observer fieldwork. While that is the hallmark of the discipline and, in my opinion, a worthy and relevant way to study disability in any cultural context, it was not possible for me to undertake this kind of project. After the birth of my daughter, I had to change the way I studied Japanese culture. When she was very small it was relatively simple to travel with her, but we had problems with medical insurance, because we could not obtain a policy that covered 'existing conditions' (in other words, her normal state of being – her disability). As she grew older and her health stabilized, we discovered that she was most settled and happy in a stable routine, so it was not in her best interests to be taken from her set school and home practices for any length of time. Therefore we would travel for two or three weeks at most, meaning that my interaction with Japanese society and disability in the past decade has been in sporadic bursts rather than in sustained fieldwork.

Even considering the drawbacks of intermittent visits versus the benefits of sustained fieldwork, I have still had a significant experience of disability in Japan. As Panitch writes, 'abled' caregivers have a unique experience of disability, that of 'relational' identity. I did not have the benefit of spending months studying special schools or social movements, but neither did I observe disability distantly or externally during those visits to Japan. I lived with disability twenty-four hours a day (in Japan as in Australia). Being in Japan highlighted some of these experiences, such as the common difficulty of persuading a child with a disability to sleep, but further complicated by the need to stay on a futon rather than in an enclosed bed. I knew what it was like to push a wheelchair through a crowded Japanese train station and I knew the frustration of going back and forth between doctor's visits, to ensure the seemingly vast amount of medication was 'just right', when my daughter came down with a respiratory infection in suburban Yokohama. I felt a flare of anger at dehumanization when, in a crowded café, other customers stepped over her legs as she sat in her wheelchair, rather than walk around her, in their haste to secure an empty table. I understood the difficulty (frankly, the impossibility) of trying to find supervision for her while the rest of the family attended my mother-in-law's two-day Buddhist funeral. Unable to find respite care, I could only participate in the services in bits and pieces. The most vivid memory I have of the funeral and the subsequent memorial services is bundling my daughter out of the temple, and walking around with her in the wheelchair, stumbling over the uneven paving and scratching mosquito bites while listening to the priest's intonation of chants within. It is my hope that these sporadic but intensely direct experiences give me the insight necessary to interpret archival data in a productive way. At the same time, I hope that this book will also effectively 'tread the line' between 'writing subjectively and exposing things', so that our family experience sheds light on the data but does not result in the impression that 'disability [is] an individual, intensely personal problem' (Oliver 1996: 3).

I am also mindful that in disability studies there is a significant awareness of the differences between the contributions of scholars with a disability and those without. Oliver, Shakespeare, Garland Thomson, Kasnitz, Titchkosky and Wendell write with authentic voices as a result of their impairments; Davis, as the hearing son of two deaf parents, also has experienced impairment in a direct and meaningful way. My experience is relational, as previously stated, but is further complicated by my position as a parent; a colleague of mine advised me of the difficulty of breaking into disability studies as a parent, a social role that is often seen as one that exerts oppression just as powerfully upon the person with a disability as strangers do. Speaking with people with disabilities, I have been told that in their struggles to live independently the first and often the most difficult obstacle was their parents' wishes for them to stay *dependent*; for many it was psychologically easier to 'battle the system' than to fight with their mother. I am wary of exerting my 'parental' (in other words, 'controlling', 'conservative' and 'patronizing') role as a disability studies scholar, but I also am convinced that in the case of my daughter's disability (severe intellectual disability with no verbal communication and limited sign language) I am the only authentic voice that she has, and I am bound by that duty to express these ideas for her, which I know to be true from our lives closely lived in both time and space.

The last concession is about fieldwork. There was some irony in the intimate connection between the research topic and the reason why sustained fieldwork was untenable; in other words, the fact that relational disability impeded my study of disability. Despite this, some fieldwork was conducted: sections of the chapters on the lifecycle and caregiving, and all of the accessibility research, can be considered distinctively 'anthropological' in that they rely heavily on direct ethnographic experience. On the other hand, the other chapters are based on critical readings of primary and secondary sources on disability in Japan, drawing on sociolinguistic, legal and social welfare disciplinary models to interpret the data. Still, I believe my personal ethnographic experience contributes a reflective quality to all aspects of the research presented here. Reflexive anthropology has been described as the researcher having an 'engagement in the lives of those being studied'; it also 'fully acknowledge[s] and utilize[s] subjective experience as an intrinsic part of research' (Davies 1999: 4–5). The anthropological task as described above – to understand difference – was crucial to my reading of any kind of disability texts in Japanese and English, whether the topic is legal policy, medical statistics, language debates, the sociology of welfare or architectural plans. More importantly, this project shows how anthropological thinking and disability studies can be truly interdisciplinary in scope: television shows, legal documents, medical journal articles and demographic statistics are all important elements in our understanding of disability.[10] Anthropologists' quests to understand the 'other' in order to learn more about themselves should not be overly romanticized, however; the intellectual baggage that accompanies the desire to cross cultural boundaries is that of 'relativism and certainty' (Goodey 2003: 554), where in the former, the desire to understand blots out significant values, and in the latter, the scientific certainty attributed to the researcher.[11]

I also hope that this book takes some of the progressive ideas that come from disability studies writing and mainstreams them into 'area studies', or more specifically, Japanese studies. The *naruhodo!* ('I see!') moment I experienced reading books by Michael Oliver, Lennard Davis, Tom Shakespeare and Rosemary

Garland Thomas reminded me of similar eye-opening experiences I had as a university student in the 1980s reading feminist works by Carol Gilligan, Nancy Chodorow, Germaine Greer and Peggy Sanday, which demonstrated to me the congruence between the two social/political/intellectual movements. I regret that disability studies has lagged behind feminism (and race) in its impact on my intellectual development, but I am grateful that it has sprung into my way of looking at Japan, and hope that it continues to frame future understandings of Japanese society.

2 Disability in the Japanese context

Impairment is always understood in a social context that affects the individual's experience of disability. While the primary focus of this book is on postwar and contemporary Japan, this chapter includes a brief cultural and social history of disability in Japan, considering the attendant historical beliefs regarding bodily and mental difference that lead to current disability issues. We then turn to demographic information on the experience of disability in Japan, specifically looking at the ways disability is defined by the government and thus recorded (and funded). The chapter finishes with a section on disability activism, from the political and social movements of other marginal groups in Japan as well as the international disability rights community.

Ideologies of disability in Japan, past and present

A detailed history of disability in Japan could fill an entire volume; here I wish rather to visit some relevant 'traditional' beliefs about disability, to understand how they have influenced contemporary ideas. 'Tradition' and 'traditional' are always problematic terms in scholarly discourse, but here I am using them with reference to a set of practices, customs and ideas embedded in the spiritual, cultural and social spheres seen as strongly associated with historical images of Japan. Furthermore, there is a self-consciousness, or an internal gaze, in the creation and maintenance of these 'traditions', as they function most often as 'an attempt at self-definition … in relation to other national and cultural entities' (Bestor *et al*. 2011: 5). Traditions tell foreigners what it means to be Japanese just as much as they instruct the Japanese, especially those who might perceive a degree of discontinuity between the 'past' and current experiences.

Japanese religious stories include representations of disability, which in turn can both 'contribute to or help break down the myths and stereotypes about disability' (Charlton 1998: 65). Broadly speaking, there are two major religious traditions in Japan exerting influence on ideas about disability: Shinto and Buddhism. Shinto is often referred to as an 'indigenous religion' (Inoue 2003: 2), but it is perhaps better described as a set of ritual practices and beliefs that were only codified after the introduction of Buddhism, which first came to Japan via Korea in the sixth century AD (Yoshida 2006: 145). It is important to remember that the borders between the two religions were fairly porous until the Meiji Restoration in 1868, when Shinto was formalized into a more distinct, organized religion that centred on the divine figure of the emperor, 'whose ideology, symbols, and rituals promoted the ancient mythology of Shinto as the origins to the imperial order and the state' (Mullins 2011: 64).

Both religions have made significant and lasting contributions to the Japanese 'worldview', which includes attitudes towards physical and mental wellbeing and disability. Congenital disability is explicitly present in the creation myths of Shinto. The first gendered deities, Izanagi and Izanami, who were technically brother and sister as well as husband and wife, created the Japanese islands (Mori 2003: 30); after they created the land, they also created a number of deities to be 'lord[s] of the universe', giving birth to the high-ranking Sun and Moon goddesses. However, '[n]ext they produced the leech-child, which even at the age of three could not stand upright. They therefore placed it in the rock-camphor boat of Heaven, and abandoned it to the winds' (*Kojiki*, as translated by Tsunoda *et al*. 1958: 14).

The term 'leech child' (the two characters in the child's name, read 'Hiruko', have this meaning) probably alluded to the useless (or absent) limbs that prevented the child from standing upright. This plight results in abandonment; the child disappears, but he later resurfaces in another area of cultural history. A seventeenth-century text purporting to record the mythical origins of the Awaji tradition of ritual bunraku puppetry relates that the long-lost deity one day appeared to a fisherman named Hyakudayū. Confronted by the grown Leech Child, the fisherman was told:

> 'I am the Leech Child of long ago. Until now I have been floating on the waves with no hall where I can be worshiped. Build me a worship hall on the shore near Nishinomiya ...' The worship hall [Hyakudayū] built in honor of the Leech Child came to be known as Nishinomiya Daimyōjin Ebisu Saburō den ... After the priest [who cared for the hall] died, the Leech Child had no one to serve him and so grew restless and angry and caused numerous calamities on land and sea. Hyakudayū ... learned of these disasters ... and made a puppet with the face and bearing of the deceased priest ... and the child deity, satisfied that his faithful servant had returned, ceased making trouble ... This, so the Awaji legend goes, is the origin of deity propitiation rites using puppets. The text concludes with a stern warning concerning the ritual use of puppets; 'Notice: This art is for the appeasement of divine spirits. Do not take it lightly. It will weigh heavily on those who do. Those who come after this should be sorely afraid.'
>
> (Law 1998: 394)

The fierceness of these warnings not to dishonour the grown Leech Child echo the fear that envelops interactions between people with and without disabilities; cross-culturally we have seen how the mainstream may recoil from interaction with disability (as described by Murphy 1987). Meanwhile, the abandonment of the Leech Child results in fear of retribution as well as sincere regret. This notion mirrors the general belief in Japan that *kami* (deities) require enshrinement and that there may be dire earthly consequences if they are not; one cares for the *kami* who auspiciously preside over nature, but one is always mindful of the carelessness or missteps that might cause disaster. It also finds an echo in Jean Vanier's blunt assessment of a contemporary, abled fear of disability: 'the severely disabled challenge us by their existence. They implicitly ask, "Do you consider me human?" They suggest how arduous it is to be human. They remind us of death' (as reported in Rosenblatt 2011).

The abandonment of the Leech Child can be also contextualized as part of a wider social welfare strategy in pre-modern Japan, that of *mabito* (literally, 'thinning', used to refer to infanticide); the reasons for the widespread presence of *jizōsama* stone statues in the landscape, today used to honour children who have died (in accidents, from illness or as stillborn or aborted foetuses), are thought to include the desire to appease the souls of victims of infanticide, including those who were disabled (Endō 1999: 17, 22–3).

On the other hand, not all associations with disability were negative. Hiruko/Leech Child survived his abandonment and evolved into Ebisu, the god of the sea; though now limbed, he is still somewhat physically impaired and deaf. Ebisu is also considered one of the Seven Deities of Happiness, and brings good luck to those who honour him. In some ancient texts his name was recorded using the former characters for 'leech', with the meaning 'unable to stand' (Kida cited in Tada 1988: 43), reprising the ancient Shinto myth. Today Ebisu is written with characters meaning 'blessing' and 'longevity', and he is portrayed as a deity who is cheerful and pleasant, also not unlike idealistic characterizations of people with intellectual disabilities, who are often described as charmingly innocent and childlike.

Japanese Buddhism is more straightforward in its association of disability with negative karma; for example, the birth of a child with a disability was taken as a statement about the morality of the parents (Nakamura 2006: 34). The Buddhist term *in-nen* (frequently translated merely as fate, destiny or karma) encapsulates the notion that current events are related, directly or indirectly, to rightful or wrong actions of individuals or their ancestors (Kato 2010: 132). In Japan congenital or childhood disability has readily been assumed to be a kind of curse or punishment (*tatari*) traceable to a family's *in-nen*, but sometimes the same perspective can be applied to interpret the birth of such a baby (positively) as a lightning-rod for others in the family, a 'blessing ... *to erase all the bad fortune in our family lines*' (ibid.; italics in original).

Disability was also approached more pragmatically from early times, by applying appraisals of its severity and effect on functioning. Legal documents published in Japan in AD 701 categorized disability based on a perceived level of impairment which related disability directly to the individual's capacity for labour (Itō cited in Nakamura 2006: 35). This is not unlike welfare criteria today, which rank impairment based on the ability to perform daily tasks, the potential for independent living as well as economic labour. Kato does not see these religious concepts as affecting only the pious, however; rather, they are a part of 'daily vocabulary', embedded in 'ordinary' people's understandings of health and medical risks along with basic knowledge about genetics (2010: 134).

It is no surprise, then, to see fears and anxieties about potential and current disability in religious practices (shared between Shinto and Buddhist practices) known as *riyake*, a term that means both 'benefit', in material terms, and 'grace', as bestowed on an individual by a deity. *Riyake* refers to 'benefits acquired through warding negative forces to avoid bad luck – and benefits that are directly beckoned through actions designed to induce good fortune' (Reader and Tanabe 1998: 46). Some of the actions undertaken to attract good fortune – aside from 'right' or moral actions in general – include *kigan* ('praying' at shrines and temples for desired outcomes), the making of contributions to said places of worship (especially those built in honour of deities associated with the target of the prayer), and the buying of amulets, or *o-mamori*, which are meant to 'protect' the owner from bad luck and serve as physical reminders of the act of asking for divine favour for a particular event or aspect of one's life.

Reader and Tanabe list five categories of wishes commonly made to the deities in this way: 'prosperity', 'male/female relations', 'childbirth and childrearing', 'prevention of accidents and misfortune', and 'recovery or healing from illness' (1998: 47).[1] These last three categories are all relevant to discussions of disability, but here I will focus on 'childbirth and childrearing'. One of the *o-mamori* most frequently displayed for sale is the *anzan* amulet; *anzan* is translated as 'easy' or 'safe delivery', but I suggest that this includes the idea of a 'safe delivery of a *healthy* child'. While very many shrines and temples offer these amulets, Nakayama-dera in Takarazuka, near Kobe, specializes in *anzan* amulets (Reader and Tanabe 1998: 52) and special maternity belts (*fukutai*) frequently used during pregnancy to support the back and for protection of the baby and mother (Daihonzan Nakayamadera 2011).

In some ways, separating 'sacred' beliefs from the 'profane' social sphere creates an artificial boundary, for the lines between the two in Japanese society and culture have been porous and interactive over time. Traditionally, disability was seen as both an individual and a familial attribute, through individuals' membership in the *ie* (the extended family or stem family unit), a significant context for community interaction. Historically, the *ie* was not only a social unit but also an economic unit. Individuals' livelihoods were often determined by their family's mode of production; in fact, this social status and identity as conflated with economic production was encoded as law in the hierarchical *shinōkōshō* system (literally, the samurai/farmer/artisan/merchant system, also referred to in English as the 'four-class system' [Hall 1983: 178]) from the 1600s on. Legally, the individual had no status; rather, the *ie* to which the individual belonged (which was regulated by the four-class system) was the recognized social unit in the community, and that unit was supported by the contributions of its members in spiritual, social and economic cooperative activities. Depending on the level of impairment and the occupation of the household, people with disabilities could make contributions to their *ie*; in other situations, one could enter a suitable profession. The category of disability experienced had an impact on the way wider society viewed the individual and his/her ability to participate in the public sphere and gain social status. For example, blind people were encouraged to enter professions related to the arts and medicine (in particular, chanting and playing the *biwa*, a four- or five-stringed lute); they were also composers, masseurs, and practitioners of acupuncture and moxibustion (Ogawa 1999: 16; see also de Ferranti's [2009] study of blind *biwa* performers). *Goze* (blind female musicians) organized themselves in troupes, playing the shamisen and *zō* (Japanese zither) 'door-to-door' (ibid.). The recognition of the blind musicians' group as a professional guild further solidified their social and economic position (Nakamura 2006: 36). Schools such as the one established by Sugiyama Waichi (1610–94), sponsored by the fifth shogun, Tokugawa Tsunayoshi, trained blind people as acupuncturists licensed by the *bakufu*, or military government (Ogawa 1999: 16).

One might expect that Japan's view and treatment of people with disabilities would 'improve' over time, as in any developed society following a modernist trajectory away from a 'backward' way of thinking and less and less influenced by superstitions. Despite the secularization of Japanese society, we see a certain level of continuity in beliefs over time; Kato concludes that the concepts of 'religion' and 'common sense' were indistinguishable to her informants (2010: 134). Here are two contemporary examples of how disability identity is both shunned (like the 'leech child') and embraced (as Ebisu, the grown child transformed into the god of fortune), recalling these ideological arguments. After the 11 March 2011 Tohoku earthquake and tsunami, a group of children with severe intellectual disabilities living in an institution called Tōyō Gakuin, located five kilometres from the Fukushima nuclear power plant, were evacuated with the rest of the local community, but were not able to settle into one camp after they found the centre could not cope with their special needs. The director of the institution's children's unit told reporters that because of the sudden change in environment and stress of the events, the children 'just could not be accommodated with regular people' (*ippan no hito to issho no hinanjo wa muri*); they were moved three times in two and a half weeks, still looking for a safe place where the children could stay and adjust (Saitō 2011). While every evacuee was certainly facing hardship, the fact that a group of vulnerable children was moving through a danger zone from site to site looking for a place that would accept them shows how people with disabilities still struggle to be accommodated in general society.

On the other hand, in the same year it was reported by *Asahi Shimbun* that a ten-year-old boy with Down Syndrome had successfully auditioned for a role in an upcoming drama on commercial television. The article stated that he was associated with 'K-Planning', a talent agency in Tokyo which had a special talent section for children with intellectual disabilities called 'Kodomo SP Kurasu' (Children's Sp[ecial] Class). This talent agency advertises the SP Class as the 'first in Japan', with the banner 'Disabled roles will be played realistically by disabled actors' (*shōgaishayaku wa shōgaisha ga riaru ni enjimasu*) (K-Planning 2011), recalling criticism often aimed at stage, television and film producers who hire abled actors to play people with intellectual and/or physical disabilities.[2]

Sometimes shunned, yet at times made 'special', people with disabilities in Japan occupy a liminal position in society, as described by Goffman, who in his essay on stigma includes people with disabilities among those who are 'discredited' – referring to a discrepancy or shortcoming the individual presents when their disability constitutes a gap, or a failing, in social expectations (1997: 204). The more serious the discrepancy, the more stigmatized an individual is. One option open to the stigmatized person is to 'attempt to correct his [*sic*] condition indirectly by devoting ... private effort to the mastery of ... activity ordinarily felt to be closed' to him or her (208); this in turn inspires others to see stigmatized people as 'extraordinary' and 'special'. Inverting the idea that disability is a negative impairment, normate people may see people with disabilities as 'courageous or noble', but this reversal rests on the foundational idea that '[g]iven the intrinsic abnormality or awfulness of disability, anyone living a "normal" or ordinary life must be extraordinary' (Charlton 1998: 51–2). There are also contradictions in the notion of a disability identity as a discrete category; while some lingering beliefs about 'fault' or 'bad karma' may persist, owing to the rapidly ageing society Japanese people also increasingly believe that disability is *not* an individual shortcoming but 'a fact of life, [because] ... no one is free from the possibility of becoming disabled' (Iwakuma 2003: 124). Truly, disability as a marginalizing attribute is an 'equal opportunity employer' in any society.

The contemporary demographics of disability in Japan

Disability as experienced and thought about in Japan today is often first outlined in demographic terms. It is broken down into kinds of disability, as well as age brackets (which automatically separates aged disability from congenital or acquired disability). The reason this occurs is interesting because it says something about the way governments (and other public bodies) view disability: that it is a different thing for people of different ages, and in different situations, yet it is often communicated in collective and aggregated ways.

Table 2.1 presents numbers of registered users of disability programmes in Japan, calculated from the numbers of official *shōgaisha techō* (disability handbooks) issued. Individuals receive a handbook according to their categorization via a national system (*shōgai teido bungu*, or classification of disability levels) into one of three types: 'physical' (which has four 'subtypes'); 'mental' (intellectual); and 'psychological' (Suzuki 2009: 228). This is somewhat misleading, however, because in many cases, disability crosses these categories, making the classification a subjective, bureaucratic decision. Technically there are three kinds of 'handbooks': the first is the physical disability handbook (*shintai shōgaisha techō*); the second, a lengthy 'psychiatric disability public health and welfare handbook' (*seishin shōgaisha hoken fukushi techō*), caters to those assigned to the latter two categories. Both of these are legal documents, as stipulated by

Table 2.1 A snapshot (by age and residence) of the Japanese population with a disability, 1999–2006

	Total number	Number living at home	Number institutionalized
Physical disabilities	3,516,000 ⇓ 3,663,000	3,327,000 ⇓ 3,576,000	189,000 ⇓ 87,000
under 18	90,000 ⇓ 98,000	82,000 ⇓ 93,000	8,000 ⇓ 5,000
over 18	3,426,000 ⇓ 3,663,000	3,245,000 ⇓ 3,483,000	181,000 ⇓ 81,000
Intellectual disabilities	459,000 ⇓ 547,000	329,000 ⇓ 419,000	130,000 ⇓ 128,000
under 18	103,000 ⇓ 125,000	94,000 ⇓ 117,000	9,000 ⇓ 8,000
over 18	342,000 ⇓ 410,000	221,000 ⇓ 290,000	121,000 ⇓ 120,000
age unknown	14,000 ⇓ 12,000	14,000 ⇓ 12,000	–
Psychiatric disabilities	2,584,000 ⇓ 3,028,000	2,239,000 ⇓ 2,675,000	345,000 ⇓ 353,000
under 18 under 20[a]	142,000 ⇓ 164,000	139,000 ⇓ 161,000	3,000 ⇓ 3,000
over 18 over 20	2,436,000 ⇓ 2,858,000	2,095,000 ⇓ 2,508,000	341,000 ⇓ 350,000
age unknown	6,000 ⇓ 6,000	5,000 ⇓ 5,000	1,000 ⇓ 1,000

Notes: to show trends over time, two sets of figures are given in each category.

For 'Physical disabilities' and 'Intellectual disabilities', the first figure is data averaged between 1999 and 2001 (Naikakufu 2003). For 'Psychiatric disabilities', the first figure is data from the 2006 Naikakufu report. The second set of figures (Naikakufu 2009) contains data from 2005 and 2006.

a The later surveys used a different cut-off date for determining the age of minors, so some of this increase can be attributed to this change.

welfare laws (see Chapter 4). People diagnosed solely with intellectual disabilities (that is, not in combination with a physical disability) are issued with a third document, called the *ryōiku techō*, which literally means 'rehabilitation handbook'. This document is part of a system that was established based on local (prefectural) educational administration guidelines.

Physical disabilities are relatively straightforward in their categorization: 'motor dysfunction (limb and body)', 'visual disability', 'hearing and speech disability' and 'internal organ disorder' (which could include cardiac, renal, respiratory, bladder, rectal or intestinal disorders). Meanwhile, each of these categories has several grades of severity – as many as seven for some (Okuno 1998). Holding the physical disability handbook is also a 'pass key' for people with disability to access purpose-built facilities in public places and can be a threshold requirement for accessing other in-home services (Stevens 1997: 59).

On the other hand, intellectual disability in Japan has no legal definition. Nishida Kazuhiro, Professor of Social Welfare Law, writes that

> There is no clear definition of intellectual disability in the Law for the Welfare of People with Intellectual Disability. The reason why there is no definition in the welfare law is because there is no unified and established method or standard by which we [in Japan] judge intellectual disability. Until now, cases have been handled without an established definition. [The drawback to putting] such a definition in place, is that it will cover a different range of the population, [and] consequently might disadvantage others concerned. Even considering this, there has been a move to create a definition of a person with intellectual disability, even in the case of enactment of the Supports and Services for People with Disabilities Act. So, what standard is used for Japan? Usually, it is the 1992 AAMR definition. It uses [the definition of] mental retardation as a combination of any of these three components: (1) mental functioning below IQ 70 to 75; (2) a disability of 'adaptive behaviour'; and (3) onset of intellectual delay before the age of 18 ... [Yet without a legal definition], and even in genuine cases of intellectual disability, there are many people who are not able to receive appropriate welfare services because the person might not have acquired a rehabilitation handbook, or because the presence of the disability is unnoticed (because of its [mild] degree).
>
> (2011a)

Nishida believes that the lack of a legal definition means that screening processes are subjective and inconsistent. The inadequacy of the screening process for intellectual disability is demonstrated by the high percentage of prisoners diagnosed with intellectual disability:

> Today, it is said that nearly 30 per cent of people imprisoned in Japan have an intellectual disability ... this is a problem, but it is not [widely] regarded

as a problem [because] people with intellectual disabilities are said to be more likely to commit crimes [anyway].

[We use this category,] a 'person with an intellectual disability', yet we don't really consider what that means – if we don't know what it is, how can we judge it? Young people become adults and commit crimes without knowing they have an intellectual disability ... If they had been granted proper welfare services early on, we could say that they wouldn't have committed these crimes, and the rate of re-offence would go down as well.

The Japanese welfare policy for people with disabilities is wholly centred on the development of welfare for people with physical disabilities, and so it is really insufficient in the area of intellectual and psychiatric disabilities.

(ibid.)

The large numbers of people with physical disabilities in Japan and the attendant welfare structure that supports their needs arguably creates a somewhat skewed view of what disability means, and what policy priorities should be. For example, the current vital statistics posted on the government website divide information based on disability (physical versus intellectual); this is a logical arrangement, but while there are seventy-two files of statistical information on people with various physical disabilities from all age groups in Japan (see e-Stat 2007), there are only four files of information on people with intellectual disabilities, and the files have not been updated as recently as those for people with physical disabilities (e-Stat 2001). This demonstrates that the government is making much more finely grained studies of physical disability while restricting its consideration of issues concerning people with intellectual disabilities. The reason for this is unclear, but I would infer that it has to do with funnelling resources into majority causes (there are simply more people with physical disabilities than those with intellectual disabilities in Japan, although numbers of people with psychiatric disabilities are much higher) and with lingering prejudices about people with intellectual disabilities being unproductive members of society, and therefore not meriting much public concern (or funds) for their rehabilitation.

Facilities for people with disabilities include residential care, day care and a variety of educational institutions. As the Cabinet Office reports, a significant number of people with disabilities live in institutions, either full time or part time; others use the facilities on an outpatient basis. In 2009, the Ministry of Health, Labour and Welfare conducted a nationwide survey of public institutions that cater to people with disabilities, giving an idea of the scope of this project: there were 9,459 facilities for the care of the elderly; 3,673 for people with disabilities in general; a combined figure of 1,137 facilities for people with physical disabilities;[3] 2,738 for people with intellectual disabilities; and 673 for people with psychiatric disabilities (MHLW 2009b). With regard to education, the numbers of educational institutions are split between those wholly devoted to special education (995 schools) and special classes in a further 30,921 local schools (National Institute of Special Education 2004).

The public face of disability in Japanese society is also on display in public events and holidays that have been instituted in the Japanese calendar, partly as a result of international influences. The 1964 Paralympic Games, which followed the Tokyo Olympics, helped to raise awareness about disability and ability in Japan in the 1970s; this was followed by the UN International Year of Disabled Persons in 1981, the International Decade of Disabled Persons (1983–93) and the United Nations Declaration on the Rights of Disabled Persons in 1995 (Sakamoto 2006: n.p.). Japan currently observes two calendar days related to raising the awareness of disability: it recognizes the United Nations International Day of Disabled Persons on 3 December (established 1982, following the International Year of Disabled Persons) as *shōgaisha dē* ('persons with a disability day') and the Ministry of Health, Labour and Welfare has further designated 9 December as *shōgaisha no hi* (which has the same meaning as the name for the 3 December, but uses the Japanese word for 'day').

The statistics and the awareness campaigns given above do offer some idea of the demographics of disability in contemporary Japan, but these figures are limited in communicating the detailed situation. For example, they do not include people with learning disabilities, or debilitating illnesses such as HIV/AIDS, chronic alcoholism, epilepsy or rheumatism. This relatively exclusive approach to defining disability means that Japan declares a lower rate of disability in the general population than more inclusive countries such as Germany, the USA or Sweden (Heyer 1999: 7). Citing data for 2000, Iwakuma notes that while the United States records approximately 20 per cent of its population as having a disability, Japanese society only records 4.8 per cent. She notes that the definitional basis for the calculation is 'quite similar' in the two countries, and observes that '[t]his large discrepancy in numbers indicates that "disability" is not a discrete, objective category. Rather, disability is an interpretative status based on social convention' (2003: 126).

Therefore, while statistics give us a general picture of what the state of disability in Japan may be quantitatively, social attitudes too must be examined for the role they play in shaping the data. Why would a person with a disability not disclose his or her status? Social conventions, as Iwakuma writes, are important. According to a 2010 survey conducted by the Cabinet Office, 68 per cent of people with disabilities say they have experienced discrimination, with 11.4 per cent saying this experience is constant and a further 50.9 per cent that they feel discriminated against 'sometimes'. In other words, people with disabilities feel significantly that their experience is different from that of the normate population. Even more interesting were the results of a separate internet-based survey conducted earlier in 2009; when the general public were questioned, 91.5 per cent felt people with disabilities were discriminated against (Kyodo News 2010). In other words, the vast majority of people without disabilities feel that individuals who have a disability are treated like second-class citizens. Arguably, this perception plays a major role in many individual decisions not to disclose disability in contemporary Japanese society.

Disability activism in Japan

> What unites disabled people within the movement is that not only do we think our lives could be better, we know they should be.
>
> (Oliver 1996: 162)

Around the world, disability activism has followed other social movements such as those supporting people oppressed on grounds of age, race and sex or gender (Marks 1999: 2). Jaeger and Bowman write that 'individuals with disabilities have faced particularly harsh treatment throughout history, and have gone unacknowledged for a longer period of time than most other disenfranchised groups' (2005: 25). Disability activists are relatively new to the global activism scene, following the civil rights movement and women's liberation in the USA; in Japan, ethnic-based minority groups such as the Burakumin Liberation League preceded the start of the disability movement as well. Activism is deemed an integral part of the disability identity, as attested in James Charlton's critique of the anthropologist Robert Murphy's widely acclaimed book, *The Body Silent*:

> Murphy's orientation is markedly different because of his lack of involvement with the [disability rights movement]. His isolation is evident in a defeatism that senses disability as a unidirectional assault on identity and a necessary dislocation or separation from family and community [...] On a personal level Murphy misses what is (potentially) gained from disability in terms of identity, insight, and comradeship.
>
> (1998: 57)

So important is activism to Charlton that he believes Murphy might have written an entirely different book if he had been a part of the disability rights movement. Activism creates and sustains these communities, much like those of feminists and ethnic minority groups, and has the capacity to change the way the individual views his or her identity.

If this activist community is so important, why has disability rights lagged behind race, ethnicity and gender rights, not just in Japan but also around the world? Lennard Davis, in his book *Bending over Backwards: Disability, Dismodernism and Other Difficult Positions*, explains why 'ableism' (2002: 65) is not considered on the same level as racism or sexism; it is because 'the public paternalistically imagines that people with disabilities are usually treated with kindness. This rationalization is then used to invoke happenstance to explain practices that harm people with disabilities' (155). Put bluntly, the mainstream wants to believe that abled people are 'nice' to people with disabilities, so when bad things happen, it is an *accident* or a *mistake* rather than a *premeditated action* or a *result of* 'ableism' (discrimination against people with disabilities). To expose this fallacy, people with disabilities – as well as those without – have taken public action to highlight the inequities that they face in an 'ableist' society.

The idea of a 'social claim' as instigator for, or a result of, a movement is an interesting way to frame the social and political phenomenon of activism. Irwin discusses 'social claims' with respect to welfare and employment (2001: 20), noting the difference between privileges (or rights or status) that are 'naturally rewarded' and those that have to be 'claimed' (ibid). Claiming is a political action (22), and the disability rights activists' claims tended to follow chronologically claims made by people of colour and women in Western societies (23). Claiming as a social and political process shows us the historical trajectory of human rights, or 'the differential ability of groups, at different historical junctures, to press claims more or less effectively' (24).

Disability rights activism is marginal to mainstream politics because it critiques the status quo; it asks for a reorganization of society based on its values; and it is not limited to a single national context (Oliver 1996: 157). Oliver observes that social movements can be distinguished by their priorities for change: in early movements, economic outcomes were privileged (e.g. 'resource allocation'), while in more recent movements, a change of the 'values on which such allocations are based' or change to 'post materialist' values is sought (158–9). The disability movement is one based on the latter priority, of changing values rather than access to resources. Post-materialist movements tend to 'emphasise relative needs and particularistic interests' rather than 'universal needs' (Hewitt cited in Oliver 1996: 159), and in relation to this Oliver notes that 'particularistic social movements cannot rely on universalistic political processes', giving the example of failures of the disability movement when it linked to 'broad left politics' (ibid). Shakespeare recognizes certain affinities between activism in protest against 'ableism' (or 'disabilism', as he refers to it) and against sexism or racism, but warns that we should not be quick to conflate these social problems:

> There are parallels between the theorisation of disability, and the theorisation of race, gender and sexuality, as the many citations of other oppressions within disability studies literature demonstrate. Yet the oppression which disabled people face is different from, and in many ways more complex than, sexism, racism and homophobia.
> (Shakespeare 2006: 41)

In other words, he suggests that if there were no social oppression regarding the colour of one's skin, gender or sexuality, these '-isms' would cease to exist, but even if there were no oppression regarding disability, hardship arising from impairment would not disappear. Therefore, Shakespeare sees the strong affinity between social movements to be dangerous and clouding the real issues at the heart of disability: '[t]here is no symmetry. These examples imply something important about the difference between disabled people and non-disabled people. Disabled people have less flexibility and fewer choices than non-disabled people' (51), no matter their colour, gender or sexuality.

The international community has played a role in providing direction for the Japanese disability movement. British activists created and engaged with the social model (which focuses not on individual impairments but on the social and physical environment which is not made for people with disabilities), and American activists, amongst others, were distinctive in not just looking at oppression from an economic and structural point of view, but also prioritizing the psychological 'exclusion' that arises from disability (Marks 1999: 5). Given these specific issues of 'ableism', social and political action has been seen as the first step in making change in Japan. While there are common issues in these movements, the Japanese movement is of course distinct in that it is operating in a social, cultural and historical context which includes a lingering attachment to religious beliefs pertaining to disability, and a particular set of demographics in a rapidly ageing society, as detailed above. This section looks at some of the disability movements in the context of these issues, focusing on how (and why) the movement attempts to implement social change.

Marginality, activism and passing

Japanese disability activists, much like those working for ethnic or gender equality, are protesting against the marginal status they experience in mainstream society. James Valentine, writing specifically about social marginality in Japan, suggests a number of categories that constitute marginality, the most common being 'foreign blood', 'foreign contact', 'pollution through illness/damage', and 'deviance: criminal and/or ideological' (1990: 40–1). People with 'mental illnesses', disabilities and chronic illnesses necessitating care such as HIV/AIDS are grouped under the third category, 'pollution through illness/damage' (41). Valentine then proposes that marginalized people in Japan have found three ways of 'coping' with their marginal status: 'passing', 'support groups' and 'compartmentalization' (44–7). The first two strategies are of relevance to a discussion of activism. Passing means to forgo a marginal identity to live publicly as a mainstream individual; this, of course, is only possible when the marginality can be made invisible (Valentine uses the example of resident Koreans who are visually and linguistically indistinguishable from ethnic Japanese). This can come, however, at a 'high psychological price' (44) for those who feel the price is too high. Meanwhile, those who wish to identify publicly can join groups that provide mutual support and the 'feeling of belonging' that is lacking in other parts of their lives (45).

While such groups provide various kinds of mutual support, in many cases these collectives also provide a setting where activism can take root. Valentine's discussion of 'coping strategies' focuses on one important step in the process of moving towards activism: simply, the motivation of individuals to make the decision to participate. After the decision is made, the individual crosses a line from living a social role where disability can be relegated to secondary or almost invisible status, to one where disability becomes a more primary identifier, and is publicly projected – even as far as to become the person's *raison d'être*. This transformation usually involves a turning point when personal subjectivity ('I'm working through *my* experience or view of disability') turns into critical consciousness ('I'm working to change society's view of disability'). Panitch defines this as an ability to 'stand apart from [one's] own personal everyday experience ... recogniz[ing] the need to take these concerns to the public arena' (2008: 73). Panitch's informants felt that the transforming 'moment' was instigated by an experience of discrimination (85). The subjective dialectic between an internally focused concern and an externally projected conviction for them resulted in a call to service. For some, however, the call does not come, and instead the concerned person works and lives 'within the system'. For others, stigma associated with both the identity attribute (disability here, but also valid in other activist contexts such as lesbian identity, black identity and so on) as well as the social mode (activist as 'troublemaker') means that some choose to fly below the radar, 'passing' as normate members of society.

Passing is also described in Titchkosky's semi-autobiographical book on living with disability, which includes a section entitled 'Mapping normalcy: a social topography of passing' (2003), and claims that people with disabilities attempt to 'pass' owing to a 'spoiled identity' (Goffman cited in Titchkosky 2003: 70). She believes passing is not 'faking' or 'copying', but involves a *'deviant individual's* techniques which he or she employs in order to negotiate a stance in the land of normalcy ... Passing is a way to work with cultural knowledge while achieving normalcy or competency' (70–1, emphasis in the original). She speaks of her partner's 'passing project', to which she is a contributor, which includes both 'privilege' (of knowledge) and 'anxiety' (of exposure) (71). This further definition of passing is helpful because it creates a foil by which we can understand its opposite, and all the grey area in between. Instead of using *passing* as a way to work *with* cultural knowledge, *activism* is a way to work *against* cultural knowledge with the aim of achieving normalcy or competency. Passing, however, is not always an option for everyone. Some consider it is only possible for those with non-visible conditions, noting that the difference between visible and non-visible impairments is that with the latter the person with the disability has control over its 'known-about-ness' (Marks 1999: 120–1).

In the case of Japan, passing is a frequently chosen strategy for a variety of socially marginalized people. Taking control over cultural knowledge about the individual is seen by Valentine as a way to reclaim mainstream status, but the costs include 'doubts about one's own identity, ... continually hiding and having anxieties of discovery, and ... having to distance oneself from, and perhaps be shunned by, those who proudly proclaim their [alternate] ... identity' (1990: 40). Valentine argues that support groups are particularly important: 'If marginals do not form or join support groups, this may mean that they remain or become all the more marginal not only because they continue to defy insider-outsider status, but because they defy the common Japanese perspective which views people as existing in groups or networks'(1990: 45). In other words, a marginal person who does not join a support group, but does not pass either, is thus marginalized as well for his/her 'un-belongingness', or anti-sociality. Identity is a personal attribute that must be shared to be recognized and effective in affirming the self.

Prominent movements in Japan

Japanese disability movements, as influenced by groups in other countries, focus on 'rights, equal access and disability pride' (Heyer 1999: 16). I have written elsewhere about the processes of political and social activism in my research on volunteers in low-income neighbourhoods, and argued that certain kinds of volunteering (which is a form of activism) were a response to social marginality, both of self and of other (Stevens 1997: 234–7). Activism in Japan has also been defined in causes other than the disability movement as a 'mobilization to defend everyday life' from encroaching forces such as private industry and government influence (Takabatake cited in Avenell 2006: 90).

The disability rights movement in Japan began in the 1960s, roughly contemporaneous with *ūman ribu*, or the 'women's lib' movement (Hayashi and Okuhira 2001: 859). Early disability rights activists were parents rather than people with disabilities themselves (857). Human rights as a universal expression of respect and dignity formed much of the discourse around their activities, which mostly addressed demands for improved residential and medical care for children with disabilities in institutions, and for an end to the physical and mental abuse they experienced there (857–8). For example, one of the forms of abuse was the sterilization of disabled females, undertaken under the guise of unburdening the patient (and the staff) of menstruation (857); this was linked to the specific clauses in the Yūsei Hogo Hō (The Eugenic Protection Law; replaced by the amended and renamed Botai Hogo Hō [Law for the Protection of the Maternal Body] in 1996) which limited the reproductive capacity of people with disabilities. The early movement experienced conflict as it gained momentum, centring on the role of abled people (which would include parents), the question of welfare reliance, and gender-based discrimination within the group (862).

Probably the first and largest postwar group was the Nihon Shōgaisha Rihabiritēshon Kyōkai (Japanese Society for the Rehabilitation of People with Disabilities, or JSRPD), which was established by a group of World War II veterans with disabilities in 1964 (Heyer 1999: 5; JSRPD 2004). They were not seen as path-breakers, however; that role was reserved for other groups which broke with social convention about what many thought it meant to be a person with a disability in Japanese society, namely, passive about expressing their disability identity and needs and compliant with wider social norms.[4] Rather, Aoi Shiba no Kai (literally, 'the Association of Green Grass'), a group of people with cerebral palsy, was seen as the significant break with this kind of patronage mindset. Formed in 1970, Aoi Shiba no Kai is thought to have 'inspired the birth of disability studies in Japan' (Nagase 2008); in its first year of existence the group stated its political and social 'platform' in what were radical terms for the time:

- *We identify ourselves as people with Cerebral Palsy (CP).*
  We recognize our position as 'an existence which should not exist' in the modern society. We believe that this recognition should be the starting point of our whole movement, and we act on this belief.

- *We assert ourselves aggressively.*
  When we identify ourselves as people with CP, we have [the] will to protect ourselves. We believe that a strong self-assertion is the only way to achieve self-protection, and we act on this belief.
- *We deny love and justice.*
  We condemn egoism held by love and justice. We believe that mutual understanding, accompanying the human observation that arises from the denial of love and justice, means true well-being, and we act on this belief.
- *We do not choose the way of problem solving.*
  We have learned from our personal experiences that easy solutions to problems lead to dangerous compromises. We believe that an endless confrontation is the only course of action possible for us, and we act on this belief.

(translated by Nagase 2008)

There were several notable activist beliefs embedded in this declaration. First was the explicit criticism of mainstream society in the first and fourth items: that disability creates an incompatible physical and social status ('an existence which should not exist'), suggesting that without intervention and assistance, people with disabilities would not be accepted in mainstream society; furthermore, this assistance often leads to 'dangerous compromises', implying that trust in social intervention is misplaced. Another departure from social norms at that time was the adoption by people with disabilities of an 'aggressive' stance, one that disparaged claims of 'love and justice'. This counteracts the idea, held not only by Japanese, that people with disabilities are social entities deserving the pity, sympathy and compassion of others, recalling Kasnitz and Shuttleworth's statement that a disability is only handicapping 'dependent on management of societal discrimination and internalized oppression, particularly infantilization and paternalism' (2001: 20), and Charlton's observation that 'attitudes about disability ... are, with few exceptions, pejorative. They are paternalistic and often ... hypocritical' (1998: 51). Paternalism is rejected by these activists, for reasons explained well by Charlton: 'Paternalism lies at the center of the oppression of people with disabilities. Paternalism starts with the notion of superiority: We must and can take control of these "subjects" in spite of themselves, in spite of their individual will ...' (1998: 52–3).

I use Charlton's quote because of the felicity of his choice of words – 'in spite of their individual will' is echoed in the proclamation of Aoi Shiba no Kai who said (in Nagase's translation), 'When we identify ourselves as people with CP, we have ... [the] *will* to protect ourselves.' Lastly, the repeating refrain 'and we act on this belief' underscores this will and the active role that the group members intend to play in wider society; they are not satisfied to sit back and let their 'fate' be played out according to external values and decision-making processes. We can say that this subjective transformation is aimed at some of the social and cultural values listed in the first section of this chapter; no longer will the person with a disability in Japan be seen as hostage to fate ('we assert ourselves aggressively') or jovial and agreeable like Ebisu ('we deny love ... we believe [in] endless confrontation'). The radicalism of this stance was not always well received; activists were 'considered "ungrateful" and "extremist" by the greater society' (Hayashi and Okuhira 2008: 417). One of their activist goals was to promote independent living, which in turn generated another kind of movement, as detailed below.

The 1981 United Nations International Year of Disabled Persons may not have had a significant influence on Japanese legislation, but it did have a meaningful impact on the disability movement itself, generating 'a new kind of activism that looks to disability movements in the United States as examples of defiant disability pride' (Heyer 1999: 1). Ishikawa writes that people with disabilities became increasingly aware of their human rights following the initiatives taken by the Aoi Shiba no Kai in the 1970s, and other disability movements developed thereafter, with the launch of the Independent Living Movement in the 1980s and the strengthening of the Deaf Culture Movement in the 1990s. These groups later focused on change in the areas of accessibility in transport, architecture and information as well as on anti-discrimination legislation (Ishikawa 2004).[5] Common cause has been one of the more powerful instigators in their formation, in contrast with the tendency among many postwar groups to focus on a single disability category, such as the Japanese Federation for the Deaf (Nihon Rōa Renmei), the Japanese Federation for the Blind (Nihon Mōjinkai Rengō) and the Japanese Federation of Organizations of [Physically] Disabled Persons (Nihon Shintai Shōgaisha Dantai Rengōkai, or Nisshinren) (Nakamura 2009: 85). DPI-Japan (the acronym for the Japan National Assembly of Disabled People's International, founded in 1986 under the auspices of the international organization Disabled People's International) is an umbrella organization of institutional members that works to coordinate some of these activities; it is a cross-disability group 'including [people with] physical, intellectual and psychiatric disabilities as well as chronic illness. All membership organizations work actively to realize [a] normalized society where persons with disabilities enjoy community living on an equal basis with other citizens' (DPI-Japan 2008).

Another prominent postwar activist group is the 'National Federation of Families with Mentally Ill People' (Zenkoku Seishin Shōgaisha Kazokukai Rengōkai, or Zenkaren) (Heyer 1999: 16). Part of their power and clout in the political arena has rested on large memberships of 'singular disability' members, but over time 'cross-disability' groups rose in prominence as they proved to be more effective (Nakamura 2009: 87).[6] We might say that the Independent Living Movement was one such group, because it appealed to people with a variety of physical as well as other kinds of disabilities who wanted to live in the community rather than in institutions or group homes. It also called for strengthening the agency of people with disabilities, allowing them to have more say in how their living situation was managed. In other words, '[t]he notion of independent living ... represents the shift from the medical model, which places decisions about care and welfare provisions in the hands of rehabilitation specialists ... to what [is] termed the "independent living model" which places control back in the hands of the consumer' (Heyer 1999: 16).

While independent living had been an aspect of disability activist work since the early days, after the 1980s this shifted from 'protest-oriented' work to more 'business'-like services; the Japan Council of Independent Living Centres (JIL), with international connections to counterpart organizations, was launched in 1991 (Hayashi and Okuhira 2008: 418). The US model of independent living centres (ILC) as places to coordinate and support individuals living outside custodial or institutional care began taking root in the early 1980s in Japan (417) with the first ILC founded in the Tokyo suburb of Hachiōji in 1986 (Zenkoku Jiritsu Seikatsu Sentā Kyōgikai n.d.a). The support provided by these centres includes 'personal assistant referral', 'peer counselling', 'housing services' and 'independent living skills training'; there are about 125 such centres in Japan, primarily concentrated in the two urban areas of Tokyo and Osaka, and scattered more thinly between Hokkaido (where there are four) and Okinawa (with two) (ibid).

While much of Japan's disability movement's history portrays it as following international leads (such as the American or Scandinavian trends), one important development is that today Japan plays a more active role in the region's disability movement; activists from the above-mentioned Japanese branch serve in the international organization the DPI (Disabled People's International), which was founded in Singapore in 1981 and has about 130 national members (Priestly 2001: 6). Currently headquartered in Canada, its members are grouped into five regions (Africa, Asia Pacific, Latin America, Europe, and North America and the Caribbean); in 2010 a Japanese representative led the Asia Pacific region in its Executive and World Councils (DPI 2010). The JSRPD has an international training unit (Hayashi and Okuhira 2008: 417), funded by the Japanese corporation Duskin, which brings people with disabilities from around the Asian region to Japan for an annual ten-month training course. One could argue that this programme promotes Japanese disability movement values around the Asia Pacific with some success; when I visited an ILC in Taipei in 2009 with my colleague Karen Nakamura, we met two young female ILC members there who spoke in excellent Japanese and favourably about their year spent in Japan. While Japanese disability activists are understandably critical of their position in wider Japanese society, at the same time people from other countries in the region look to Japan as an Asian model for progress in their own societies.

Conflict and resolution

Avenell, writing about other kinds of groups in Japan, observes that there are several 'myths' about activists, which include that 'they are democratic, they are against the state, they are cosmopolitan, and they are progressive' (2008: 715). While it is to be expected that activists would come into conflict with aspects of the wider society against which they are protesting, conflict within the groups also often constitutes a significant obstacle to the achievement of their goals. I certainly found this to be true in the social activist groups I studied in Yokohama in the 1990s; in particular, disagreements about decision-making processes based on class identity plagued the groups and their capacity for social change

(Stevens 1997: 206–28). The disability movement too has experienced such difficulties; disagreements over disability and gender identification are frequently observed. Conflict can also occur based on differing individual interpretations of the group's manifesto, as occurred with the potentially provocative declaration by Aoi Shiba no Kai that 'We deny love and justice' (cited above).

People with different kinds of disabilities have different experiences of their impairment, leading to different interpretations of how disability identity is formed and should be addressed; women have not always seen eye to eye with their male counterparts who tend to dominate the groups. For example, Kwok, Chan and Chan's study of self-help organizations across the Asia Pacific region found that in Japan, most of their survey respondents were men with physical disabilities (2002: 93), implying that the voices of women with disabilities are not as prominent in this particular area of social activism in Japan.[7] It is also the case that people with learning or intellectual disabilities are few and far between in these groups. Hayashi and Okuhira documented the postwar disability rights movement and discussed the troubles it had grappling with gender as it attempted to break down discriminatory ideas and practices in wider society associated with the care and the perception of people with disabilities.

> When a mother killed her disabled child, the disability movement saw mothers as enemies. 'Mothers, do not kill!' was their slogan, not 'Parents, do not kill!' The disability movement failed to acknowledge the intersection of sexism and ableism in this incident. When women could validate their social status only as mothers who bore 'healthy' children, those who bore disabled children were condemned to live in shame with the children ... By ignoring other oppressions in society, the movement became an uncomfortable place for many.
> (2001: 862)

Another area of gender-based conflict within the disability movement has been between disability rights activists and feminists with regard to reproductive rights. Since its 1947 promulgation, both feminists and disability rights activists have fought against the Yūsei Hogo Hō, which only prohibited the sterilization of people with disabilities as recently as 1996, with the enactment of the Botai Hogo Hō. Feminists were particularly concerned that these laws did not give women a 'choice' but instead supported a top-down strategy of population control (Tsuge 2010: 113). While both groups agreed in their opposition to the government's legislation imposing control over their bodies, the details of the argument differed significantly: disability activists saw the feminists' 'right to choose' as a 'healthy person's egoism' (Ogino cited in Tsuge 2010: 114). Feminists countered, saying that their right to choose was not one of morality (or of 'escaping morality'), but of choosing 'not to give birth under [the] inauspicious circumstances we live in' (Tsuge 2010: 115).

One disability support group that is specifically concerned with this aspect of prenatal testing is the Japan Down Syndrome Network, which represents a group of individuals (and their families) who carry one of the genetic disorders for which foetuses are most frequently screened. On its information web page, the organization provides detailed information on what kinds of prenatal testing are available in Japan, what they look for, and what the results might mean. In conclusion, it offers a gently worded but still firm message to parents: 'The birth of a child with whatever kind of disability is actually very common. Please prepare yourself for a baby as he or she is without drawing a line between a child with a disability and one without a disability' (JDSN 1998).

Despite this diplomacy, Kato finds that disability activists and feminists still treat each other as adversaries.

> The disabled people's movement suspects that women ... would ultimately choose to abort a disabled child in the name of women's rights. Equally, the women's movement has been sceptical about the disabled people's movement, which is mainly represented by disabled men, who sometimes demonstrate an ignorance about the experiences of abortion, believing that women simply opt for abortion if a pregnancy is not convenient. This mutual distrust remains unresolved.
>
> (Kato 2009: 21)

In the end, we might say that a truce has been called, with the disability movement having a slight edge in the outcome: a joint professional body of obstetrics in Japan recently issued a guideline that doctors are not under any 'obligation' to inform patients about specific tests for irregularities[8] in ultrasound scans (Tsuge 2010: 117; Nishi Nihon Shimbun 2008), owing to fear of criticism from disability groups and fear of claims of wrongful birth (or wrongful termination; this debate will be explored in more detail in Chapter 5).

Conclusion

This chapter has outlined some of the traditional beliefs regarding disability in Japan and the contemporary statistics that describe a demographic picture of people with disability in the country. Both of these descriptive sections – of the past and present, of ideas and empirical facts – give us a sense of how disability has been perceived and experienced over time. Various conclusions can be drawn: for example, the fact that empirical data in Japan are heavily skewed towards people with physical disabilities suggests both a utilitarian approach to public policy (e.g. that attention and resources go to the greatest numbers) and a lingering sense of priorities based on the belief that people with physical disabilities are more likely to have the capacity for rehabilitation into social (and possibly economic) productivity. People with intellectual or psychiatric disabilities are still seen as 'difficult', in the sense both that their disabilities are hard to define, and that their social potential is unclear, so government surveys are less rigorously carried out on their numbers and needs.

Of the various issues listed in the activist section (consciousness, passing and conflict), that of disagreement is perhaps most instructive for our understanding of the future of disability identity in Japan. Conflict within activist groups is common, whether their basis for solidarity is ethnic, racial, gender or disability; in the case of disability movements, interests rooted in the specific disabilities may exclude others' participation. While any conflict which slows the cause would be regrettable, it is important to understand it for two reasons: first, because it can identify those setbacks that are unrelated to its moral imperative to protest and demand change, and thereby shield the movement from misdirected criticism. Second, conflict between competing interests (whether in terms of impairment, approach or other personal attributes such as gender) is instructive because it shows us where disability as a personal attribute interacts with other marginalizing attributes. In the examples shown above, disability identity is vulnerable to conflict based on gender, both in terms of the history of male activists taking precedence over the contributions of female activists, and in terms of clashing with the feminist movement. Yet, most activists, from Japan and elsewhere, would agree that ideally '[d]isability is not a category that should be obliterated by race or gender. Rather, all these forms of oppression should walk, or wheel, side by side' (Davis 2002: 157). It is by examining these conflicts more openly that we can hope to resolve them. The three disparate strands of this chapter – tradition, demographics and activism – can be drawn together if we see them related as the past, present and future: a future where traditions are understood in context and in ways that benefit rather than punish people with disabilities, and where support programmes include those who have formerly been overlooked. Activism, like scholarship, is one path towards that future.

3 Disability, language and meaning

> Discourse is more than about language. Discourse is about the interplay between language and social relationships, in which some groups are able to achieve dominance for their interests ... Language is a central aspect of discourse through which power is reproduced and communicated.
>
> (Hugman 1991: 37)

Language is the symbolic expression of a shared understanding; it merits our examination and reflection because of its primary place in everyday life. It serves to communicate not only our basic needs but also nuanced, abstract meanings about our selves and the world around us. The ways we use language are just as political as they are functional; they have 'become subject to an enforcement of normalcy, as have sexuality, racial identity, national identity, and so on' (Davis 2002: 104–5). This is why activists from various social and political movements around the world often target language use as a first step in instigating social change. Words, and the way they are used, are important to many disability issues addressed in this volume; for example, many protests associated with the groups described in Chapter 2 explicitly addressed the use of language in the public sphere. Disability policy and law, summarized in the next chapter, are also shaped by the concepts behind the language used to describe them. Furthermore, the language used in textbooks needs to be carefully chosen, because it has the power to shape a generation's thinking; the mass media also projects visual and aural messages with similar potential for public influence. In these contexts, questioning language also allows us to reflect on ideology; through this questioning and reflection, we can start to unpack how disability is internalized in our understanding. Through this questioning, it remains a negotiated concept, one that can, and should, respond to change.

Charlton, writing specifically about disability, suggests that language is not merely ephemeral words melting into air: '[w]hen a term is used over and over again, it establishes a meaning, an image, a reality' (1998: 66). This reality is often divisive; Coleman remarks that language, as 'speech', is one of the fundamental ways that 'people communicate social rejection' (1997: 224). Marks concurs, and states that 'language plays an important role in removing disability from mundane experience, and treating it as radically "Other"' (1999: 137). With reference to the Japanese language, Valentine writes that there are cultural preferences in the ways one communicates difference:

> [t]he acknowledgement of difference within Japan is held back by circumspection in naming the other within: direct designation is frequently shunned. Names and their avoidance must be acknowledged as a crucial aspect of identification of self and other in every society: whether, how and what we call others says much about our selves.
>
> (2002: 214)

Here we see that spoken language is not the only tool for expressing Japanese identity; silence is just as important as a communicative strategy, as are the 'euphemisms' which are used to sidestep the awkwardness that explicitly recognizing difference creates. Disability has long been a prickly and thus uncomfortable area in Japanese public discourse, not unlike other discussion topics concerning ethnic minorities in Japan, such as the Burakumin (outcast) group. Unsure what term to use (and who might be offended, and why), commentators in the Japanese public sphere often avoid specific mention when discussing disability (and therefore, people with disability); it is even reasonable to suppose that some speakers and writers prefer to remain silent on the topic precisely because it is easier and safer to say nothing than to say something that is offensive. Hesitation regarding 'political correctness' in public language is not limited to Japan, but the linguistic and historical particulars of this case, as we will see below, make Japan a good example of the juncture, and possible disjuncture, between language, ideas and disability.

This distancing of descriptive language from reality, through either silence or euphemism, is also addressed in English language critiques of the social model, where it has been wryly noted that '[t]he social model of disability appears to have been constructed for healthy quadriplegics. The social model avoids mention of pain, medication, or ill-health' (Humphreys cited in Oliver 1996: 42). Language, whether used to describe the disability, the person with the disability or the corpus of knowledge around understanding disability, is a two-edged sword – while it pleases some, it excludes others. Omission, however, is rarely complete and silence does not blanket every social interaction. When discriminatory words arise periodically in public discourse, debate ensues, and activists for movements supporting minority ethnic and religious groups as well as people with disabilities continue to protest about the use of discriminatory language in the mass media, public policy and other forms of everyday usage. Not all may be in agreement on the extent to which this language is offensive or discriminatory, and conflicts with other interest groups often set up obstacles to the wider public acceptance of activist views.

When a debate about language arises, frequently this is between disability rights and civil rights proponents. For example, in January 2010, the American media was flooded with expressions of public dissatisfaction and condemnation after the *Wall Street Journal* published a story about the White House Chief of

Staff Rahm Emanuel using the term 'f—ing retards' to describe lawmakers opposed to the White House's programmes. The ensuing media fallout demonstrated divisions within society in the reception of words referring to people with intellectual disabilities; some said that the use of the 'r word' was offensive (Shriver 2010), while others claimed freedom of speech privileges (Fairman 2010), as enshrined in the US Constitution. (Of course, what was most objectionable was the use of a word associated with disability, coupled with the expletive, as an insult.) Notably, within a few months the protests died down, soon after the constitutional phrase 'freedom of expression' was invoked, and the public silence regarding the American English use of the term 'retard' was restored. In the American case, the juxtaposition of disability rights and constitutional rights regarding 'freedom' created an insurmountable conflict of interest. In Japan, freedom of speech is also upheld in the Constitution's Chapter III, article 21; therefore, language used by the Japanese mass media and wider use of colloquial expressions are notionally protected, reflecting some of the issues at stake in the Emanuel incident in the USA.

Constitutional debates aside, overly zealous protests may result in an overly oppressive environment, where people feel unable to speak about topics that need discussion merely for fear of offending others. Further clouding the issue is the fact that while some words clearly offend, others are less provoking. Nevertheless, people's interpretations of terms can certainly differ; even when the terms are agreed upon, some can convincingly argue that an acceptable term may be used in an unacceptable way. With respect to silence or omission, what may be thoughtful in one person's eyes is restrictive in another. The objective understanding of a word can be obscured in the subjective choice of wording, context and nuance. In response to these concerns, the use of certain words and phrases has been discontinued in a range of publications in Japan, a development which has in turn been deemed objectionable by those who see it as part of *sabetsu yōgogari* ('discriminatory word hunting') or *kotobagari* ('word hunting'), an oppressive witch hunt for speakers or writers who use terms that offend activists. For some this invokes unwelcome memories of a not-too-distant past when censorship was used as a tool of repression. This chapter explores this conflict for the purpose of identifying yet another context where disability identity causes social division.

What constitutes *sabetsu yōgo*? Certainly there is ongoing debate about which words offend, how they are used, and why. Gottlieb defines *sabetsu yōgo* as not only the words themselves but also how they are used in conversation and writing; it is 'the use of language which label[s minority groups] as in some way inferior to other members of those societies' (2005: 100). As social problems arise and fade from public view, the parameters of acceptability also change: according to Yuasa, what qualify as 'discriminatory phrases' in Japanese are in constant flux (1994: 3). Where once *sabetsu yōgo* consisted of words predominantly referring to minorities such as the Burakumin, resident Koreans, the Ainu and people with disabilities, now the term is informed by a wider consciousness about any kind of language which is demeaning, including references to people

Disability, language and meaning 47

of African descent, women and people with HIV/AIDS (ibid). Gottlieb further distinguishes between the use of particular words that are offensive and 'linguistic stereotyping', where the terms may not be offensive in isolation but nevertheless manage to cast groups in an unflattering light (2006: 3). A subtler example of linguistic stereotyping, in English, would be something like 'a person confined to a wheelchair' or 'wheelchair bound' (which focuses on restriction and limitation) or a person who 'suffers from a rare genetic disorder' (this is despite the fact that Down Syndrome, as trisomy 21, is not necessarily painful). Colloquially, we hear the term 'lame' to refer to something 'uncool'; the more obvious example of this kind of usage would be the above-mentioned Rahm Emanuel incident in 2010, where a disputed term was combined with foul language to create an insult.

This chapter first outlines the Japanese terms both past and present used to refer to people with disabilities and the efforts of the disability activists to abolish discriminatory language. This gives some background to the dilemma at hand, in effect the tension between respectful acknowledgement of people with disabilities and freedom of speech. This tension is further complicated by the ways in which stakeholders manage the dilemma, namely media self-regulation, or self-censorship (*jiko kan'etsu*), which some suggest has merely replaced state censorship (Yōgo to sabetsu o kangaeru shimpojium jikkkōiinkai 1976: 214). Through an examination of the discourse and protests, we can see that this ongoing conflict reveals a continuing ideological division between people with disabilities and those without.

Disability discourse in Japan

Japanese, like all languages, is constantly evolving, creating new words within its indigenous parameters as well as absorbing new words from other languages to describe new phenomena. Historically, a variety of words and phrases were used – directly and indirectly, and with varying levels of controversy – to refer to people with disabilities. An essay posted by a disability service provider gives some examples of pre-war language relating to disability: in 1874 the phrase '*haishitsu ni kakari kyūhaku no mono*' (廃疾ニ罹リ窮迫ノ者) was used in public documents to refer to people requiring public aid; literally, this means 'distressed people who are suffering from disablement/deformity' (Niji Zaitaku Kanwa Kea Sentā 2003). *Haishitsu* (disablement, deformity) is a compound comprising the characters for 'to become useless' (Nelson 1985: 367) – or 'abandon, abolish' (O'Neill 1986: 164) – and 'disease' (250), implying that disability occurred when, through disease, an individual was 'abandoned' by his or her body. These people, consequently, would be 'distressed' by their physical abandonment, but obviously this was not an acceptable descriptor to many people with disabilities.

When thinking about these terms in Japanese, it is important also to determine their sociolinguistic context. Joy Hendry has written about the Japanese language in terms of 'wrapping', where the choice of a mode of communication, involving different kinds of vocabulary, conjugations and expressions, can change a basic sentence's formality as well as meaning (1993: 52–69). With specific reference to disability terminology, Valentine uses Hendry's notion of 'wrapping' to describe the euphemistic ways that language distances interlocutors from the harsh realities of social life (2002: 213). In other words, we can 'wrap' the ideas that make us feel uncomfortable in 'nicer' sounding terms so that we can protect ourselves from social criticism (Hendry calls this 'language as a form of self-defence' [1993: 62]). By doing this, we can shield ourselves from the discomfort or sorrow that is associated with the unpleasant idea, in this case, the 'pain' of disability. This need for distance between social expectations about language and the reality to be expressed is also described by Ivry in her research on medical discourses in Japan. She noted a distinction between the *omote tatemae* and *ura/honne* (front/'formal expression' and back/'true feeling') uses of language: '[there] is a gap between the way [doctors and patients] actually feel and what they feel is acceptable to say about people with disabilities' (2010: 115).

It is within this sociolinguistic context that the generic word for 'disability' itself (*shōgai*) has undergone a transformation in form (and meaning) in the past two hundred years. More recently it has become the subject of debate among activists; the problematization of *shōgai* demonstrates the real ambivalence embedded in Japanese language regarding disability. The most widely used version of the term is made up of two Chinese characters: *shō* 障, meaning 'be a hindrance (to), have a bad effect (on)' (O'Neill 1986: 170), and *gai* 害, meaning 'harm' (83). Some have suggested replacing 害 with the character 碍 – meaning 'obstacle' but also pronounced *gai* – instead, thereby communicating the difficulties a disability presents without the negative nuance of the former. Another option to replace 害 is the character 礙, meaning 'obstruct' or 'hinder'. This suggestion is made because the character 害 contains a 'calamity' or 'catastrophic' nuance, while 礙 can refer factually to a boulder blocking one's path (Niji Zaitaku Kanwa Kea Sentā 2003).[1] This debate, and ongoing movement towards neutral terms to describe disability, is not idiosyncratic to the Japanese language, but is similar to the questioning and the gradual discarding of the English term 'handicap', as it is thought to be associated with begging ('cap in hand') (Jaeger and Bowman 2005: 4; *Tōkyō Shimbun* 2010). (See Table 3.1.)

Sensitivity regarding the appropriate use of kanji has caused some people to avoid using 障害 *shōgai* altogether; increasingly, the katakana loanword ディスアビリティ (*disabiriti*) is being used by reporters, activists and others to distance themselves from the controversy, but use of this loanword risks giving the impression that Anglocentric views of disability are to be accepted uncritically, a position which is itself uncomfortable for many.[2] There have been several recent examples of the use of English loanwords to forestall arguments over perceptions of discrimination in available Japanese equivalents, such as *disabiriti* over *shōgai* (regardless of the kanji chosen); other loanwords increasingly used in Japanese discourse are *eru dii* ('LD' or learning disability), *niizu* ('needs', in the context of social welfare policy), *nōmaraizēshon* ('normalization', also used in policy documents) and *bariafurii yunibāsaru dezain* ('barrier-free universal design'), to name a few. The singer/songwriter Mizukoshi Keiko refers to her son as a

Table 3.1 Sabetsu yōgo (discriminatory terms related to disability)

Japanese term	English translation	Disability category	Examples in use	Revised term
障害者 shōgaisha	person with a disability	general		障碍者 shōgaisha Note: the following phrases can replace the three kanji compound: 1 障害を持つ人 shōgaisha o motsu hito / kata (a person with a disability; literally, to 'hold' a disability) 2 障害のある人／方 shōgaisha no aru hito / kata (a person with a disability)
気違い（気狂い）kichigai	mad, lunatic	psychiatric disability	気違い/狂人に刃物 = incredible danger (to give a sword to a lunatic)	精神障碍者 Also 精神障碍者
野放しの精神異常者 nohanashi no seishin ijōsha	a mentally 'abnormal' person left to him/herself	psychiatric disability	Nohanashi refers to letting cattle out to graze	精神障害者 Also 精神障碍者
跛 bikko	cripple	physical disability		身体障害者 Also 身体障碍者
片端；片輪 katawa	crippled, deformed; 'incomplete [human being]'	physical disability		障害者
盲 mekura	blindness, illiteracy	physical disability	群盲 = blind/ foolish masses 群盲象を評す/なでる = the mediocre have no right to criticise the great – implies blindness as 'foolishness'	目が見えない者 me ga mienai mono (a person who cannot see)

(Continued)

Table 3.1 (Continued)

Japanese term	English translation	Disability category	Examples in use	Revised term
聾 tsunbo	deafness	physical disability		耳が聞こえない者 mimi ga kikoenai mono (a person whose ears cannot hear)
唖 oshi	muteness	physical disability		口がきかない者 kuchi ga kikanai mono (a person whose mouth does not …)
片手落ち kataochi	literally, 'one hand dropped (missing)'; used to mean one-sided, impartial, unfair	physical disability	手 (te) refers to the compound 手段 (shudan) which means way, means or measure. With only one 'hand', there is only one 'way'	障害者
不具 fugu 不具廃疾者 fuguhaishitsusha	deformity; distortion; disability; cripple	physical disability	fugushaishitsusha was one of the first terms requested for deletion from public use by the Shinanomachi Municipal Government in Nagano Prefecture, October 1980	障害 障害者
馬鹿 (バカ) baka	idiot	intellectual disability	Widely used in colloquial language; problematic when attributed to people with disabilities	
薄鈍 (ウスノロ) usunoro	half-wit, simpleton	intellectual disability		

Table 3.1 (Continued)

Japanese term	English translation	Disability category	Examples in use	Revised term
白痴 hakuchi	idiot	intellectual disability		Suggested phrase in 1981: 精神の発育の遅れた者 seishin no hatsuiku no okureta mono (a person with delayed psychological development)
精神薄弱者 seishinhakujakusha	mentally 'feeble' person; 'feebleminded' person	intellectual disability	Used in the Japanese Constitution; the fifth law of the Six Laws of Welfare (福祉六法), to allocate benefits to people with intellectual disabilities. Terminology altered in 1998. This word was instituted to replace the term 白痴 (hakuchi) in legal documents in the 1980s	知的障害者 chitekishōgaisha (a person with an intellectual disability) Also 知的障碍者

Sources: examples and definitions taken from the Japanese Constitution; Jim Breen's WWWJdic (available at www.csse.monash.edu.au/~jwb/cgi-bin/wwwjdic.cgi?1C); Gottlieb 2005; Takagi 1999; Yōgo to sabetsu 1976.

'*handei o motsu musuko*' (a son with a 'handy', abbreviating the English word 'handicap') (ODIK 2011). In April 1994, *Asahi Shimbun*, one of the three largest nationally circulated daily newspapers, declared it would no longer use the phrase '*shōgai o motsu*' ([a person who] 'possesses a disability') and instead use the phrase '*shōgai ga aru*' in its reporting on disability issues in Japan (Niji Zaitaku Kanwa Kea Sentā 2003). The '*ga aru*' suggests merely that a 'disability is present' and is considered to have a more neutral tone, as the verb *aru* communicates a more abstract existence of the disability than the more personalized *motsu* (to hold or possess). Some years later, another major newspaper took a different stance: *Tōkyō Shimbun* published an editorial proposing to discard the term 'disabled person' (障害者) in favour of its preferred phrase 'a person with a disability' (障害のある人) (*Tōkyō Shimbun* 2010). Much like *Asahi Shimbun's* statement, these editors wished to portray people with disabilities as people first, but people whose experiences are coloured by the existence of a disability. Lastly, an 'e-book' published by the casual clothing retailer UNIQLO features disability on each page, and the word *shōgai* is written using the traditional 障 character, but its authors have chosen to bypass the 害/碍 controversy (while still using the Japanese rather than English term) by substituting phonetic *hiragana* for the second character, resulting in 障がい. In this way, the original sound of the word is retained while the symbolic meaning is suppressed. While these examples of change may be seen as progressive by some, others regard such euphemistic expressions as a token stopgap which only delays real action to secure the social change that needs to occur.

Examples of discriminatory language in the public sphere

If we accept that the term *shōgai* is already a problematic expression, it is no wonder that the language often used to describe various impairments is similarly fraught. This section looks at the way some of the terms listed above have been used, specifically in public discourse (in the scope of this chapter, this is limited to the discussion of language in public documents and the mass media), to illustrate how language frames and negotiates social relations involving people with disabilities in Japan. This section addresses the language used in these two powerful areas of the public sphere – government and the mass media – for several reasons. The language used in public documents is extremely important because of the political legitimacy that is associated with the power to rule as well as the power to allocate public resources (in the form of welfare and pension payments). The second area of the public sphere, the mass media in Japan, is powerful not only economically (in part owing to a variety of tie-ups between print, television and film media, creating mega-media corporations) but also ideologically. Many of the instances of discrimination documented below are drawn from examples of television broadcasts, and here it is important to note this medium's unique place as a source of information and imagery in the Japanese public sphere. Mainstream television in Japan is a 'para-culture', which is at the same time fictional and abstract (as a source of 'entertainment') and also non-fictional and representative (with respect to its purported role as 'newscaster'); nevertheless, both aspects of television content and their associated roles and functions in society are based on a supposedly shared set of values. Japanese contemporary society is one of the most media-rich in the developed world; Japanese citizens are bombarded with a multitude of media messages all day, every day. This includes not just the traditional media such as print, radio and television, but also the internet, with multi-media advertising available in nearly every possible environment, from the street billboard to the commuter train screen of 'news' and advertising.

In Japan, awareness about words or phrases that cause discomfort to people with physical disabilities began in the 1980s, building on the work in the 1970s by other minority groups and supported by the designation of 1981 as the United Nations International Year of Disabled Persons (Takagi 1999: 120).[3] One of the first areas to see change in the public sphere was that of legal terminology. In 1980 the word *fuguhaishitsusha*, a term noted in Table 3.1, was replaced by *shōgaisha* in the Self-Defence Forces Law Enforcement Order with reference to the treatment of injured soldiers. The Ministry of Health and Welfare in the same year moved to remove the terms *tsunbo*, *oshi* and *mekura* (derogatory terms for deaf, 'dumb' and blind) from disability and welfare laws under its jurisdiction (Takagi 1999: 121). In July 1994, the Ministry of Education withdrew its newly approved *Kokugo I* (*Japanese 1*) textbook after protests by the Nihon Tenkan Kyōkai (Japan Epilepsy Association). The textbook had contained a fictional story about a robot policeman, an officer in a force which searched out people with epilepsy; this policy was justified on the grounds that 'people who are prone to seizures are dangerous drivers, so any [drivers] with abnormal EEGs should be taken to the hospital before they have a seizure' (cited in Yuasa 1994: 47, 48).

While there are discriminatory words related to all kinds of disability, the most commonly occurring transgressions seem to be in the area of intellectual and psychiatric disabilities. As an indication of the frequency of the use of these terms, Takagi notes that over the years activists have requested apologies for disparaging remarks about people with intellectual and psychiatric disabilities from just about all the major media outlets in Japan: TBS, NHK, Asahi and Fuji television networks; newspapers *Mainichi Shimbun* and *Kyōto Shimbun*; and radio broadcasters Mainichi Hōsō and Shin'etsu Hōsō (1999: 102–6). Physical disability is also an issue, however; Takagi found that mainstream media organizations such as NHK, TV Asahi, Mainichi Hōsō Radio, TBS, *Asahi Shimbun*, Kadokawa Publishing Co., and *Shūkan Shinchō* (a weekly magazine) were all targeted by activists seeking apologies concerning language used in portrayal of people with physical disabilities (107–12). Among the specific examples given was the 1988 ad campaign by the athletic shoe company Asics which proclaimed '*Aruku kara ningen*' ('Because I walk, I am human') (112). In 1993, Sanyo Electronics withdrew a campaign for cordless phones after a negative response to its jokey dialogue on technological mobility: 'Aren't you overlooking the feelings of people with physical disabilities?' (*teashi ga fujiyū na shōgaisha* [literally, disabled people with 'unfree', or impaired, limbs] *no kimochi o hairyo shiteinai no de wa nai*

54 *Disability, language and meaning*

no ka?) (115). There are also examples of problematic language with respect to people with chronic conditions such as epilepsy and Hansen's disease. For example, the Japanese Epilepsy Association protested when, in 1993, Nintendō posted strongly worded 'warnings' on its video games regarding PSE (photosensitive epilepsy; *hikarikabinsei tankan*), concerned that this warning would cause discrimination against children with epilepsy and prevent them from participating fully in physical education and other school activities (Takagi 1999: 118).

Many of the examples of media offences involve broadcast *jidaigeki*, or historical dramas, which include *sabetsu yōgo* in their dialogues. For example, the television series *Kōya no Surōnin* (*The Masterless Samurai of Kōya*, starring the famous actor Mifune Toshirō as the lead) broadcast by NET*kyoku* (now Asahi) was an early example (Takagi 1999: 102) that was criticized, but the producers countered that they were merely using 'authentic' language to portray historical drama to a contemporary audience. In other words, the historical distance of the fictional setting was used to distance the producers from any responsibility in offending people in today's moral context. Through this distancing technique, producers have been able to justify the continuing use of these terms and thus historical drama remains problematic.

Examples of discriminatory language in the media persist into the twenty-first century. Even though the term *jakusha* (weak person), as in the phrase *seishinhakujakusha* ('feeble-minded' person), was phased out of legal documents, it still persists in descriptions of people with disabilities. *Seishinhakujakusha* was replaced by *chitekishōgaisha* (a person with an intellectual disability) in social welfare laws in 1998, but the term *jakusha* as a suffix identifying disability as 'weakness' is still in use in the media. The lead story on television channel NHK1's 7 p.m. news on 5 May 2010 identified the emergence of a new social problem when it profiled '*kaimonojakusha*' (literally, people who are weak at shopping). The background was the increasing market dominance of large chain stores edging out small, family-run local shops located near the residences of elderly people, one result of which was the unavailability of fresh food for sale within a reasonable walking distance of where they live (one kilometre). The newscast estimated that there are approximately six million *kaimonojakusha* who have trouble walking long distances and climbing stairs, and stated that the proliferation of large-scale shopping centres which edge out smaller local businesses has made daily life more difficult for these people, especially with regard to procuring perishables. The provision of fresh, healthy food to an elderly population is a crucial public health issue for urban planners and local government as well as geriatric health-care providers, but one cannot help but ask why the network did not term them *kaimono de komatta mono* (people who are troubled by shopping) or *kaimono shizurai to omou hito* (people who find shopping difficult). The use of *jakusha* as a suffix recalls the 'feeble-minded' label for people with intellectual disabilities which is no longer in use for public policy documents, demonstrating the lag between different kinds of language use.

While changes in the symbols used to write the gai' of *shōgai* (害/碍/がい) in the mass media demonstrate an increasing level of public awareness regarding

Disability, language and meaning 55

the relationship between words and disability in Japan, these changes are not entirely linear (e.g. a shift from the use of discriminatory language to its eventual disuse, and abandonment). Words may go out of use, and then arise in the public sphere again: this suggests a more complicated symbolic media landscape, not infrequently subject to global influences. An example of the reintroduction of terms via a transnational context is seen in the role-play animated video game *Katawa Shōjo* (this translates literally into English as 'Cripple Girls', but it often appears in English as 'Disability Girls'), created by Four Leaf Studios in 2007. The creative process by which this game came into being, its popularity and reactions to it show the ongoing tension between artistic expression and respectful engagement with disability. *Katawa Shōjo* is described as a 'visual novel' (Four Leaf Studios 2007–12), which unfolds through a role-playing computer video game. In it, the gamer takes the role of Nakai Hisao, a boy who has just transferred to a *shōgaiji gakkō* (literally, a 'school for children with disabilities', a more colloquial term, in contrast to bureaucratic terminology such as *tokubetsu shien kyōiku* or *yōgo gakkō* used to describe 'special education' and its institutions in Japan). The main character suddenly acquires a disability identity through the diagnosis of a heart condition, and is transferred to the Yamaku High School after his release from treatment at a rehabilitation hospital. While the game's synopsis refers to uplifting aspects of his experience meeting his new classmates and fitting in at his new school (e.g. he and his classmates are said to '*shōgai o norikoete*' – they 'overcome their disability'), the goal of the game is for the player, as Hisao, to decide which of the five main female classmates should become his girlfriend. The game software requires a declaration of age (18+ rating) at download, though there is a game option to play without erotic content. The game was developed collectively by a group of amateur artists (*dōjinshi*), thus the name 'Four Leaf Studios' (a reference to the transnational, anonymous and controversial website '4chan'; no named individual takes artistic credit for the production) (ibid). While 4chan is a US-based website focused on Japanese popular culture, it is a transnational and anonymous online community; therefore, we cannot know for certain who the artists are and can only guess the game is a collaboration between Japanese and US artists. The website, however, states that '[t]he origin of the name is of course Japan itself, with Raita [the pseudonym of a Japanese 4chan user] and his original concept' (Four Leaf Studios 2008). The story is said to have been inspired by real events in Japan, posted to the website by a male nurse in a rehabilitation hospital (Alexander 2010).

Reactions to this game have been mixed. One Japanese gaming critic notes the potential for controversy but normalizes the gaming experience with a favourable response: 'The name [makes you think] "huh?" but [*nēmingu wa chotto are desu ga*] the content seems normal and interesting [*futsū ni omoshirosō desu yo*]' (Okamoto 2012). In fact, one of the 'normalizing' techniques the designers used was to write the word *katawa* in feminized, curved *hiragana*, rather than the Chinese characters usually used (shown in in Table 3.1). In an online review, an English-speaking gaming critic defends the game, but agrees that '4chan users may be a perverted collective, and the way in which they objectify a wide range of people from the safety of anonymity can be shocking to many' (Alexander 2010). One of the developers responds in an interview that s/he and colleagues set out to create a game that, amongst other things, 'tell[s] a story about something that people don't normally talk about' (*futsū katareru koto no nai monogatari o tsutaeru*) (Hirunuma 2012). Notably, both the designers and the one reviewer cited above use a word (*futsū*) signifying 'ordinary'/'normal' to describe how they think the game should be received. I wonder if this game poses more questions about the place of disability in Japan than it provides answers, but these questions remain provocative. Is disability still something to be juxtaposed against 'normal'? Does bringing it into the public sphere through the video game help, by using this term, to 'normalize' it? Or does the fantasy aspect of this game push the disability issues too far into the realm of the imaginary, unrealistically romantic and even fetishized?

Why does the use of these terms persist, despite the external protests of disability groups and the internal pressure from broadcasting companies to conform? Certainly in some cases the 'fictional' aspect of dramatized dialogue provides a measure of legitimation. Preserving the historical 'flavour' of dialogue, or the fantasy element of a video game, can constitute a reason for the maintenance of discriminatory words in fictional or artistic work. The other role of the media, however, as 'non-fictional' and ideally impartial presenter of current news and events, means that producers cannot always claim artistic licence when justifying themselves in the face of protests. In these cases, broadcasters must make a decision about whether to exercise the company's right to free expression in presenting the 'facts'; often in such situations they resort instead to self-censorship, described below.

Kotobagari and freedom of expression

As noted in the introduction to this chapter, some of the negative outcomes attributed to an increased awareness of language are an increased level of public censorship, or self-censorship, and the loss of freedom of expression.[4] There is a certain 'catch 22' conundrum in this context that could dissuade people from actively pursuing change. On the one hand, some might feel strongly the need to protest against certain representations; but on the other hand, publicly naming those who are believed to have infringed the human rights of the disadvantaged or oppressed recalls Japan's pre-war and wartime censorship policies. Demonstrations against discriminatory language carry with them a fear of being associated with an outdated political position with strongly negative associations that are incongruent with contemporary Japanese society.

Postwar accusations of *kotobagari* were not the first time language had been constrained for political ends in Japan. Earlier examples of politically motivated language censorship began during the isolationist policy of the Tokugawa Period, when foreign (mostly European) terms were banned, but this practice was relaxed after the country 'opened' during the mid- to late 1800s. The government banned the use of English in wartime Japan (Yue 2008: 29), as there were many English language words that had been adopted into Japanese after the Meiji Restoration; they were avoided because it was thought, as *tekiseigo* or 'hostile language' (Hashimoto 2008: 34), they represented the presence of the enemy on native soil. After the war, state censorship continued, but this time in the form of US-dominated Occupation policy which was concerned with creating a mass media free from references to the militaristic past (Kersten 1996: 13). National and commercial station broadcast policy, as well as newspaper publication policy, since the 1970s relies on voluntary self-censorship (*jiko kan'etsu*).[5]

To prevent the potential for *kotobagari*, reporters and announcers have adopted the practice of avoiding certain words, relying on lists of taboo terms (*kinkushū*) and of acceptable substitutes (*iikaeshū*, 'saying in other words') drawn up by their employers. Gottlieb writes that some of the earliest lists were made in 1973 by two major commercial networks, NTV and TBS (2006: 102). In 1975 a collective called the Hōsō Hihyō Kondankai (the 'Consulting Group of Broadcast Critics') published a book entitled *Tsukaenai Nihongo – Hōsō Tabū no Jittai* (*The Japanese You Can't Use: How Words are Tabooed on Air*), but today for the most part anonymous bloggers are those who most vigorously debate these conventions. NHK, the Japanese 'national' television and radio broadcasting service, conducts and publishes research on broadcast terminology through its Hōsō Bunka Kenkyūjo (Broadcasting Cultural Research Institute), and a glance through its reports on the 'correct' use of terminology by its broadcasters shows much thought is put into the speakers' choice of words: the documents clarify the subtle differences between similar kanji characters, the difference between using the particle *ga* versus *o* in a verb phrase, and so on (NHK Broadcasting Culture Research Institute 2011). Another NHK report, entitled *Hōsō genba no gimon shichōsha no gimon* (*Doubts of the Broadcaster – Doubts of the Audience*) offers advice on how to refer to people infected with HIV, but the text is more concerned with proper nomenclature than privacy issues or discrimination (NHK Broadcasting Culture Research Institute 2009).[6] Research reports related to people with disabilities are primarily concerned with accessibility for people with visual and hearing disabilities, and the efficacy of broadcasts during emergencies (e.g. Sakai 2005, 2006); none of these publications are proactively discussing the terminology used or the associated issues of its use.[7] These media handbooks are confidential and not for public circulation, but there have been some leaks on the internet; for example, a Japanese blogger using a pseudonym has reproduced sections of *Yomiuri Shimbun's* handbook; s/he notes that terms are generally divided into three categories: '(A) not to be used; (B) best not to use except in certain circumstances; (C) in most contexts, best not to use' (Hanagoyomi 2002). Because of these shifting and uncertain expectations, researchers on the news media in Japan have more recently argued that some reporters have voluntarily abandoned coverage of stories on difficult topics (which include ones concerning ethnic minorities such as the Ainu, the Burakumin or resident Koreans) because of fear of lawsuits (MacLachlan 2001: 124). Clearly, this kind of self-censorship can lead to the difficulty that '[s]ince discussion is ... taboo, people cannot be expected to understand what the problem is' (Yorō cited in Gottlieb 2001: 986).

58 *Disability, language and meaning*

Silence can be just as excluding as the use of discriminatory language. For many people with disabilities, 'passing' (see Chapter 2), one of the key strategies in belonging to the 'silent majority', is just not possible, unlike the options available for other groups who can function independently and 'invisibly' in Japanese society. Furthermore, media self-censorship 'may contribute to the continuing stigma against these groups by simultaneously contributing to a stereotype of the Japanese population as ... homogeneous' (MacLachlan 2001: 125), which is not in the interests of disability activists.

Self-censorship does give journalists the opportunity to reflect on their influence on the way ideas are framed in the public sphere, and can encourage reporters to take responsibility for the way they express these ideas. On the other hand, self-censorship, if it results in avoidance and omission, results in a bland or even incomplete media landscape. Some have even argued that the Japanese media tends to portray people with disabilities in a positive light, to counteract the 'too serious, ugly, frightening and/or depressing' picture of disability in a media landscape that in general is more focused on beautiful and positive imagery (Kohama cited in Iwakuma 2003: 130), suggesting there is disagreement internally as to how people with disabilities should be portrayed in the mass media. Should the image of people with disabilities be purposefully positive (a necessary counterweight to the many negative portrayals), or should realism be consciously used to help communicate the difficulties people with disabilities face, with the hope of improving their situation through awareness raising?

Conclusion

While fighting the media over words may seem petty, it is through small choices of language that mainstream values are expressed, maintained and protected in this most representative of public spaces. The media in Japan can be seen as amplifiers of the values of different groups of people, both those of the mainstream and those of interest groups such as disability activists trying to change the status quo (Iwakuma 2003: 130). This is why activists target television and newspapers in Japanese society: not just to amplify their own message, but also to undercut the influence of messages already in circulation that put people with disabilities in an inferior position. Some might feel that the insistence on making some of the above changes regarding the use of language is trivial, but again it is important to put these into a longitudinal context. Disability studies scholar Lennard J. Davis writes about public backlash in the United States, stating that this has arisen because the public sees complaints based on disability rights as disruptive: disability court 'cases tend to be about rather small matters. A series of small matters may add up to a large matter ...' (2002: 129). Furthermore, 'most complaints made in such cases are going to be seen by people without a disability consciousness as "trivial"' (130) and 'the plaintiff will appear overly concerned about ... details, petty, narcissistic' (151). Paralleling this perspective, Gottlieb writes, regarding discriminatory language and stereotyping in Japan, that '[m]uch of the general discussion, however, relates specifically to semantics'

Disability, language and meaning 59

(2006: 100), which could be interpreted as a dismissal of its importance – a mere quibbling about words. The temptation to dismiss complaints is further supported by fears of unjust witch hunts of *sabetsu yōgogari* (discriminatory word hunting) or simply *kotobagari* ('word hunting'). Words can be seen as unimportant in the light of larger issues such as medical care and pension funds. Critics proffer this perspective: what do the words matter – isn't it more important that people's needs are met? Fighting about words can seem to be a waste of time when practical issues need addressing.

But there are important reasons to keep up the fight. The language used to describe people with disabilities is often conflated with who they are, so much so that it is at times difficult to distinguish between the two: 'The disability itself primarily informs the conception most people have about individuals with disabilities. Their humanity is stripped away and the person is obliterated, only to be left with the condition – the disability' (Charlton 1998: 54).

Language is also a mirror on history: changes in terminology reflect changes in societal attitudes, but it is not enough merely to condemn past language without looking on what is happening today. Just because government policy and the mass media are not using certain offensive terms anymore does not mean contemporary language is 'value neutral':

> New inoffensive terms often function as euphemisms, and it doesn't take long for previous offensive connotations to 'catch up' with new 'politically correct' terms ... Thus we should not be so confident of the oral superiority of contemporary language. A more valid way of assessing past values is to engage in historical research which assesses the specific meanings attributable to 'impaired people' in previous historical eras ... contemporary beliefs, practices and structures shaping the treatment of disabled people may not always represent an improvement on the past.
>
> (Marks 1999: 29)

As an example of this, we have seen that even when a negative term is replaced by a new word or more acceptable euphemism, other linguistic 'habits', like linguistic stereotyping, remain. But not all awareness about discriminatory language is restrictive or meant to enforce an unnatural 'political correctness'. Marks believes that 'defiant self naming' is an important empowerment tool:

> [i]n much the same way as the gay community has reappropriated the term 'queer' to refer to a specific strand of gay culture, disabled people might call themselves 'crips'. Such language rejects positive euphemism. It also contains an important element of 'in-your-face' confrontation with non-disabled people.
>
> (1999: 147)

Marks observes that 'denigrating previous ways of speaking, people can take a superior stance that prevents them from looking critically at themselves and the complex ways in which language functions' (1999: 148–9). Yet, the re-emergence of the term '*katawa*' in the *anime*/video game *Katawa Shōjo* does not seem to be a 'defiant self naming' device; furthermore, its use in the marginalized gaming community means that any attempt to bring disability issues into the public sphere is tainted through its association with its accompanying impressions of anti-social behaviour.

To what extent does the kind of change described above really represent social progress? In the case of Japan, Valentine points out that the search to replace a discriminatory term with a socially acceptable term usually goes through more than one stage (2002: 219). For example, the term *mekura*, as noted in Table 3.1, 'has given way to *mōjin* [blind person] ... [but] is now regarded by many sighted people as too direct and is coming to be replaced by the more lengthy euphemism *mōmoku no hito*' and the even longer *me no fujiyū na kata* and *shikaku ni shōgai no aru kata*, which similarly place the disability further away from the person (the argument is that this distance is lacking in the original euphemism *mōjin*, where the two characters – 'blindness' and 'person' – are joined together). Valentine critiques the ongoing changes in terminology, not to detract from the importance of naming, but to point out that 'recent labels are not necessarily more accurately descriptive or less stigmatizing' (ibid.). Longer (and more opaque) terms merely replace the shorter ones, while the place that people with disabilities hold in society is unchanged. While there is some merit in making linguistic changes, clearly the path taken needs to avoid the twin evils of using old terms that exclude groups of people and creating new terms which in reality merely perpetuate the status quo. The fear of repercussions, as well as the distaste for 'witch hunting', motivates writers and speakers in Japan to ignore (or pretend to ignore) people's disabilities, yet silence is an outcome that few disability activists would support. Japanese society must balance the need to defend free exchange and the need to protect and respect the human rights of people with disabilities, consulting stakeholders along the way.

4 Disability policy and law in modern Japan

> The twin myths of bodily wholeness and bodily lack that underpin a compensation model of disability structure the history of public policy toward the extraordinary body. The concept of able-bodiedness and its theoretical opposite, disability, were continually reshaped as the state attempted to qualitatively distinguish between people whose physical or mental conditions legitimately prevented them from obtaining wage labor and people who simply refused to work ... The history of public and private distribution of resources to people termed the 'disabled' has been tinged with the punitive and the paternalistic as well as the compassionate and the just.
>
> (Thomson 1997: 49–50)

This chapter[1] examines Japan's record of 'public and private distribution' of funds and services to people with disabilities with reference to disability policy and law. The relationship between policy and law is a complicated one. Policy is the broader term of the two; it 'can be generally defined as a system of laws, regulatory measures, courses of action, and funding priorities concerning a given topic promulgated by a governmental entity or its representatives' (Kilpatrick 2000). Policy directives are not necessarily 'enforceable', but are still important because they can alter the way a minister or government official interprets an existing law, resulting in changed delivery of programmes – even though the legislation is unchanged. Disability policies in Japan are primarily aimed at finding ways to support the social and financial needs that impairment gives rise to, in the form of assistance, special services or extra funding. This interaction between policy and law, while not a relationship unique to Japan's jurisdiction, is significant in this cultural context because some have argued that the close link between the two is coloured by the strong position bureaucrats (as opposed to elected officials) enjoy within the executive government (see Johnson 1982 for early analysis of this, and Wright 1999 for a more recent view).

Public policy and welfare law can also be seen as symbolic of collective attitudes. For example, Thomson observes that in US disability policy there has been a practical move away from 'compensation' to more of a focus on 'rehabilitation', which occurred in postwar Japan as well. According to Thomson's understanding of the compensation model, when disability is seen as a cause for reimbursement, it 'then becomes a personal flaw ... [and d]ifference thus translates into deviance'. Shifting the emphasis to accommodation, she argues, however, 'suggests that disability is simply one of the many differences among people and that society should recognize this by adjusting its environment accordingly' (Thomson 1997: 49). The key difference between these terms is the tension between bringing the person with a disability into line with society (rehabilitation) and bringing society into sync with the needs of a person with a disability (accommodation).

The concept of reimbursement colours much of the logic encapsulated in many disability policies. This is because in post-capitalist societies such as Japan, the USA and Australia – where individual productivity is highly valued – disability almost always equates to some kind of economic disadvantage. Therefore, disability welfare laws in Japan are frequently expressed as providing financial payments for living expenses, as well as funds and/or direct support for medical treatment and specialist equipment. While there are other laws concerning disability in Japan that involve protection from discrimination and the provision of social equity, a very significant aspect of most disability-related laws is the provision of day-to-day welfare services. Understandably, with fundamental daily needs at stake, much debate revolves around how these services are determined and how they should be distributed, and to whom.

Adults and children with disabilities are eligible for schemes according to the guidelines in basic welfare laws; specific programmes are created and operate in accordance with their provisions, and are subject to the periodic review, revision and rewriting of laws. As an anchor for understanding how these laws sit relative to one another, Figure 4.1 gives a map of the laws covered in this chapter (and further laws discussed in Chapters 5 and 6).[2]

It is important to note that the interaction between policy and law, and its resultant impact on law through change, is not *directly* reflected in the Constitution itself, because the Japanese Constitution has never been formally amended (Piotrowski 2005: n68). Change can be perceived, however, through the creation of complementary laws that 'sit' acceptably within the Constitution's framework, through the courts' variable interpretation of law, and by government officials in their actions and applications of the law.[3]

Generally, the goal of social welfare for people with disabilities can be simply put: it is to provide services (or extra funding) that cover the extra needs that impairment creates. In terms of a specific policy for welfare law, Yōda argues for a system in Japan that includes 'the provision of goods and services, in the form of income guarantees, housing assistance or educational, medical and other livelihood assistance, [which] should be designed as systems for use by as many people as possible' (2002: 13–14). The latter part of her statement makes explicit the general accessibility of the welfare system as a determinant of its success; considering the prevalence of disability in the general population, if only a few utilize it, then how can it be called successful? While this is a logical response, it unfortunately opens up further debate about appropriate intake: to meet as many people's needs as possible, how will applicants be judged? Which needs should be met and to what extent?

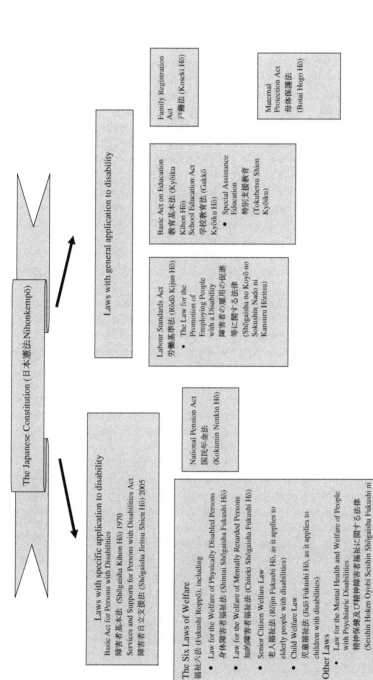

Figure 4.1 A conceptual chart of Japanese laws related to disability

No discussion of disability policy and law in postwar Japan can be complete without the inclusion of two key concepts, neoliberalism and normalization, which drive change in many areas of the Japanese welfare system. Generally speaking, neoliberalism is a particular sensibility or imagining whereby problems and solutions are defined in economic terms, and behaviours are moulded in terms of business interests. In other words, neoliberalism projects a 'business model' on to schools, universities, hospitals and other kinds of institutions which have been traditionally thought of as separate from the economic sphere. Japan has not always embraced this kind of thinking: Chomsky writes that in the early postwar era, Japan 'rejected the neoliberal doctrines of the US advisors' in their industrial sphere and instead gave the state more power, but gradually this changed as Japan's bureaucrats realized its potential for global economic success beyond reconstruction (1999: 31). Taken to another, and even more critical, conclusion, neoliberalism in Japan has also been seen as an 'ideology ... that sanctions greed of the rich and the propertied and places the blame for poverty on the poor and the non-privileged' (Ikeda 2004: 379).

The other influential concept, normalization, is a term first used in the 1960s in Sweden as a response to the segregation of people with disabilities from the rest of society (Heyer 1999: 9). Tom Shakespeare refers to it as an aspect of the 'Nordic relational model' (2006: 25), which he finds helpful to bridge the gap between the medical and social models of disability (that is, disability defined as, respectively, a biological, medical and individual condition, or as the social discrimination and hardship experienced as a marginalized person). Normalization is a powerful term that presents a utopian vision of an inclusive society. Normalization also has its critics, however, because few can agree on what the 'normality' is. Heyer observes that positive notions of 'self-determination and self-advocacy' came to the disability rights movement from the normalization movement (1999: 10), but the baseline to which people with disabilities are 'normalized' still may be out of synchronicity with the reality of many people's experiences and may even legitimate 'normal' life as the status quo.

Neoliberalism and normalization can be seen to align in curious ways in more recent developments in welfare policy. These concepts are apparent in the nomenclature used in legal documents; for example, if we look at the recent terminology used in revised legislation – such as in the naming of the 2005 law, Shōgaisha Jiritsu Shien Hō (the Services and Supports for Persons with Disabilities Act),[4] as detailed in the next section – we find the word *jiritsu* (independence) making a first appearance. This was in response to requests from disability activists promoting a more self-sufficient identity for people with disabilities through independent living in the community ('normalization'). While many see this as progress, there are, however, many who have criticized using these terms as a cover for a neoliberal shift to a 'user pays' system that puts more of a burden on the welfare recipient. Independence is not a term easily defined; it is associated with 'normal' life, yet it comes with many responsibilities. Independent living, in the ideal sense, is defined as 'living in an accessible home and the availability of accessible environments and services and information' (Shakespeare 2006: 139),

Disability policy and law in modern Japan

and is contrasted with the model of adults with disabilities living with their families until they are placed in an institutional setting, which recalls the isolationism of previous generations. Independent living is the ambition of many people with disabilities; yet, for some, living independently can result in social isolation as well, especially if there is little community support and public services are receding. In this light, the term *jiritsu*, as part of normalization, must be viewed critically. This chapter, by identifying the pros and cons of normalization and neoliberalism in disability policy and welfare law, argues that Japanese welfare reality does not always match the policy ideals. It is important to note, however, that a discussion of Japanese government policy (as reflected in legislation) engages with only one view of disability in Japanese society, and this view is often a conservative one. Clearly there are many alternative views, as disability studies scholarship and activism both in Japan and elsewhere suggest. Despite the tendency towards a monolithic, homogenized understanding of disability through government policy, this 'official' view has real, concrete ramifications for people's lives. It is this potential – where policy and law have significant impact on the everyday experiences of people with disabilities – that makes this chapter important in understanding the meaning of disability in Japan.

This chapter first outlines the history of welfare policy in Japan, which initially focused on rehabilitation to restore productivity, and the 'professional management' of a medicalized condition through separation. This is followed by a description of the legal structure of welfare and employment laws pertaining to people with disabilities in Japan. These laws are presented in chronological order and my analysis focuses on the shift from professional management to integration in welfare policy. In particular, one important example of how this has happened is found in the establishment of new, complementary laws such as the Shōgaisha Jiritsu Shien Hō. The last sections look at issues such as paternalism and external pressure on welfare policy, and the contemporary trends of 'normalization', 'integration with the mainstream' and neoliberal attitudes.

Welfare policy for people with disabilities in the twentieth century

At the turn of the twentieth century, Japanese welfare policy was focused on treatment for disabling medical conditions; in these cases, rehabilitation was important – welfare recipients were to be rehabilitated from 'illness' to 'health'. Disease and disability were to be 'managed', and the best way to do this was through separation and rehabilitation. From the early modern period, sanatoriums for illnesses such as tuberculosis and Hansen's disease functioned to 'control' just as much as they 'treated' their patients ('*iryō yori kanri*'; Ozawa 1999: 128). Part of that control was of course related to fear of contamination, resulting in isolation of patients, even if they were not an imminent threat to the public (Hansen's disease constituting the most misunderstood illness in this respect). Ogawa writes that the third most frequent cause of death in the late nineteenth century was tuberculosis; after 1911, infected people were institutionalized as part of the government's public health policy (1999: 75). Medical treatment was 'modernized' in twentieth-century Japan, and accordingly this treatment was seen as best delivered in an institutional setting. Residential medical treatment combined with education for '*shitai fujiyūji*' ('handicapped children') began in the Taishō Period, with the first fully residential facility for children with disabilities established in 1937 (ibid.), implying that before that time children with high medical and special educational needs were cared for outside the public system. The management of children with physical disabilities as per the medical model was not uncommon considering that children with scoliosis were hospitalized as well as those with infectious diseases such as tuberculosis (ibid.: 86). Separation was common for those with physical disabilities as well as intellectual disabilities, though commonly children with disabilities were housed together. The first dedicated institution for children with profound intellectual disabilities (*jūshō seishinshōgaiji*) was opened in 1961 (ibid.: 75, 92).

The other significant welfare policy focused on injury rather than debilitating illness or congenital disability. Before 1945, with compulsory military service and troops actively deployed across the Asia Pacific, many early Japanese policies on disability dealt with the immediate needs of wounded service personnel. Hayashi and Okuhira found that early postwar lawmakers were also primarily concerned with (male) ex-servicemen: 'disabled *veterans*' who needed '*rehabilitation*' in order to return to civilian life; people with disabilities other than returning soldiers were not specifically provided for (2001: 856, emphasis added). Not surprisingly, considering the stress on the extended family as a social unit, Japan's welfare focus during the late nineteenth and early twentieth century was on supporting soldiers' wives and children, who were struggling because, in many cases, the family's main breadwinner was absent in combat, had been killed in action or disabled (Endō 1999: 123, 127, 130). This is in line with the priorities of disability legislation in the United States, which tended to overlook 'people with congenital disabilities and disabled women ... because they could not lose a hypothetical advantage they never had' (Thomson 1997: 49).

Commonly held notions of productivity also coloured the way the laws were interpreted. This view was not unlike those held in other developed societies; for example, Jaeger and Bowman note that industrialization of American society actually helped raise awareness about physical disability after the increasing mechanization of factory work created new risks for workers and a class of people with newly acquired disabilities (2005: 38). Such concerns also confronted Japan as it embraced heavy industry during the early modern period. A male-focused and vocation-driven ideology skewed the postwar welfare system's outcomes to disadvantage not only females with disabilities but also carers (most often female as well) who were responsible for children and other relatives who did not fit into the requirements of earlier schemes.[5] This also meant that the early postwar welfare system tended to focus on people with physical disabilities (such as soldiers who had lost their sight or limbs in the war) rather than intellectual (such as those diagnosed with mental health issues or intellectual impairments).[6]

Both of these historical precedents – the management and supervision of chronic illness, and rehabilitation of the wounded soldier – refer to the public management of the individual who is deemed unable to support him- or herself. Disability welfare programmes were then meant to assist the person to be a 'productive' member of society. The value of productivity refers to beliefs in the individual's relationship to wider society as an economic contributor (to oneself first, as in earning a living, but indirectly as well as a taxpayer), for it is this activity that is compensated for in many of these welfare schemes. The phrase 'welfare philosophy' refers to our understanding of the boundaries of our moral responsibilities to others; in other words, it is the view that wealth should be distributed in ways that rectify disadvantage, as long the recipient 'plays by the rules' that are set out to discourage 'welfare cheats' or other disingenuous uses of public funds. Yōda refers to a number of welfare mindsets at work in Japan, including the 'common sense view' (which relies heavily on specialist or medical advice for decisions on who should receive what and how much) and the 'residual welfare model' (which puts the family as primary caregiver; the state is to supply funds or services for anything not met by the family's efforts) (2002: 3, 9). It is also possible to consider that under this model it is not in the state's interest to provide support that might serve as a disincentive for families to provide care. Following this logic, we can conclude that, according to the 'residual welfare model', it is likely that the individual with a disability is still seen as dependent on someone, whether it is his/her parents or the state (or both). This does not sit well with disability activists, who have critiqued the system and its implementation in the context of recognizing the person with a disability as an independent adult. They argue that welfare policy forces the recipient into an unequal, dependent and ultimately subjugated role.

The Japanese legal structure

This section provides a descriptive overview of Japan's main disability laws. The legal system in Japan is highly developed and intricate,[7] so here I will focus on the basic laws of disability rights and welfare. Other laws related to disability (such as selective abortion, special education, family registration and employment) are included in Chapter 5, 'Disability and the lifecycle'; policies such as those that include the needs of carers will be discussed in Chapter 6, 'Caregiving and the family'.

As noted in Figure 4.1, the Constitution of Japan lies above the other laws as an overarching document that not only outlines the 'rights and obligations' of its citizens but also those of its government, and is designed to provide procedural reference for all matters of the state.[8] While the Constitution is a distant ideological statement with respect to concrete welfare benefits, it is worth mentioning with reference to ideology. Oda and Stickings write that the Japanese Constitution has 'three underlying principles... the sovereignty of the people, pacifism, and the guarantee of human rights', all of which are seen by some to be 'imposed' by the US-led Occupation of the first seven years after Japan's defeat in 1945 (1997: 1–2). Human rights, in this instance, is perhaps the most relevant principle with respect to disability policy.

Disability policy, as a set of laws, priorities and actions, is grounded in the legal framework that begins with the overarching postwar Japanese Constitution (promulgated 1946; effective 1947). It was enacted to implement the processes of demilitarization and democratization as set out by the Occupation (Herzog 1993: 218; Caprio and Sugita 2007: 12). From the time of its ratification, the Constitution only recognized people with disability implicitly; this is notable in the absence of an explicit reference to people with disability in constitutional articles related to human rights. The articles that outline the Japanese citizens' human rights, individual equality, standards of living, access to education and jobs can be found in Chapter III, 'Rights and the Duties of the People':

Article 11. The people shall not be prevented from enjoying any of the fundamental human rights. These fundamental human rights guaranteed to the people by this Constitution shall be conferred upon the people of this and future generations as eternal and inviolate rights.

Article 13. All of the people shall be respected as individuals. Their right to life, liberty, and the pursuit of happiness shall, to the extent that it does not interfere with the public welfare, be the supreme consideration in legislation and in other governmental affairs.

Article 14. All of the people are equal under the law and there shall be no discrimination in political, economic or social relations because of race, creed, sex, social status or family origin ...

Article 25. All people shall have the right to maintain the minimum standards of wholesome and cultured living ... the State shall use its endeavors for the promotion and extension of social welfare and security, and of public health.

Article 26. All people shall have the right to receive an equal education correspondent to their ability ...

Article 27. All people shall have the right and the obligation to work ...

(House of Councillors 2001; JSRPD 2007–9)

These six excerpts from Chapter III's 103 articles outline fundamental social, political and economic areas of concern applicable to people with disabilities who are disadvantaged in respect of these 'rights and duties' compared with people without disability. The first three (Articles 11, 13 and 14) encompass identity and justice issues: Article 11, for example, says that everyone is guaranteed basic human rights. Although 'sex' is addressed, at the time of writing, disability status is not included here, but legal scholars consider this not a 'restricted list' of groups that must not be discriminated against, but merely an 'illustrative example';[9] in other words, Article 14's wording does not mean that people or groups not written into it are not included. In response to this, however, we can see that this absence creates a need for explicitness under the Basic Act for Persons with Disabilities (Shōgaisha Kihon Hō). Articles 25 to 27 relate to the rights of all Japanese citizens to basic standards in housing, education and employment.

Accordingly, the laws discussed in this chapter have all been put in place to meet these basic 'rights and duties of the people [with disabilities]'.

The Six Laws of Welfare (Fukushi Roppō) (1947–64) and other related laws

Before the implementation of public welfare, people generally provided welfare and social insurance to each other through *sonraku kyōdōtai no sōgo enjo* (mutual reciprocity in the village community) (Endō 1999: 24). This usually involved labour exchange, but also included social support and disaster relief (ibid.: 24, 36). As large numbers of the Japanese population moved from a village-based social system to an occupationally diverse and urban social system, social safety nets were put into place to ensure a certain level of social stability in Japan's growing cities.

The first 'umbrella' set of welfare laws in the postwar era that dictate the eligibility criteria and actual benefits for people with disabilities and their carers is the Fukushi Roppō, the Six Laws of Welfare. They provide the main framework by which social benefits are distributed to the entire public, not just those with disabilities. The six laws are, in order of their enactment:

1 the Child Welfare Law (Jidō Fukushi Hō, enacted 1947);
2 the Law for the Welfare of People with Physical Disabilities (Shintai Shōgaisha Fukushi Hō, enacted 1949);
3 the Public Assistance Law (literally, 'Livelihood Protection Welfare Law', Seikatsu Hogo Fukushi Hō, enacted 1950);
4 the Law for the Welfare of People with Intellectual Disabilities (Chiteki Shōgaisha Fukushi Hō, enacted 1960, renamed 1998);[10]
5 the Senior Citizen Welfare Law (Rōjin Fukushi Hō, current law enacted 1963); and
6 the Law for the Welfare of Mothers and Children, and Widows (Boshi Oyobi Kafu Fukushi Hō, enacted 1964).

In the immediate postwar period the first laws set up were the 1947 Child Welfare Law and the 1949 Law for the Welfare of People with Physical Disabilities, which was 'focused on policy for wounded soldiers' (Sakamoto 2006: n.p.), illustrating the most pressing needs at the time and the priorities of the government in addressing social problems. The fourth law, for the welfare of people with intellectual disabilities, came later. The fifth law, for the welfare of senior citizens, does not explicitly refer to 'disability', but because increasingly disability is seen as concomitant with ageing in Japan, in practice it is invoked in a large number of applications for welfare by people with disabilities. Similarly, it is important to note that many people with disabilities can fall into a number of categories from a legal perspective, and thus be eligible for benefits under more than one of the laws; for example, children with disabilities receive funds from the Child Welfare Law until they reach the age of eighteen. The persistent application and

70 *Disability policy and law in modern Japan*

the creative packaging of a number of programmes to supplement the single disability payment is the best way of creating the best outcome from the client perspective (Stevens 1997: 78); this is also true for carers. In this sense, welfare laws that support carers are also important to the integration of disability status in wider society.

These set criteria for receiving welfare benefits are vigorously debated. The question 'what are the needs of a person with disability?' is much like the rhetorical phrase 'how long is a piece of string?' For each person, there will be a different answer; furthermore the answers will vary even for the same person over his or her lifetime. But to meet criteria for welfare programmes as stipulated by the law, there has to be a measurement tool. One way to measure disability is to take a mundane example of a daily activity, and then assess the complexity of the situation for a person with a disability; most commonly medical and nursing professionals are relied upon to make these evaluations. The phrase 'activities of daily life' (ADL) is used to set standards by which medical professionals can rate a person's impairment (the ADL scale, adopted by many nations' medical associations, is based on research conducted in the USA and the UK; it has been implemented in Japan, using the original acronym ADL to refer to '*nichijō seikatsu dōsaku*', or literally the 'actions of everyday life').

ADL tasks are defined as those 'necessary to maintain physical well-being, personal appearance, hygiene, safety and general functioning in one's home and community' (Sotnik and Jezewski 2005: 29). Furthermore, a further set of skills called IADL (instrumental activities of daily life) are assessed to check on other aspects of life such as housekeeping, finance and cooking (ibid.). If ADL scores are very low, clients are considered to have a more severe impairment (and thus need greater support). But there is so much more to it than the mere 'tasks' that require physical and intellectual coordination. The ADL and IADL are set against a very complex social background. Take, for example, the action of cooking and eating a meal. Professionals look for the ability to use cooking equipment safely and the ability to hold cutlery, for example, as indicators. Yet these skills can be further seen in a wider social context. In the late-capitalist urban society that the bulk of Japanese citizens inhabit, meals can be taken at home or publicly in a restaurant or similar location. Even if the context is private, this act takes on many dimensions that require external physical, intellectual and social skills. In most cases, individuals must have an income to pay for the ingredients and have the ability to shop for food: these abilities precede the ability to prepare one's own meal and then to consume it in the privacy of one's home. All of the actions require physical and intellectual connections between a person with a disability and an abled[11] economic and social context. It is these connections, when broken, disrupted or impossible, that frame social problems that arise from disability. Social policies attempt to address these disruptions by supplementing or replacing the connections. While many welfare systems (such as those of Japan and the USA) focus on tests such as the above, it is quite confronting to think of how individuals may sit outside these categories: for example, the British physicist Stephen Hawking, living with ALS, who presumably has low ADL and IADL scores, has been a highly productive member of society with a long list of books and scholarly articles authored. Hawking's remarkable example is not one most people can realistically aspire to, but it throws into relief the dilemma of what we ought to consider a task, ability and disability. The ability to perform a task such as cooking does not guarantee that the individual can participate in a market economy to obtain the ingredients; nor does the inability to perform a task such as cleaning mean that the individual cannot contribute to society.

The Law for the Welfare of People with Physical Disabilities and the Law for the Welfare of People with Intellectual Disabilities are most explicitly related to disability welfare policy, so next we will look at them in detail. Under their regulations, benefits for disability clients are handled through local government offices. These two laws, as Yōda notes, heavily rely on a medical/individual model for classification. An individual is ranked according their ADL and IADL scores, and the 'disability certificate' (or issuance of the *shōgaisha techō*, as per Chapter 1) is based on these test outcomes (Suzuki 2009: 227).

The Law for the Welfare of People with Physical Disabilities

Now we turn to the relevant welfare laws under the Six Laws of Welfare umbrella, focusing on laws relating to physical disability and intellectual disability. The Law for the Welfare of People with Physical Disabilities, enacted in 1949, has undergone many revisions,[12] but today its general provisions read:

> Article 1, The Purpose of this Act:
> This Act, coupled with the Services and Supports for Persons with Disabilities Act, aims to enhance the welfare of persons with a physical disability through the necessary protection and the support of people with physical disabilities to promote their independence and participation in social and economic activities.
>
> Article 2, Endeavours towards Independence and Guarantees of Opportunity:
> All people with physical disabilities must strive to be able to participate in social and economic activities, by overcoming their disability of their own free will, and by making the best of the practicalities of their abilities.
>
> All people with physical disabilities, as members forming our society, will be given the opportunity to participate in social, economic and cultural activities.
>
> Article 3, The Responsibilities of the State, Local Governments and its Citizens:
> The State and local governments, aiming for the realization of the ideals in the preceding article, must work to put in place comprehensively the necessary support for and protection of (hereafter, 'rehabilitation') people with physical disabilities to promote their independence and participation in social and economic activities.

The Japanese people, based on the principle of social solidarity, must work to cooperate with people with physical disabilities in overcoming their disability and in their efforts in participating in social and economic activities.

(Shintai Shōgaisha Fukushi Hō, translation by the author)

In discourse terms, the inclusion of the term '*mizurasusunde*', which I have translated above as 'of their own free will', is notable. In this passage, people with physical disabilities are called to act 'freely', or 'voluntarily', to 'overcome their disability' to be part of mainstream society. While social inclusion is a multilateral process, it is striking that the wording uses the rather stronger *mizurasusunde* (which puts focus on the will of the individual) rather than more collective phrasing such as 'working together [with others] to overcome their disability'. 'Independence' and 'participation' as more active words balance out the more passive terms 'protection' and 'support', which appear frequently throughout the passages.

Word choices aside, the activist group JSRDP has set up a website entitled Disability Information Resources, which summarizes some of the more concrete outcomes of this law:

The following is carried out to promote independence and participation in society of physically disabled persons. [This includes:]

- Issuing of physically disabled persons' handbook.
- Various counseling services.
- Grant of prosthetic appliances such as wheelchairs, canes, hearing aids and artificial limbs.
- Provision of technical aids for daily living such as bathtubs, toilet facility, beds and communication aids (e. g. talking machines and word processors).
- Rehabilitation training.
- Provision of services necessary for participation in society such as sign language interpreter, translation Braille, guide helper and modification of motor vehicles.
- Provision of work opportunities.
- Provision of specialized facilities for nursing care.
- Provision of place for living.

(JSRDP 2007–9)

The law, as stated above, provides home-based assistance ('home help services', *hōmu herupu sābisu*) for clients. The home-care business is a growth industry, for Sakamoto records that between April 2004 and April 2005 the national number of clients receiving this service rose from 100,000 to more than 180,000, with requests from people with physical disabilities staying relatively stable, but applicants with an intellectual disability and those under the age of twenty as the two growing groups of home-care recipients (2006: 2).

The Law for the Welfare of People with Intellectual Disabilities

Some passages of this law (first enacted in 1960) are identical to the Law for the Welfare of People with Physical Disabilities, but there are important differences. The first three articles of the Law for the Welfare of People with Intellectual Disabilities read:

Article 1, The Purpose of this Act:
This Act, coupled with the Services and Supports for Persons with Disabilities Act, aims to enhance the welfare of persons with an intellectual disability through the necessary protection of and the support for people with intellectual disabilities to promote their independence and participation in social and economic activities [*This article is identical to the law for people with physical disabilities.*].

Article 1, part 2, Endeavours towards Independence and Guarantees of Opportunity:
All people with intellectual disabilities must work to be able to participate in social and economic activities, by making the best of the practicalities of their abilities.

All people with intellectual disabilities, as members forming our society, will be given the opportunity to participate in social, economic and cultural activities. [*This article is also the same except that in the first section people with intellectual disabilities are* not *asked to work hard to 'overcome' their disability* (shōgai o kokufuku suru).]

Article 2, The Responsibility of the State, Local Governments and the Citizens:
The State and local governments, aiming for the realization of the ideals in the preceding article, and while deepening the public's understanding of the welfare of people with intellectual disabilities, must work to enforce comprehensively the necessary support for and protection of (hereafter, 'rehabilitation') people with intellectual disabilities to promote their independence and participation in social and economic activities. [*This article includes a clause asking for public understanding, suggesting that intellectual disabilities are 'harder' to understand than physical disabilities.*]

While deepening the public's understanding of the welfare of people with intellectual disabilities, Japanese people, based on the principle of social solidarity, must work to cooperate with people with intellectual disabilities in their efforts to participate in social and economic activities. [*Again, no mention of overcoming disability, and again the emphasis on 'understanding'.*]

Article 3: Obligatory Cooperation between Related Personnel [*kankeishokuin*]:
According to this Law and the Child Welfare Law [Jidō Fukushi Hō], the personnel of the state and local organizations who implement and direct

rehabilitation programmes must work together to provide relevant rehabilitation for people with intellectual disabilities from childhood to adulthood.

(Chiteki Shōgaisha Fukushi Hō, translation by the author)

As noted, there are small but important differences in these two laws: the first is the emphasis on 'deepening public understanding' about intellectual disabilities. While all people with disabilities are concerned with the public's understanding of the reality of their impairment and the difficult social situations that arise from impairment, the inclusion of this phrase in this law accentuates the wider misunderstanding of intellectual disability compared with a relatively more advanced acceptance of physical disability in Japanese society. Another difference is the omission of the word *mizurasusunde*; people with intellectual disabilities are not asked to exercise their will in 'overcoming disability', which could suggest that intellectual disability is not something against which one can successfully struggle. Lastly, the mention of the need to coordinate services between welfare schemes ('from childhood to adulthood') suggests the perceived permanent nature of intellectual disability, and the infantilization of people with intellectual disability.

According to the Disability Information Resources website, the concrete benefits available under this programme are:

The law carries out necessary support in promoting independence and participation in society of mentally retarded [*sic*] persons.

- Specialized counseling provided by Social Welfare Offices and Rehabilitation Consultation Centers.
- Various training for independence.
- In-house services such as home helper, day care and short stay programs, etc.
- Provision of technical aids for daily living such as electric toothbrush and special type mat, etc.
- Provision of living space such as welfare home and group home, etc.
- Provision of specialized facilities to help daily life. For instance residential facilities for rehabilitation, nonresidential facilities and so on.
- Handbook for people with mental retardation is issued to enable easy access to various services. Information and consultation services are available at Social Welfare Offices (in cities and prefectures) and Counseling Centers for the Rehabilitation of the Mentally Retarded Persons as well as Section in charge of Disabled Persons in local governments. In each local government, there are counselors for mentally retarded persons appointed by the prefectural governor.

(JSRPD 2007–9)

Prior to the 1960 promulgation of this law, there was no legislation that clearly addressed the needs of people with an intellectual disability. In some cases, intellectual disability is part of a medical condition where physical disability or chronic illness is also present, meaning that people with diagnoses of intellectual disability can be eligible for benefits under the Law for the Welfare of People with Physical Disabilities, but there are also significant numbers of people with impaired intellectual abilities whose needs are not met through those programmes.

Delays in policy and welfare programme implementation, and continuing loopholes in programmes for people with an intellectual disability, are most likely a result of the fact that mainstream society views intellectual disability as more complicated and difficult to understand and deal with than physical disability. During fieldwork in Yokohama in the 1990s, I observed many examples of this: physical disabilities were seen as less 'threatening' to the social fabric; people were especially sympathetic to those disabilities which were congenital (in other words, 'no-fault' acquired disability). Physical assistance could be seen as a relatively concrete task that, when appropriately provided, could allow the person with a physical disability to join mainstream society on many levels. The comparative deficit in sympathy for those with intellectual disability was a result of the fact that such disability was seen as disruptive, primarily in response to the phenomenon of impaired communication and unpredictable (and possibly inappropriate) behaviour, which are not as easily externalized as the special medical or accessibility needs of those with physical disabilities. People with an intellectual disability are seen as erratic, and even dangerous, in mainstream society. In fact, because of the perceived unpredictable nature of the behaviour of intellectually impaired people, welfare services are sometimes revoked. This usually happens not because the client is maliciously disruptive, but when the services do not match the needs of the client, but the client cannot express his or her desires. Rather than shifting the service to meet the client's needs, the person is 'suspended' from the services, or privileges in the service are revoked, both of which are punitive.

Another issue affecting welfare policy for people with an intellectual disability is the idea of the individual's capacity for productivity: people with physical disabilities are seen to require concessions no more onerous than wheelchair ramps, guide dogs, Braille signage and so on (mobility and communication arrangements, in other words) to ready them to make a contribution to the economy. People with intellectual disabilities, especially in the moderate to severe range, are not expected to contribute in wider society. They are forever children, first to their parents and later to the welfare state. Their ability to make decisions (*handan nōryoku*) is impaired, so they are placed in an even more vulnerable social position than people with physical disabilities. Thus psychologically and physically sheltered, even restrained, their existence becomes even more remote from the mainstream public, and in the absence of regular interaction they come to represent the 'unknown' side of humanity.

Under both laws for people with disabilities, a disability identification card or 'handbook' (*shōgaisha techō*) is issued to people who qualify under the criteria framework described in Chapter 2. *Shōgaisha techō* benefits include pension payments – 'over $1,700 per month' in the case of severe disability (Nakamura 2006: 19) – free or reduced fares on public transport, medical and rehabilitation treatment, and special aids and equipment. Further to these two laws are other programmes and payments made to those deemed 'disabled' under these state guidelines that involve criteria concerning sight, hearing, movement and mental functioning. Parents or carers of children with disabilities receive between ¥30,000 and ¥50,000 a month (depending on the severity of the disability) in the form of a 'Special Child Rearing Allowance' (JSRPD 2007–9). Another example of further grants is the *tokubetsu shōgaisha teate* ('special allowance for people with disabilities'), a payment system for both intellectually and physically impaired people over the age of twenty who require extra care on a daily basis but are not living in a public or private institution and have been hospitalized for less than three months per annum. It is administered on the local level (from the municipal government offices, like many welfare programmes) and is paid on a quarterly basis (Shōgaisha Jiritsu Shien Hō 2005). At the time of the law's inception, the payment was ¥26,440 a month.

Other related laws

Elderly people, like people with disabilities, are often deemed 'unproductive' members of society, but in most cases the elderly are perceived to have 'earned' their share of social security by paying into the scheme throughout their 'productive' years as workers. The national pension system was 'inaugurated' in 1961 (Hayashi and Okuhira 2001: 856), but this was a scheme aimed at the general population, not just those with disabilities. The *shōgai kiso nenkin*, as the 'basic disability allowance' (Yōda 2002: 10), was introduced in 1985 as part of a total reform of the pension system (OPIPA 2004: 4). The disability basic pension mainly targets those who have been diagnosed with a 'permanent disability before reaching twenty years of age' (16). Recent figures for this pension were ¥82,758 per month for grade one disabilities (more severe) and ¥66,208 per month for grade two disabilities (JSRPD 2007–9). Pensions are paid bi-monthly; the national Pension Bureau calculates an annual disability basic pension ranging from ¥797,000 up to ¥996,300 depending on the severity of the disability and whether there are dependent children (OPIPA 2004: 11, 17).

As noted above, twenty years of age is significant because at that age an individual is considered an adult, independent of their parents. After a 1986 reform, payments were made directly to the adult individual and not the family (Yōda 2002: 10). Yet Hayashi and Okuhira observe that the pension is always income-tested against the person's family's financial circumstances (2001: 856); thus one can argue that the government views the individual with a disability as an extension of a family rather than as an individual, and this nearly always puts the person with a disability in the position of a dependent child rather than an independently functioning adult. Income testing also puts stress on the individual, as Japan's welfare mindset has always been to provide financial support 'only after all other personal and public resources have been exhausted' and that 'public assistance should be provided to a household rather than to an individual' (Yōda 2002: 10). This results in some people with disabilities remaining dependent on their families for financial reasons in cases where it may not be in their best interest and their overall quality of living suffers (11).

The Mental Hygiene Law, or Seishin Eisei Hō, was enacted in 1950, revised in 1954 and revised again and renamed in 1987–8 to become the Mental Health Law (Seishin Hoken Hō). These changes involved the strengthening of the human rights of people diagnosed with psychiatric disabilities through changes to institutional admission processes and hospital practices (Heyer 1999: 12–13). These reviews were instigated by a breaking-point incident in 1983 at the Utsunomiya Hospital, where two patients were killed while admitted at a psychiatric hospital, having been beaten with pipes by nurses. When this information became public in 1984, Japanese activists brought in the United Nations Commission on Human Rights to investigate, and this international pressure brought about reform, although Ohnishi et al. have critiqued the effectiveness of these changes on the basis of a list of newspaper reports of ongoing human rights violations in hospitals from 1987 to 2005 (Ohnishi et al. 2008).

The Law for the Welfare of People with Psychiatric Disabilities, Seishin Shōgaisha Fukushi Hō, sits beside the two welfare laws for physical and intellectual disabilities, and its articles reflect the other laws' ideals of inclusion, participation and 'understanding'. One notable difference is the wording in Article 1, which mirrors the other two welfare laws' wording except for the emphasized additions:

> Article 1, The Purpose of this Act:
> This Act is to provide medical care and protection for people with psychiatric disabilities, and coupled with the Services and Supports for Persons with Disabilities Act, *aims to prevent the occurrence of such disorders*, and to enhance the welfare of persons with psychiatric disabilities through the necessary protection of and the support for people with psychiatric disabilities *to promote their reinstatement in society*, as well as their independence and participation in social and economic activities.
> (Seishin Shōgaisha Fukushi Hō, translation by the author)

'Psychiatric disabilities' are defined in Article 5 as conditions such as 'schizophrenia, disorders arising from [alcohol or drug] addiction, intellectual disability or mental illness [psychosis]'. The law here refers to this disability as a 'disorder', which implies an adherence to the medical model and that a psychiatric disability is an illness to be treated and even cured, rather than a state of being; having schizophrenia is not akin to being blind, or deaf, or having cerebral palsy.

Considering this stance, the Law for the Welfare of People with Psychiatric Disabilities is the only law that aims to prevent the occurrence of a condition, again aligning it with the 'medical model' rather than with the 'social model' that accepts disability as part of life. Unlike the intellectual disability law, which considers this impairment as present from childhood to adulthood, the psychiatric disability welfare law views such individuals as having lost their place in society as a result of their illnesses, though capable of being 'reinstated' (*fukki*) through protection and support. The inclusion of 'intellectual disability', creating an overlap between this law and the intellectual disability welfare law, probably stems from the order of the laws' enactment: that on physical disability enacted in 1949, followed by that on psychiatric disabilities in 1950. Until 1960, the welfare of people with intellectual disabilities would have been addressed under the Law for the Welfare of People with Psychiatric Disabilities.

The Law for the Promotion of Employing People with a Disability

Among Japan's many labour laws, the Law for the Promotion of Employing People with a Disability (Shōgaisha no Koyō no Sokushin nado ni Kansuru Hōritsu)[13] stands as one that highlights the productive capability of this sector of the population. This capacity for contribution was not acknowledged in the Six Laws of Welfare, but is stated in this labour law, as well as in the wording of the newer Services and Supports for Persons with Disabilities Act.[14] The Law for the Promotion of Employing People with a Disability was first enacted in 1960; it has been revised many times in its fifty-year history (the last time in 1992), and is part of Japan's ratification of International Labour Organization Convention 159, or the 'Vocational Rehabilitation and Employment of Disabled Persons' (Naikakufu 2003). In the early years of implementation, this law focused on retraining individuals in new vocations, but suffered from a lack of 'substantive progress in the welfare [of those employed under this law]' (Endō 1999: 165). As with the precursors of other laws like the Basic Act for Persons with Disabilities, the earlier version of this employment law in its title specified people with 'physical disabilities', which excluded those with intellectual impairment (Heyer 1999: 6; Matsui 1998), pointing to explicitly formulated notions about who, amongst those with disabilities, should and should not work. Ideas about work for people with disabilities are, however, changing; Kyōgoku Takanobu, scholar of demography and social security, warns that Japan's falling fertility rate, coupled with an ageing society, means that labour shortages may impede Japan's economy. One way to remedy that situation is to facilitate the participation of people with disabilities in the workplace to take advantage of every person's ability to contribute to the economy (Kyōgoku 2005a).

The first version of the employment law, which focused on people with physical disabilities, established a quota to be implemented in 1976 (Heyer 1999: 7); as Matsui observes, this was achieved by changing the quota from a 'moral obligation' to a 'legal requirement' (Matsui 1998). People with physical disabilities were to be allocated jobs through Public Employment Security Offices throughout the country. These offices assisted not just people with disabilities but also other sorts of people looking for work, as per the Employment Security Law (ibid.). Furthermore, other employment laws complement the Law for the Promotion of Employing People with a Disability. For example, the Employment

Countermeasures Law (1966) is meant to do this by providing and improving 'vocational training' to clients and assisting with job placement. Another example is Article 16 of the Employment Security Law, which states that

> The Minister of Health, Labour and Welfare may establish necessary standards concerning the implementation of employment placement and vocational guidance for the physically or mentally disabled, those seeking to newly enter employment, middle-aged and older unemployed persons and others in need of special consideration with respect to obtaining employment.
> (Shokugyō Antei Hō 1947)

Today's Law for the Promotion of Employing People with a Disability refers to people with both physical and intellectual disabilities and specifies quotas for employees with a disability in a variety of settings. These quotas are said to be set in response to 'the number of disabled people who wish to work and are able to do so' (Zenkoku Jiritsu Seikatsu Sentā Kyōgikai 2001). The current quotas are:

1.8 per cent employment in 'private sector firms' [more than 200 regular workers]
2.1 per cent in 'governmental corporations' [*tokushu hōjin*]
2.1 per cent in 'national and local public entities' [NGOs/NPOs]
2.0 per cent in 'designated education commissions' [prefectural level]
(Hasegawa 2007:47–8)

Levy forms are to be submitted by companies that employ more than 200 'regular' employees (JEED 2010: 9). Awards are made to companies that exceed the quota, with smaller companies receiving ¥21,000 a month and larger companies ¥27,000 a month (ibid.). This 'levy and grant system' means that those that do not hire the quota are to pay into a fund which is then redistributed as awards for those that do, and the Japan Association for Employment of the Disabled handles these exchanges (Matsui 1998).

This association is supposed to collect ¥50,000 a month per person below the quota from large companies; this forms a pool to provide the grants listed above (JSRPD 2007–9). If these quotas are not met, fines may be imposed; one well-known example of this is the case of Japan Airlines, which was charged in 2001 with not meeting its quota, although the case was settled out of court. In the end, Japan Airlines did not pay a fine, but instead agreed to increase the number of employees with a disability to the required quota by the end of March 2011, and publicize the actual numbers of people with disabilities employed on its company website (Zenkoku Jiritsu Seikatsu Sentā Kyōgikai 2001).

In general, industry, mining and manufacturing companies are more likely to meet the quota while tertiary industry does not; furthermore, small companies fared better in their hiring of people with disabilities overall, and of people with intellectual disabilities (Matsui 1998). Still, about half of registered private companies do not meet this quota (Shimizu cited in Iwakuma 2003: 126), and while the quota exempts small firms, it is the smaller companies that tend to comply most closely because they cannot afford to pay the infringement fines (Iwakuma 2003: 126). Matsui observes that the lingering recession since the early 1990s meant that the reduction in the overall workforce of companies that were restructuring spared such companies from having to hire more employees with disabilities because the overall numbers of their employees were contracting (1998). In Japan's continuing sluggish economy, the absolute numbers of people with disabilities in employment may not be increasing.

The Japanese employment environment is still very segregated, especially for those with intellectual impairments (Heyer 1999: 14), which reflects the original law's delineation between people with disabilities who can work and those who should not. Part of the reason for segregation is a reliance on *jusan shisetsu* ('sheltered work programmes'), also sometimes referred to using the more generic term *sagyōba* ('workshop'), for employment of people with intellectual disabilities. These programmes are important in that they give adults with intellectual disabilities a sense of daily routine and purpose. Because these programmes are subsidized by the government, the wages paid by the company are lower than ordinary labour costs. Furthermore, such programmes keep their members out of wider unemployment (and regular employment) statistics. In Kotobuki-chō, an underclass area in central Yokohama, I worked occasionally in the mid-1990s with members of the Roba no Ie, a workshop for adults with mild to moderate intellectual and psychiatric disabilities. The workshop was crucial in providing training and social interaction, but its employees were still segregated from mainstream society, first by virtue of their employment scheme and second owing to the workshop's location in a marginalized section of the city (see Stevens 1997: 88–90).

Although these employment laws appear to be progressive in the eyes of activists who promote independent lifestyles, in some cases they act as an impediment to the full participation of people with disabilities in the labour force. The law itself discriminates against different kinds of disabilities as its scope does not extend to 'persons with psychiatric disabilities' (JSRPD 2002–7), and while grants are paid to employers taking on employees with 'mental retardation', no employer is required to do so (Matsui 1998). Rather than treating all people with disabilities as equal, the system privileges companies that have employed people with severe disabilities by letting them count one such worker twice for the quota requirement (ibid). Furthermore, Nakamura learned in interviews that these laws influenced people's decisions, discouraging some from going on to higher education that would have resulted in a higher probability of them obtaining more prestigious or higher-paying jobs. She writes that high school graduates of deaf school were unlikely to go on to university, even if they were capable of doing so, because '[t]he disability job quotas enacted by the government actually exacerbate the situation since even high school graduates are pretty much assured a job, even if it were a dead-end "window-seat" job' (2006: 89–90).

Implied here is that students from special educational institutions, such as those for the deaf or blind, have been funnelled without distinction into low-paying jobs, instead of being encouraged to seek further training to reach their full employment potential. Despite this, for those for whom university training is not appropriate, the disability job quota is an important support pathway into an adult placement (this programme is also important for family carers, so that they are given a reprieve from their caring duties during their children's or siblings' working hours).

Another structural impediment to instituting equitable employment practices for people with disabilities in Japan is the various legal loopholes that allow indirect discrimination in hiring practices. For example, the presence of a disability can mean the government can withhold licences needed for certain categories of work (Heyer 1999: 18–19). One typical example of this is the provision that people who are deaf and people with intellectual or psychiatric disabilities cannot obtain a driver's licence. While this situation is a practical necessity, indirect discrimination occurs because it thus possible for employees to advertise for workers using a *kekkaku jōkō* (disqualifying clause) that allows the employer to request any medical records.

The employment environment for people with disabilities is not entirely bleak, however. One company that not only meets the quota but also advertises its quota as a selling point is the ubiquitous budget clothing retailer UNIQLO. Established in 1984, it became popular in 1998 marketing casual clothing for men, women and children and currently has 703 shops across Japan.[15] In 2001, the company began a campaign of *ichitenpo ichimei ijō* ('more than one person per store'), and within one year changed its employment rate of employees with disabilities from 1.27 per cent to 6.35 per cent. In 2010 approximately 90 per cent of UNIQLO stores had an employee with a disability, exceeding the 1.8 per cent minimum with an 8.04 per cent employment rate (Fast Retailing Co. 2010), up from 7.42 per cent in 2007 (*Yomiuri Shimbun* 2007).[16] The company's website reveals that there is diversity within this group: of the 763 people employed in 2009, 10.9 per cent had a psychiatric disability, 12.8 per cent had a mild physical disability, 14.7 per cent had a severe physical disability, 28.9 per cent had a severe intellectual disability and 32.7 per cent had a mild intellectual disability (ibid.). This figure of more than 700 employees is set against the total employee figure of about 11,000. In 2007, UNIQLO received the *saicharenji shien kōdō hyōshō* (a prize for public service awarded by the Prime Minister's Office) in recognition of its efforts to diversify its workforce. In an email message, I asked the company's customer service section to illuminate the webpage statistics, asking exactly what kind of work its employees with a disability performed, and the response was:

> As for the specifics of the work, while it is mainly work done outside of business hours cleaning and putting out products in the backroom, there are also cases where we have them work inside the store, attending to customers.
>
> Furthermore, at our company, all staff who work at a store for more than 100 hours a month become 'associate employees' (*junshain*); those working

less than 100 hours are casual, while the rest are 'associates'. When we appoint a person with a disability, at each store we appoint [them] as a rule as [an] 'associate employee', and, we consider their disability with regard to their work. Furthermore, we offer as much guidance as possible to store managers who are hiring new staff to help them follow [their employees' progress] while exhibiting [core values of] consideration, watchfulness and attention.

(personal communication, 9 July 2009)

For more personal stories from this company, see Chapter 5 for an explication on what it is like to be a young adult with a disability in the workplace.

The Basic Act for Persons with Disabilities (1970) and the Services and Supports for Persons with Disabilities Act (2005)

As a defining standard, functioning in a similar way to Chapter III, 'Rights and the Duties of the People', in the Japanese Constitution for the general population, the first chapter of the Shōgaisha Kihon Hō (mostly simply translated as 'Basic Act for Persons with Disabilities' by the Ministry of Justice, but it has also been translated as the 'Fundamental Law for Countermeasures for Mentally and Physically Handicapped Persons') sets out a parallel text of human rights. Of particular interest in the discussion of human rights are this law's Chapter I, Articles 3, 4, 5 and 6 (Shōgaisha Kihon Hō 2010). The third line of Article 3 states that 'no one may discriminate against disabled persons by reason of disability nor disturb their rights and benefits'. Articles 4 and 6 discuss the 'responsibilities' of the 'central government', 'local public entities' and the 'nation' to 'advocate' and 'advance the welfare' of people with disabilities. Article 5 calls for 'necessary measures to increase the proper understanding of the nation in regard to disabled persons' (translation by JSRPD, 2007–9). Chapter II of this law treats the welfare of people with disabilities in an abstract sense, and notes that it is the responsibility of the state and the local government (*koku oyobi chihō kōkyō dantai*) to meet their needs. Chapter III is entitled 'Fundamental Measures regarding the Prevention of Disability' while the last chapter is entitled 'The Committee for the Promotion of Policy for People with Disabilities' which calls for the Naikakufu, or the Cabinet Office, to form a committee to plan future disability policy in Japan (Shōgaisha Kihon Hō 2010). This role for the Cabinet Office was established in response to the UN's International Decade of the Disabled Person (ending in 1992) (Heyer 1999: 9).

The Basic Act for Persons with Disabilities was established in 1970, when it carried the title Shintai Shōgaisha Kihon Hō (Basic Act for Persons with Physical Disabilities), but the word *shintai* (physical) was deleted in 1993 to extend the law's scope to include people with intellectual and psychiatric disabilities (Heyer 1999: 11). The DINF (Disability Information) website (sponsored by the JSRPD) considers the following seven articles (of the total twenty-nine) in the Basic Act for Persons with Disabilities to be most important:

- Article 2 (Definition): 'Disabled persons' as used in this Law means persons whose daily life or life in society is substantially limited over the long term due to a physical disability, mental retardation or mental disability.
- Article 3 (Fundamental Principles): The dignity of all disabled persons shall be respected. They shall have the right to be treated accordingly. All disabled persons shall, as members of society, be provided with opportunities to fully participate in such a manner.
- Article 4 (Responsibilities of the State and Local Public Entities): The State and local public bodies shall be responsible for promoting the welfare of disabled persons and for preventing disabilities.
- Article 5 (Responsibilities of the Nation): The nation shall, on the basis of the principle of social solidarity, endeavor to cooperate in promoting the welfare of disabled persons.
- Article 6 (Efforts to Achieve Independence): Disabled persons shall endeavor to participate actively in social and economic activities by making effective use of the abilities they possess. The family members of disabled persons shall endeavor to promote independence of disabled persons.
- Article 6–2 (Disabled Persons' Day): Disabled Persons' Day shall be established for the purpose of raising the public awareness to the welfare of disabled persons and stimulating disabled persons' desire to actively participate in social, economic, cultural and other areas of activity.
- Article 7 (Fundamental Policies): The measures regarding the welfare of disabled persons shall be carried out according to their age and to the types and severity of disabilities.

(JSRPD 2007–9)

In 2005, a new 'umbrella' law, the Shōgaisha Jiritsu Shien Hō, or the Services and Supports for Persons with Disabilities Act, was established with the intention of improving and systematizing the content and delivery of services to clients regardless of their disability (Kyōgoku 2005b: 7–9). According to the government, this law is based on five reforming principles:

1 centralization of services;
2 improving society's capacity to give work to people with disabilities;
3 'relaxing regulations' or allowing local governments to be more flexible in delivering their clients' specific needs;
4 transparency and clarity in procedures and standards; and
5 strengthening the sense that a growing welfare service sector needs to be funded fairly and properly, acknowledging private and public contributions (in other words, balancing individual or family contributions with government support).

(Kyōgoku 2005b)

The first paragraph of this law (the 'purpose') sets out the specific laws underneath it, such as the two laws discussed above (the Law for the Welfare of People with Physical Disabilities and the Law for the Welfare of People with Intellectual Disabilities) as well as laws concerning people with psychiatric disabilities and the welfare of children, to the extent that it applies to children with disabilities (Shōgaisha Jiritsu Shien Hō, 2005). The first few sections that follow are concerned with stakeholder roles; Chapter II lists the services for which payments can be received, application procedures, and the process of disability classification.

The most striking change instituted with the promulgation of this law is found in Article 28 item 3 of this chapter; it sets out the level of client co-payment for welfare services, which was originally set at 10 per cent of the cost of the service:

> (3) An amount of nursing care payment or payment for training, etc., shall be equivalent to 90/100 of the expenses calculated pursuant to the standard specified by Minister of Health, Labour and Welfare by each expense normally needed for designated welfare service, etc. for every kind of welfare service for persons with disabilities.
>
> (ibid.)

Standards for services and facilities are set by ordinance, and the process for 'naming and shaming' the service providers that do not meet minimum standards is also stated. Grant approval, as well as conditions under which a grant may be withdrawn, is spelled out in Chapter III, while Chapter IV outlines the proper structure for a variety of welfare 'businesses'. Chapter V, Article 87 states that the Minister of Health, Labour and Welfare will 'consolidate welfare service for persons with disabilities and consultation support, and provision systems for municipal and prefectural life support services, and ensure smooth operation of services and supports for persons with disabilities payment and community life support services (hereinafter referred to as "basic guidelines")' (ibid.).

Of interest here is the specification of 'consolidation' and 'smooth operations', which were the cause of common complaints under the previous system. After further discussion of roles and responsibilities, processes and appeals, the law provides for its own review in five years' time (outlined below).

Taking the above information into account, there are approximately five major areas of reform introduced by the Services and Supports for Persons with Disabilities Act.

1. Collapsing the distinctions between the three major disability categories (physical, intellectual and psychiatric disabilities); this means that people with different kinds of disabilities can equally access facilities which may have been established primarily for others (e.g. allowing a person with intellectual disability to use a facility for physical disabilities).
2. Streamlining programmes and facilities to help cut waiting times; for example, instead of thirty-three different kinds of facilities, six categories will be

available. Formerly facilities were divided by disability, severity of impairment and age of client. The reform helps to separate out hospitals for medical treatment from facilities to be used for long-term care. Terms for access to these facilities are found in the Law for the Welfare of People with Physical Disabilities, the Law for the Welfare of People with Intellectual Disabilities and the Law for the Mental Health and Welfare of People with Psychiatric Disabilities.
3   Strengthening the vocational programmes including, but also beyond, sheltered work programmes and welfare workshops.
4   Promoting transparency in the decision-making process.
5   Stabilizing the source of funds for individual payments (such as those for home services) through making them uniform throughout Japan; making policy at local and state levels consistent.

(summarized from Sakamoto 2006: 6–10)

The main problems with this new legislation are:

1   The introduction of the levy system, where after a contract is drawn up, the user then pays 10 per cent of the fee. What this meant in practice was that the more services a client utilized, the more costly it was for the individual, which discouraged users from applying for all the services for which they were eligible. Because of this criticism, the levy has dropped to 3 per cent.
2   Responsibility and accountability in 'individual care management' (*kobetsu shien keika*). In the former system, the 'unilateral administrative decision' was made by the local government, and represented a 'top-down' decision-making process. While this was disempowering, it was also clear where responsibility lay.
3   Persistence of bureaucratic discretion: while the application process has been made more transparent by these changes, it is not clear whether the standards by which decisions have been made are equally transparent.
4   The myth of the contract: while the notion of a mutually agreed contract is more empowering of the client than the former 'unilateral administrative decision', in reality some of the contracts are little more than decisions made by bureaucrats.[17]

Shakespeare, though writing about the West, offers an applicable critique of the 'user pays' model embedded in the Services and Supports for Persons with Disabilities Act:

Anti discrimination law and independent living solutions seem to suggest that the market will provide, if only disabled people are enabled to exercise choices free of unfair discrimination. But market approaches often restrict, rather than increase, choice to disabled people ... An individual, market-based solution, by failing to acknowledge persistent inequalities in physical and mental capacities, cannot liberate all disabled people.

(2006: 66)

Why these changes? While a need to rein in budgets is surely a contributing factor, a desire to match global standards has also been attributed to some of the changes in Japanese law (Heyer 1999: 3–6; *Japan Times* 2007); hence, international comparisons are useful in contextualizing the policy that drives this area of Japan's legal system. Japan is not alone in its struggle to deal with these difficult issues; many situations in other countries are substantially comparable. The most relevant might be disability law in the United States, owing to the historical relationship between the two legal systems (considering the significant US involvement in the drafting of the Japanese Constitution). Looking overseas, the Japanese Constitution recognizes 'treaties and customary international law'; while the Japanese government does not necessarily implement 'international instruments' (such as UN Declarations), they do have symbolic value (Heyer 1999: 4).

The Americans with Disabilities Act (ADA) provides an interesting comparison with the Basic Act for Persons with Disabilities. Passed in 1990 and amended in 2009, it first guarantees people with disabilities freedom from discrimination, as per Section 12101 (see ADA 2009: appendix ii). The ADA follows Section 504 of the Rehabilitation Act (1973), which gave people with disabilities 'full social participation as a civil right', but both were deemed ineffective because 'specific regulations and guidelines regarding requirements and enforcements' were not immediately put into place (Jaeger and Bowman 2005: 40). The ADA promises more through 'prohibit[ing] discrimination and requir[ing] equal opportunity in employment …government services, public accommodations, commercial facilities and transportation' (41), and 'provides a mechanism for legal protection and remedies' (42). Davis, however, warns that general American sentiment is not truly supportive of this law: approximately 95 per cent of cases brought against employers under this Act are lost in favour of the employer defendants (2002: 24, 148). Heyer distinguishes the ADA's wording as a law that 'views disability from a civil rights perspective and mandates neutrality, or "blind justice", in decisions regarding protected groups' (1999: 3). Australia has its 1992 Disability Discrimination Act, which is meant to 'eliminate, *as far as possible*, discrimination against persons on the ground of disability' (Commonwealth Consolidated Acts 1992, emphasis added).

In March 2012, the Japanese Cabinet announced its decision to instigate a three-year reform process for the 2005 Services and Supports for Persons with Disabilities Act, as a response to calls from disability activist groups to restore 'in-principle cost free access to welfare services' (*fukushi sābisu no riyōryō no gensoku muryōka*), using a method of deciding services based on needs rather than other, possibly irrelevant criteria (NHK 2012). This development is accompanied with warnings that reforms need to include people with chronic illness, who might be left out of benefits if their illnesses (however acutely disabling) do not meet criteria for disability status, creating a 'chasm in the system' (*seido no tanima*).

The laws listed above have come about in a particular chronological order, and now sit in a particular relationship to each other (see Table 4.1). Yet today, they are implemented based on a series of bureaucratic decisions that result in a

Table 4.1 The relationship between the major laws concerning people with disabilities in Japan

Basic principles 原則 (*gensoku*)	Services and Supports for Persons with Disabilities Act *Shōgaisha Jiritsu Shien Hō*			
Exceptions 例外 (*reigai*)	The Welfare Law for People with Intellectual Disabilities *Chiteki Shōgaisha Fukushi Hō*	The Welfare Law for People with Physical Disabilities *Shintai Shōgaisha Fukushi Hō*	The Welfare Law for People with Psychiatric Disabilities *Seishin Shōgaisha Fukushi Hō*	(Others)
Concepts, ideals 理念 (*rinen*)	Basic Act for Persons with Disabilities *Shōgaisha Kihon Hō*			

nesting of laws that work in different contexts; the newer laws do not replace the older laws in every situation. Welfare applications are presented either as fitting in with basic principles or as exceptions to the rule.[18] The way these laws came into being, and how they now interact with each other, can certainly be attributed to policy shifts from recompensation to normalization, and even from a socialist welfare attitude to a more neoliberal view of welfare.

In Table 4.1, the laws in the middle row (the 'exceptions') came first (from 1947 to 1964); in this sense, they were the earliest and, at that time, the only laws for people with disabilities. These laws addressed immediate and practical needs without much concern for human rights principles, thus focusing wholly on 'recompensation'. The existence of the newer 'basic principles' in the top row, however, does not overrule any of the Six Laws of Welfare; rather, the six laws remain there to handle 'exceptions' brought up when cases do not fit neatly into the programmes of the Services and Supports for Persons with Disabilities Act. The new 'basic principles' are a result of normalization principles (read: independent, integrated) influenced by the 'user pays' model, found in many neoliberal policies affecting many aspects of governance. This can be demonstrated in the process by which individuals apply for and receive benefits under the new scheme.

The main difference between the processes in the 'principles' category and the processes in the 'exceptions' category is the nature of the relationship between the client and the service provider. In the principles category, the welfare client is thought to be more empowered than in the exceptions category, which was in fact, prior to 2005, the way all cases were handled. This difference has been termed, in Japanese, '*sochi kara keiyaku e*' ('from administrative measures to mutual contract'). Under each of the Six Laws of Welfare, the relationship between client and service provider is described from the standpoint of '*sochi*', literally meaning 'measures', but this term can be more fully understood as an 'unilateral administrative decision'.[19] Decisions about welfare services (e.g. what service is needed, how often it is accessed, where it takes place and who will deliver it) were made by an administrator on behalf of the client, and in some cases clients understandably felt powerless and confused by the process. Under the Services and Supports for Persons with Disabilities Act, however, the relationship between client and services is conceived as a contract (*keiyaku*) between two mutually agreeing parties. For example, under this scheme an applicant makes a request to their local government for disability services; consultation follows, and the client makes a decision as to which services s/he would like to engage. Accordingly, a contract is drawn up with the provider to engage with its services, and the client then pays a levy (*chōshū*) of between 3 and 10 per cent. In cases where an individual is deemed unable to make decisions about which services s/he wishes to access, however, the case reverts to the 'sochi' mode and the client's services are determined (and paid for) by authorities.

When disability benefits are requested, the applicant is repeatedly scrutinized (evidenced by pages and pages of text on application, and then later upon review of grants, or appeals of the rejection or reversal of grants); the connection between the individual and the state is amplified. In exchange for more benefits to the welfare recipient, the responsibilities of the citizen are also heightened: processes of evaluation, compliance and accountability all weigh heavily on welfare recipients. As the system diversifies through the creation of more specific programmes, or is supposedly simplified as per the Services and Supports for Persons with Disabilities Act, the welfare recipient's condition as well as character is more closely scrutinized to prevent abuse of the system. The scrutiny begins with classification, and then 'appropriate' applications to programmes; as the individual ages and/or the condition changes over time (as per the lifecycle) some programmes no longer apply and new applications to programmes with new criteria must be made.

Issues

Certain issues have been identified concerning the workings of the legislation. For example, Karen Nakamura, an anthropologist who has researched the deaf community as well as the comparative politics of severe physical and psychiatric disabilities, writes that Article 25 of the Constitution, while forming the foundation of Japanese policy regarding disability, is 'paternalistic in the best and worst sense of the word' (Nakamura 2005: 58). The paternalism that she refers to is the control of the 'minimum standards' of social welfare through the allocation of services and funds. The problem relates to who determines what these minimum standards are, and how they are to be achieved by the individual. For people with a disability, especially those who have communication and/or intellectual impairments, expressing an opinion about minimum standards is very difficult and they may rely on another person to decide what constitutes satisfactory living standards. Here we see both the 'common sense view' and the 'residual model' in action: medical professionals often dictate 'minimum standards', and if recipients are independent of their families, the state steps in and tries to behave as if it were a parent. This is reflected in the perceived need for change in the delivery of disability welfare benefits in the 2000s, as discussed later in this chapter with regard to the ideological shift from 'administrative measures' to 'mutual contract', illustrated in the move from the Six Laws of Welfare to the Services and Supports for Persons with Disabilities Act as the 'normal' legal structure that supports people with disabilities.

Another influential factor affecting both policy 'trends' and decisions about welfare law in Japan over time is *gaiatsu*, 'foreign pressure', on Japanese lawmakers. The role of foreign pressure on executive and administrative decision-making in Japan has been longstanding and has proved difficult to resist in many cases. We can discern the influence of an external gaze on many aspects of postwar Japanese society. Nakamura refers to *gaiatsu* in her account of the disability activist backlash against funding programmes that supported independent living: '[i]n confronting the government, Japanese disability advocates have tried to play into the insecurities of the politicians and bureaucrats by showing how far behind Northern European countries Japan is in its disability welfare policies' (2005: 58). It is apparent with respect to Japan's treatment of not only people with disabilities but also other minorities such as the Ainu, Burakumin, resident Koreans and gendered groups. International pressure has been identified as a cause of both legal changes (e.g. revisions to the Mental Hygiene Law in the late 1980s and the establishment of domestic labour laws as part of Japan's ratification of the International Labour Organization Convention) and initiatives such as the establishment of barrier-free design in urban planning in the 1990s.

Normalization and neoliberalism

As noted in the introduction to this chapter, 'normalization', with its main objective of encouraging integration into mainstream society, has been a major policy directive in Japanese disability policy discourse. In a 'user-friendly' manual published by the Ministry of Health and Welfare, the goal of services for people with disabilities is said to be to ensure 'that people with disabilities may live with the same rights as those without disabilities; and to embody the ideal of "*normalization*" which aims at a society of *action*...' (1995: 95, emphasis added).

Striking in the original is the katakana term '*nōmaraizēshon*', borrowed from English, which suggests that abled life constitutes 'normalcy' and 'action' to which people with disabilities must aspire. The government consciously adopted normalization as a policy principle in the early 1980s (Heyer 1999: 9). A government Social Welfare Handbook defines normalization as 'aiming towards a society of participation' (*katsudō suru shakai o mezasu*) for people both with and without disabilities (MHW 1995: 95). The government's white paper on The Law for the Promotion of Employing People with a Disability also uses the term *nōmaraizēshon* to communicate this idea of adapting the person with a disability to a non-disabled lifestyle through employment (Naikakufu 2006). Postwar Japanese welfare policy has frequently relied on the notion of having people with disabilities conform to mainstream expectations first, rather than modifying ableist society. This is, as Thomson writes, a mindset where the overriding principle is 'rehabilitation' (away from 'compensation', but not yet 'accommodation')

(1997: 49). Yet normalization apparently has limits, as it seems to align with issues concerning certain disability groups while ignoring others. For example, Heyer critiques the Japanese normalization principle for overlooking the needs of people with intellectual disabilities while focusing on the more practical needs of those with physical disabilities (1999: 9).

The impact of policy trends on Japanese law is demonstrated in the way laws are interpreted, revised and implemented, resulting in changes in the means by which recipients apply for and receive benefits, as well as changes in the way they view the 'system' and how they interact with it. This section looks at specific outcomes resulting from the impact of normalization and neoliberalism in the postwar era.

Normalization can be seen in the most fundamental legal document, the Japanese Constitution. It creates a baseline of understanding of what it means to be recognized as a citizen in Japan, and accordingly what 'rights and duties' are encompassed in this status, and in Article 25 the Constitution aims to bring all people, regardless of background, 'the right to maintain the minimum standards of wholesome and cultured living. In all spheres of life, the State shall use its endeavors for the promotion and extension of social welfare and security, and of public health' (House of Councillors 2001).

The right to 'maintain the minimum standards of...living' can be interpreted as the right to earn a living, but recognizing that not all individuals can perform this task, the state extends 'social welfare and security'. This line, drawn between who can and cannot earn a living, continues to be divisive. Some believe that people with disabilities could earn a living if, for example, accessibility features were widespread and appropriate jobs were made available to applicants with disabilities; others might criticize people with disabilities as 'dole cheats'. When the ability to exercise one's social, economic and political power is compromised, and individuals find it difficult to participate in community life that confers social status, then their 'minimum standards of wholesome and cultured living' are more 'minimal' than those of able-bodied compatriots. In other words, their status as full-fledged citizens of the nation is reduced as compared with those who find no obstacle to the performance of such duties. Thomson reiterates this: 'In other words, people deemed disabled are barred from full citizenship because their bodies do not conform with architectural, attitudinal, education, occupational, and legal conventions based on assumptions that bodies appear and perform in certain ways'(1997: 46).

There have been some concrete advances, however, that are more accommodating than normalizing, suggesting that the 'rights' of citizenship are being considered in alternative ways. In 2000–1, the Ministry of Health and Welfare established the 'Barrier Free no Machizukuri no Katsudōjigyō' (Project for Building Barrier-Free Cities) which provided planning and incentives for local governments to choose barrier-free construction (including the widening of walkways, the elimination of stairs in entrances to public buildings, and installation of elevators and crossing signals for the seeing impaired [Naikakufu 2003], plus improvements to toilet and public phone facilities). This too was a result of international influence, and we can see the temporal lag before grassroots movements translate into policy: the international 'barrier-free' movement began in 1974, but it was not until 2001 that the term was adopted by the United Nations as part of the work in preparation for the 2006 Convention on the Rights of Persons with Disabilities. The barrier-free movement in Japan has resulted in some positive changes (see Chapter 7 for details), but at the same time these reveal further problematic notions about sharing space with people with disabilities, where able-bodied people are cajoled into giving people with disabilities preference in using these facilities rather than deferring to them as a matter of course. This reflects Heyer's observation that Japanese welfare laws tend to 'aim for equality of results by emphasizing special needs over equal rights and mandating quotas' (1999: 3), with the idea that individual needs should be addressed rather than adopting a one-size-fits-all approach to welfare benefits.

As a logical consequence of normalization, the concept of *jiritsu* (independence) has become a major element of recent welfare discourse and the main principle driving the Services and Supports for Persons with Disabilities Act. This policy shift was arguably in response to the positive requests from disability activists promoting a more self-sufficient identity for people with disabilities through independent living in the community, but related policies are often criticized instead for twisting normalization ideals into a neoliberal 'user pays' system which in reality puts more of a burden on the welfare recipient. Independent living, ideally, is defined as 'living in an accessible home and the availability of accessible environments and services and information' (Shakespeare 2006: 139), and is contrasted with the model of adults with disabilities living with their families until such time as they are placed in an institutional setting, which recalls the isolationism of previous generations. The start of the independent living movement in Japan is attributed to the formation of the Aoi Shiba no Kai (literally, the Green Grass Association) (arsvi.com n.d.; see Chapter 2), a group of activists with cerebral palsy who were influential in the 1970s and 1980s (Hayashi and Okuhira 2001: 859). Influenced by American activism in the 1960s (JIL n.d.), Aoi Shiba no Kai called for independent living (*dokuritsu shite/shita seikatsu*) in the early 1970s (arsvi.com n.d.), and support for independent living in the disability community grew in the 1980s (Hayashi and Okuhira 2001: 863).

Initiatives which encouraged independent living through the establishment of Centres for Independent Living (ILCs) were applauded, but Nakamura is critical of the policy, citing the fact that the activists who receive these services through 'welfare' protest against this label, claiming they should be termed 'salaries' (Nakamura 2005: 58). Behind this protest, interestingly, was disdain for the term 'welfare', which in Japanese society still smacks of unearned benefit, given to a child by a paternalistic parent, and this takes away from the individual's sense of independence as a part of their standard of living. A certain standard of living, as guaranteed by the Constitution, is expected. Its delivery, however, is at the root of the debate: the Japanese independent living movement desires a shift away from what Kwok *et al.* call the 'social status [of] Patient' (who is submissive and childlike) to that of 'Clients with disabilities (consumers)' (who are empowered decision-makers) (2002: 99). Independent living calls for 'the *freedom* to select the care-giving and assistance that best meet their needs' (Yōda 2002: 11, emphasis added). Independent living, while separating the individual from a residential disability community, is meant to integrate the person with a disability into the mainstream community, signalling a shift in the conceptual framework of the kind of 'community' to which a person with a disability should belong. Nakamura also recounts a policy reversal in 2003: because of the fast-growing number of applications for these programmes (and the rising accompanying costs) the Japanese Ministry of Health, Labour and Welfare announced first limits and then the end of the funding programme for ILC members' personal care attendants, resulting in protests (2005: 58).

The 2005 Services and Supports for Persons with Disabilities Act represented a major shift in the implementation of these ideas. It does not replace the Basic Act for Persons with Disabilities, but instead aims to streamline government services and supports participation in the workforce. The two laws do not conflict, nor does one overrule the other; their functions differ as they concern different levels of policy: the Basic Act for Persons with Disabilities sets general principles for policymakers, while the Services and Supports for Persons with Disabilities Act includes specific rules for administrators.[20] In other words, the Basic Act for Persons with Disabilities establishes the ground rules, which are then – in theory – adhered to and practised through other pieces of legislation. The 2005 law places more emphasis on the person's 'independence' and increasing social inclusion, but this has come at a cost, giving rise to criticisms that the new programme is merely a neoliberal disguise for legitimizing reductions in government benefits (Nakamura 2009: 86–7). Current amendments and changes to the system are, at the time of writing, still to come, demonstrating the interactive relationship between the legal system, the practical enactment of welfare programmes and the wider public response.

Conclusion

This chapter has examined issues regarding the welfare and wellbeing of Japanese people with disabilities by asking three main questions: what major policy directives have influenced social welfare law? How do recent changes affect our understanding of the overall structure of the law (and associated services) concerning people with disabilities? How do the laws themselves affect the way we understand disability? In considering these questions, I focused on the concepts of normalization and neoliberalism and how they have been integrated into policy and law, to the detriment as well as benefit of welfare recipients, while also considering how external pressure has had an effect on policy. Authorizing the individual to make personal choices in and responsibility for decisions regarding their welfare programmes can empower clients, but this also has the potential to limit the concrete outcomes of their applications for support, and increases the practical burden on the individual in the pursuit of their goals. Lastly, we have seen how the relevant laws have over time disadvantaged some groups relative to others (e.g. the criteria for laws regarding welfare and employment tend to apply more neatly to people with physical disabilities than those with intellectual or psychiatric disabilities). Clearer legislation purpose-written for these groups would benefit them, but instead a push for the streamlining of programmes (in the service of simplified management) has prevailed.

Changes in the laws, over time, serve to chart the changes occurring in society and are one example of the interactions among policy, law and public opinion. Yet some of these changes come about for multiple reasons, and result in complicated and even contradictory outcomes. For example, one could ask why the Basic Act for Persons with Disabilities was necessary if human rights were adequately covered in the Constitution in Chapter III, 'Rights and the Duties of the People'. With the benefit of hindsight, we can see that the reason why the Basic Act was necessary was because Japanese society between the 1950s and 1970s had become more sensitive to social issues regarding discrimination in a variety of contexts such as gender, ethnicity/race and ability (its enactment coincides roughly with the start of Aoi Shiba no Kai's activism), and legislators (and the bureaucrats who deliver these programmes) needed to address those changes. Similarly we can ask: why would the Services and Supports for Persons with Disabilities Act be needed when all the services were available under the existing Six Laws of Welfare? Again, the desire to 'integrate' people with disabilities as 'independent' and autonomous decision-making adults had its roots in the requests of disability activists, which stressed the independent status of the person with a disability, as a discrete adult individual, not an unproductive member of a family unit. In this sense, the Services and Supports for Persons with Disabilities Act can be seen as a logical outcome of the Independent Living Movement: both embrace the concepts of independence and self-determination. The law does not always deliver the movement's ideals; it often legitimizes cuts to funds and services. Surely the 'independence' of people with disabilities is desirable, yet this autonomy may come at too high a price for some. In fact, calls for the overarching Services and Supports for Persons with Disabilities Act to be repealed demonstrate its ineffectiveness in creating 'independence' for people with disabilities in Japan. The case of this law especially demonstrates this dialectic relationship: sometimes laws shape society, and at other times they respond to social pressures.

Throughout these discussions, we have seen how policymakers have struggled with the notion of social responsibility as a basis for reining in costs and presenting programmes to the voting constituency as financially reasonable. This leads to a further question: to what extent is a person with a disability seen by wider society as a passive recipient, or as an active contributor to society? 'Welfare dependency' is a phrase with many negative connotations, suggesting that people who receive significant welfare benefits are somehow not deserving. In a sense, the above shift to the Services and Supports model seems to address this by shifting the responsibility (and some of the cost) to the client. Yet many believe that welfare dependency is a myth; research in the United Kingdom has shown that this has its roots in the systemic segregation of young people in education, and later in employment (Oliver 1996: 64), rather than being connected directly to the experience of having a disability itself. In fact, recalling some of the debates described in Chapter 1 regarding the social and medical models of disability, Oliver notes that welfare dependency can be interpreted in two ways:

> one [is] that disability has such a traumatic physical and psychological effect on individuals that they cannot ensure a reasonable quality of life for themselves by their own efforts; the other [is] that the economic and social barriers that disabled people face are so pervasive that disabled people are prevented from ensuring themselves a reasonable quality of life by their own efforts.
> (Oliver 1996: 65)

Owing to the prevalence of the medical model in Japan to date, it is no wonder that the legal system is highly influenced by it. While the Services and Supports for Persons with Disabilities Act aims to promote independence, there is still a great reliance on the medical profession and other 'professionals' to make decisions, and as we have seen, this is especially the case for those with psychiatric or intellectual disabilities as opposed to people whose disabilities are physical. This medicalization of disability has delegated decisions about people's bodies and minds into the hands of 'skilled professionals'. In doing so, part of the 'independence' of people with disabilities – the valued part that enables them to be seen as 'successful', and a key selling point of the new programmes – is stripped from them. Their agency is diminished, and their identity is subordinated to the structural needs of welfare law. As Thomson writes:

> Medical validation of physical incapacity solved the problem of malingering by circumventing the testimony of the individual ..., eliminating the patient's ability for self-disclosure and, ultimately, self-determination.
>
> [I]n constructing this legal social group, quite distinct conditions merge into a single administrative and social identity.
>
> Yet, the new, clinically disabled category defined the person with a disability as a figure excluded from economic opportunities and therefore without free agency, self-determinism and self-possession, the ennobling attributes of the liberal ... individual.
> (1997: 50)

Recognizing that legal structures provide benefits as well as placing practical and ideological limits on the individual is crucial to the understanding of how people with disabilities fit into the larger fabric of society, as well as how their lives can be improved.

5 Disability and the lifecycle

Despite the legitimacy of the social model's quest to take our focus away from the individual and medical impairment as the defining characteristics of disability identity, its critics have argued that the real impact that impairment has on individuals' experiences is too great to discount completely. Different kinds of disability, or different combinations of impairments, give rise to different sets of issues, and demonstrate how complex the disability identity is. Needless to say, disability identity can be further complicated by different grades of the various disabilities (e.g. mild, moderate, severe and profound). These tensions are apparent throughout this book, and specifically in Chapter 4, which highlighted inequities across disability profiles, such as the dearth of services for people with intellectual disabilities as opposed to physical disabilities. This chapter similarly acknowledges the reality of disability's impact on a person's experience and identity, but rather than focusing on the definitive impairment or degree of severity, I argue for a more nuanced understanding of disability. The benefits of an age-specific approach are multiple: Irwin writes that '[a] life course orientation sensitizes us to various issues and processes and puts these at the heart of analyses of social change' (2001: 15) and 'the dynamics of individual lives in historical and social context' (17). Irwin focuses primarily on education, employment and retirement as the broad lifecycle categories with which disability interacts (18). By looking at disability at different stages of an individual's life, Irwin argues, we can better understand change in people's experiences, which can then be projected over the course of history as a change narrative. While this chapter cannot provide a comprehensive 'change history' of disability in Japan for all individuals, it is still important to address the wide variety of disability experiences in Japan, and a life-course perspective helps to highlight specific issues that might be overlooked if we focused on only one life stage when talking about disability.

In Japan, as well as in any other society that has previously subscribed to the medical model of disability, diagnosis is almost always the first step in creating a disability identity, and the time when this occurs for the individual is important. Diagnostic science inches our understanding of disability further and further back into ever earlier stages of the individual's life course. Debates about prenatal testing and selective abortion, and their use, problematize the acquisition of a disability identity. Childhood and teen disability is more focused on the ongoing issue of special or integrated mainstream education – and prognosis, or a proper diagnosis (if there is none).[1] Discussions concerning adult disability are often directed at training and employment, and the potential for independent living; while disability in the elder years also includes decisions about independence and institution-based care, there is in addition a view to end-of-life care.

Another function of this chapter is to highlight some of the issues that confront a person (either the individual with a disability or those who care for a person with a disability), which are age specific and not applicable to other common rubrics addressing disability in Japan. Because of demographic context, much research and public discussion of disability is geared towards geriatric disability and care; therefore, this chapter is intentionally skewed towards the earlier stages of the lifecycle in order to rectify this imbalance (the main life stages I address are prenatality and infancy; childhood; young adults; and older adults). Primarily, I want to show how the meaning of disability over time changes in two ways: how disability is differently experienced based on the time of one's diagnosis, and change according to the different social expectations of an individual over their lifetime. Oliver refers to the latter aspect as a 'disability career', which refers to how disability interacts with 'other aspects of an individual's total experience' (Carver cited in Oliver 1996: 138). As noted in the previous chapter on welfare policy, the timing of a person's disability diagnosis can have an effect on perceptions of his/her identity; for example, young adults impaired through an accident would be steered towards 'rehabilitation', primarily so that they could return to the role of 'productive member of society'. Meanwhile, infants diagnosed with Down Syndrome are tested for organ malformations and basic functions (hearing, sight, heart, kidneys and so on), but because there are different expectations for adult 'productivity', these children are groomed through their education to a different sort of future. This chapter, through addressing different life stages explicitly, aims to demonstrate that expectations associated with the life stage combine with other expectations (such as impairment and degree of severity) to create a more complete disability identity.

Prenatality and infancy

The diagnosis of disability for infants often comes in the form of a prenatal test, or immediately following the birth (whether traumatic or normal); alternatively, it is commonly made some time during the first year of life when developmental milestones are not achieved. This section focuses primarily on the application of prenatal diagnostic technology. What distinguishes the issues surrounding apparent disability in this very early stage from those of other stages is the ever-evolving role of medical technology, complicated further by resultant debates about selective abortion, and concerns about prognosis as an outcome of diagnosis and acquiring a full disability identity (one that requires lifelong support and care) even before the individual takes an independent breath. Pregnancy in developed countries, including Japan, has evolved into a process that is highly medicalized (Ivry 2006: 446). Therefore, the debates surrounding unborn children with disabilities, while inevitably raising social, cultural and ethical considerations, have intensified along with advances in medical technology. This section outlines the tests, the laws and attitudes about prenatal testing (hereafter, PNT) and selective abortion[2] in Japan with reference to disability (or the potential for disability).

What is PNT? Technically, it includes both prenatal screening and prenatal diagnosis. Prenatal screening can refer to the creation and analysis of family histories, maternal serum tests, ultrasound scans and amniocentesis (Sleeboom-Faulkner 2010: 14–15). Amniocentesis and CVS (chorionic villus sampling) are considered prenatal diagnosis as they are more definitive; ultrasound and blood serum screening are better referred to as 'prenatal screening', because they are merely suggestive of an underlying issue rather than giving a concrete result.[3]

One of the more widely known and utilized prenatal diagnostic procedures, amniocentesis, was introduced to Japan in the 1960s (Tsuge 2010: 113) with the aim of strengthening the labour market through encouraging the birth of healthy children (Kato 2009) during Japan's postwar economic boom (1955–73). Today, termination (including selective termination) is allowed in Japan under conditions prescribed in the Botai Hogo Hō (Maternal Body Protection Law), an amended version of the former Yūsei Hogo Hō (Eugenic Protection Law).[4] Both laws have regulated abortion, setting out the circumstances under which termination is acceptable to Japanese society.

Jaeger and Bowman define eugenics as 'the principle that only certain people [have] the right to perpetuate their genetic materials through reproduction' (2005: 34). In pre-war Japan, eugenics 'provided an avenue for the application of science to social problems, including public health, education, and hygiene'; positive eugenics was the elevation of women's reproductive health through better health and nutrition, while negative eugenics involved sterilization and abortion (Robertson 2002: 196). This continued the concerns of the Meiji Period, when, in its early encounters with the USA and UK, the Japanese government set great store by 'catching up' with the West, both technologically and militarily.[5] The latter aspect of this quest was obliged to address the putative 'inferiority' of the Japanese body; thus the government promoted stronger, healthier bodies through changes in diet and the implementation of eugenic policies (Ivry 2006: 444–5). More relevant to our discussion here is the stance the law took on people with disabilities, both as potential parents and as potential children (as foetuses). People with disabilities were discouraged from having children because they were not seen as capable of caring for them, and children with disabilities did not contribute to strengthening the nation's military.

The opening to the former Eugenic Protection Law read: 'The purpose of this law is, from the point of view of eugenics, to prevent the birth of inferior [defective] offspring, together with protecting the lives and the health of mothers' (Yūsei Hogo Hō 1948, my translation). It allowed for the sterilization of people with 'a hereditary psychopathological condition, hereditary bodily disease, hereditary malformation or mental diseases, or leprosy' (Mackie 2003: 192–3), as well as the abortion of 'defective' foetuses (Yūsei Hogo Hō 1948). Economic devastation after the war made lawmakers wary of unfettered population growth, and conditions under which abortion could be seen as 'legal' were stipulated in 1949. The Eugenic Protection Law attempted to restrict the availability of abortion in Japan, yet the inclusion of 'economic grounds' made it reasonably accessible (Mackie 2003: 138).

The Maternal Body Protection Law similarly contains language that demonstrates its departure from earlier laws: '[t]he articles of the former Eugenics Protection Law ... which were aimed at preventing the birth of people with inferior heredity ... are offensive and discriminatory toward the disabled. Therefore, the regulations that are [based on] eugenic ideology are canceled' (cited in Ivry 2006: 445).

The new law addresses issues of sterilization and abortion, and its terminology focuses on the 'protection' of women's reproductive bodies. The first article reads: 'this law is aimed at protecting the lives and health of mothers with respect to matters concerning sterilization and abortion' (Botai Hogo Hō 2006, my translation). Compared with the preamble to the Eugenic Protection Law cited above (which also included the phrase 'to prevent the birth of inferior offspring') we can say that the specific 'eugenic philosophy' of the former law was 'submerged' (Mackie 2003: 193), but Robertson has argued that the term *botai hogo* (maternal protection) is merely a euphemism for eugenics (2002: 199) and that the former law's basic views regarding elevating the 'purity' of the race remain. The Maternal Body Protection Law as listed today still shows that approximately twenty-two lines have been deleted (*sakujo*) from the original law, suggesting the lingering shadow of its precursor. Ivry reminds us, however, that '[t]he Maternal Body Protection Law reiterates a public understanding of abortion as a means of choosing when to have children rather than what kind of children will be born. Significantly, it should be remembered that the Maternal Body Protection Law disqualifies genetic, chromosomal, and other fetal anomalies as reasons for legal abortions' (Ivry 2006: 445).

Despite this disqualification, there have been calls to recognize selective abortion: anti-abortion activists have conceded these conditions (Tsuge 2010: 113) as well as proposals from the Japan Society for Obstetrics and Gynaecology (Takeda 2005: 174). The current law gives only two reasons that allow legal termination of a foetus: first, when the pregnancy or birth itself would pose a danger to the mother's health for either 'physical or economic reasons', and second, if the pregnant woman experienced violence; furthermore, the law calls for the consent of the spouse wherever possible (Article 14, Botai Hogo Hō 2006). Takeda notes that one change in the Maternal Body Protection Law is that it 'draw[s] a boundary between women who are/will be mothers and women who do not want to be or cannot be mothers, by protecting the reproductive health/rights of only one group' (2005: 173); meanwhile as recent as 1999 the Japan Society for Obstetrics and Gynaecology proposed to insert another legal reason justifying termination, one 'where the foetus has serious deficiency' (174). The current Maternal Body Protection Law does not support the termination of foetuses diagnosed with disability, illness or disorder (Ivry 2006: 448), but because of the 'economic clause', which is said to account for virtually all of the abortions performed in Japan since 1950 (Norgren 1998: 70), it is impossible to know what percentage of these terminations involve an abnormal test result.

Prenatal testing and other kinds of prenatal screening procedures are generally promoted in developed countries, such as the UK (Edwards 2003: 526) and Australia ('New test opens prenatal genetic diagnosis to all', reads a headline from *Medical News Today* [2003]). Ivry states that these tests are 'routinized in the United States and in many parts of Europe' but not in Japan, despite its 'hypertechnological' status (2006: 442–3). I found this to be true in my own experience: during my first trimester, I lived with my parents-in-law in Yokohama for six weeks where I was under the watchful gaze of my mother-in-law. She scrutinized my diet intake very carefully; she was worried that I wasn't eating enough due to nausea; she couldn't understand why I didn't want to drink too much tea, being worried about caffeine, and scoffed at my request for prenatal vitamins. I also listened to repeated advice about managing the childbirth ('Don't argue with the doctor if he tells you something has to happen'). Despite my status as an 'elderly primagravida' (I was thirty-six; the definition refers to any first-time mother over the age of thirty-five), my mother-in-law did not ask if I was going to have any prenatal screening, nor did she request that I do so, or express concern that I had chosen not to – despite the fact, at the time unknown to me, that there was a history of genetic disability in her family.

Ivry (2006) studied the use of ultrasound, AFP (alpha-foetoprotein) tests and amniocentesis in Japan to diagnosis foetal abnormalities – or, in a more positive light, to 'reassure' mothers that their foetus was normal – and included the perspectives of both the pregnant women and their doctors. Obstetricians who were otherwise seen as strongly authoritative with other kinds of instructions to the patients were 'silent' and 'vague' about prenatal diagnosis procedures with their Japanese patients (447), and diagnosis was undertaken 'in secrecy' (ibid). This is an interesting statement, for it contrasts with views in the UK, as Shakespeare notes that '[g]enetic counsellors and nurses are the least directive. Obstetricians are the most directive ... Unlike genetics professionals, obstetricians do not tend to work with disabled people directly' (2005: 231).

Attitudes of both the doctors and the patients are important. Ivry's Japanese interviewees were generally not interested in prenatal tests because, as they said, '"we have no genetic or chromosomal disorders in our families"' (451). It seems that Ivry's pool of patients (twenty-seven pregnant Japanese women) either truly had no family histories, or were at least not aware of one (for example, the possibility of asymptomatic balanced translocation, which is a cause of chromosomal abnormality believed to be a risk in 1 in 625 persons in the general population [RGI 2010]). Discussing prenatal screening and testing with a different set of patients – those with a known family history of genetic disorders or hereditary diseases – might have yielded different results. Nevertheless, for her interviewees, the tension between disability rights and prenatal diagnosis is an external issue: a problem for other people to worry about, an attitude that further marginalizes the reality of the experience of disability from mainstream society. Ivry observes that the general rate of births of babies with chromosomal abnormalities in Japan has been decreasing since the 1980s (2006: 457), which suggests that testing and subsequent termination of abnormal foetuses is being practised.

Based on interviews with mothers, Ivry concluded that despite Japan's eugenic history, there seems to be a 'greater readiness of Japanese mothers to bear less-than-perfect children' because the ideology of mothering is so 'powerful', they believe their children will eventually 'integrate in society' (2010: 251). Similarly, according to Kato's study, which involved interviews of a pool of sixty respondents, only 13 per cent chose to undertake prenatal tests, the rest being unwilling to take the risks; the majority of those who did have the tests and received an abnormal result terminated the pregnancy (2009). Matsuda and Suzumori's research similarly found that 89 per cent of women who received a result of abnormality in a chromosomal test terminated, but only 4 per cent of Japanese women over the age of thirty-five chose to undertake prenatal testing or diagnosis (2000: 12). Matsuda and Suzumori's data also showed low levels of informed consent in these procedures, implying that doctors made the decision on behalf of the patients. This is also in contrast with Shakespeare's summary of North American and European prenatal testing practice, where he states that '[t]he role of prospective parents has been largely ignored by disability rights critics of genetics. Often it is prospective parents, not clinicians, who are the active agents in choosing to terminate pregnancy' (2006: 87).

My personal experience of prenatal care is grounded in the Australian, not the Japanese, medical system, but while I was pregnant with my daughter I spent six weeks in Japan, which constituted a good part of my first trimester. We had decided to forgo prenatal testing: it didn't seem 'right' given our experience working closely with people with disabilities in Kotobuki, and a research trip finalized in the previous semester made it difficult to do the test in Australia on the earliest key dates for testing (specifically, blood serum tests and the nuchal scan/ultrasound); even if I had wanted to do the tests, I was in the wrong country and travel seemed difficult at that time. Ivry's conclusion regarding Japanese mothers' belief in the power of mothering to overcome impairment was not, I think, at work in my case; rather, I believe it was that the recognition of genetic impairment on my mother-in-law's side of the family was so firmly repressed by relatives (except, of course, for the impaired children's immediate family). While my mother-in-law may have known on some level that it was no coincidence that her brother had two impaired children, she did not seem to understand that this could affect her own children and grandchildren. This was, I learned later, likely because of the physical and emotional separation between these two branches of the family, resulting in no discussion between the adult siblings. My husband knew of the existence of these impaired children, but the details to him, as an adult, were hazy. It was only later that we learned that in the 1970s, after the birth of the second child with a disability in the family, arguments broke out between the parents and the child's grandmother over who was to 'blame' for the genetic fault, and while the parents underwent genetic testing to find the source and the details of the translocation, they did not tell their siblings, including my mother-in-law. Later, when my daughter was born and we explained to my mother-in-law about the translocation, she still did not openly discuss the matter with her brother or sister-in-law. When I asked her why, she said she did not want to trouble her older brother while he was receiving medical treatment for a liver ailment. She said it would be too upsetting to confront him while he had his own health issues. He then died, and a few years after that my mother-in-law also suddenly died of cancer; with the deaths of these two siblings so too died the answers to who knew what when, why the genetic disorder had been hidden, and what kinds of discussion had taken place.

Following my daughter's birth in 2000, it seemed that there had been very little discussion about these issues, even after her diagnosis. When my husband's aunt saw my daughter for the first time at my mother-in-law's funeral in 2005, she expressed first shock and then, perhaps, nostalgic delight in seeing an active five-year-old child so like her son, who was at that time over thirty years old and in compromised health from repeated respiratory infections and epilepsy. The ensuing discussion about the disclosure (or, more precisely, lack of disclosure) was complicated. At first it was friendly, but then it became more difficult as I learned that my husband's cousin had known for decades, and had even undergone prenatal testing before starting her family. This suggested to me a kind of double standard: for the family that knew, knowledge informed their decision-making, but non-disclosure prevented other members of the family from understanding their options.

In general, high-quality perinatal care is widely available in Japan, especially in urban areas, and this includes not only early detection of medical conditions but also intensive care provision. Nishida notes that 'after the introduction of intensive care in the 1970s', the mortality rate of children born very prematurely plummeted from 90 per cent to 50 per cent in the early 1980s, and to 25 per cent in 1989. Because of this, the 'viability limit as defined in the Eugenic Protection Law in Japan was amended from 24 completed weeks of gestation to 22 completed weeks in 1991' (Nishida 1993: 611). Nishida notes that the increase in medical intervention has not only lowered mortality rates but has also contributed, in his opinion, to an increase in the number of 'handicapped children' born in Japan. Only 17 per cent of the extremely low birth-weight babies showed 'major neurological sequelae [consequent problems]'; therefore, Nishida believes that the significantly larger number of infants surviving birth injuries or high-risk gestations means that the number of impaired children is also increasing. Of all infant mortalities, 62.4 per cent can be attributed to 'congenital malformations, deformations, and chromosomal abnormalities' as well as 'certain conditions originating in the perinatal period' outside other infant mortality factors such as infectious illnesses and accidents (MHLW 2009c: 24), but relatively speaking, Japan's overall infant mortality is quite low compared with that of other developed countries.[6] For example, Japan's infant mortality of babies less than four weeks old is 1.2 per 1,000 live births, which is lower than in the USA (4.6), France (2.4), Germany (2.7), Italy (2.7), the Netherlands (3.3), Sweden (1.7) and the UK (3.6);

Singapore is just higher with 1.4 (MHLW 2009c: 25). Research on national rates of childhood disability arising from birth trauma is scarce, but a small-scale study of 109 traumatic births resulting in nervous system disorders in Miyazaki Prefecture over a five-year period found the rate of birth injury to be the equivalent of 2 per 1,000 live births (Ikeda 2010: 12). Of these 109 cases, the most common causes were as follows: 19.3 per cent were due to restriction of blood and/or oxygen to the brain; 17.4 per cent were attributed to prematurity; 24.8 per cent were caused by 'hereditary malformations' (ibid.). While PNT does not provide diagnoses for all disorders, in this study almost a quarter of infant disorders were categorized as being caused by conditions that were (or could have been) discovered during screening or diagnosis (e.g. spontaneously occurring malformations seen in an ultrasound, or malformations related to chromosomal disorders diagnosed through amniocentesis), demonstrating the key role PNT can play in prenatal care today.

Japanese abortion laws are often viewed as contradictory; Kato (2009) notes the government's conflicting stance since the 1990s, as it wants the general population to limit the number of abortions performed (in response to the falling fertility rate), but it also wants to allow selective abortion. Disability rights activists have opposed this owing to what Kato refers to as 'past trauma', connected to human rights abuses resulting from the Eugenic Protection Law, which only abolished the sterilization of people with disabilities as recently as 1996. Kato also notes that the medical profession tends to see these tests as not against the birth of people with disabilities, but rather aimed at 'allaying' the fears of pregnant mothers and thus they are conducted to benefit the mother's health (ibid.). In the 1990s, some confusion arose around how these new technologies were being used, and how patients understood their use and meaning, so the Ministry of Health and Welfare established a Special Committee on Prenatal Diagnosis in October 1998 (MHW 1999).

An examination of views regarding disability at this life stage is so important because the technology can be seen as allowing parents and doctors to 'choose' whether or not disability is perpetuated, a highly contentious topic. Davis writes that the term 'eugenics' has become so abhorrent to contemporary society that its use is avoided, but the philosophy behind it still stands behind 'prenatal screening, which works some of the time, and genetic engineering, which has not worked ... ... so far' (2002: 21). On the other hand, Shakespeare wants to redefine eugenics more narrowly, and stresses that the issue should not necessarily be whether eugenics discriminates against certain genetic combinations, but instead whether eugenic practice is a 'voluntary action, influenced by education and advice', or amounts to 'coercive eugenics, based on legal controls or paternalistic professional practices' (2006: 88). He believes that, with appropriate parental support and choice offered, current genetic testing is mostly about 'preventing and treating genuine illness, rather than "purifying the population"' (87). Another issue is the role of legal abortion in society: if abortion is seen to be part of a woman's right to choose, and to have control over, her reproductive future, why is it acceptable to abort a healthy but unwanted foetus but not acceptable to

Disability and the lifecycle 103

abort a wanted but impaired foetus (Shakespeare 2000: n.p.)? In this discussion of the use of prenatal diagnosis in Japan, the USA and the UK, it is important to note that none of these medical systems enforces the termination or the protection of impaired foetuses; this is seen from the legal standpoint as a private decision. Jaeger and Bowman thus argue that this makes the prenatal screening and diagnosis process quite different from the eugenics of the past; by way of comparison, they cite China as a modern eugenic society, where prenatal tests are compulsory and the decision to terminate rests legally in the doctors' hands (2005: 125).

Abortion rights are usually debated between two distinct positions (the 'pro-life' stance, which recognizes human rights of all foetuses; and the 'pro-choice' position, which focuses on the mother's agency), but it is difficult, if not impossible, to position disability concerns between these two polarities. Tom Shakespeare has written openly about the contradictions arising from disability activists entering this debate. He frames the contradiction as this: disability activists tend to support (or at least are silent about) abortion for women who want to become a mother at 'a particular time and with a particular partner, but [they do] not [support] any choices which depend on the characteristics of the foetus'; Shakespeare finds this stance 'inconsistent' as disability activists rarely object to terminations involving severe medical conditions that always lead to death (Shakespeare 2006: 92–3). Despite this, Shakespeare also says that perhaps consistency is not the issue here:

> Logic and consistency and resolution are required of academic bioethics. In practice, pragmatism, feelings and lived experience may lead individuals to decide in ways that are not intellectually rigorous, and this is not always a bad thing, especially if the particular questions are not resolvable anyway. Moreover, we live in societies containing groups and individuals who hold a range of religious, cultural and ethical beliefs. It is not easy, and sometimes impossible, to reach a consensus about the morality of particular practices ... My claim is that selective termination is not an issue to which morality or rationality demands a universal response, and that it is appropriate to espouse an ethic of individual choice.
>
> (Shakespeare 2005: 218–19)

Shakespeare does concede that the concept of 'free choice' is a loaded one, and comes with the baggage of 'thousands of interactions, implicit expectations, subtle influences and restricted choices' (2006: 88). He believes that the most ethnical choice is where there is an 'informed choice', which importantly includes support for parents who wish to carry an impaired foetus to term, and a society that is 'supportive of disabled children and adults' (2005: 219).[7] It is when that support is withdrawn from parents who have received a prenatal diagnosis of impairment or when doctors portray disability to future parents as a 'pathetic' condition (226) that prenatal diagnosis is discriminatory against people with disabilities.

Childhood

At some point in their childhood, nearly every Japanese young person is observed and evaluated and given the label of 'normal' (*ijōnashi*) or 'abnormal' (*ijō*). These labels are given during checkups conducted at the local public health centre (*hokenjo*) or at other public and private doctors' offices. They are mostly thought to be a standard procedure, where the parents seek reassurance from 'professionals' that their parenting skills are adequate, their children are progressing 'acceptably', and that there isn't anything 'wrong' with them. Children undergo many different kinds of assessments; after immediate concerns about their physical and psychological development are allayed, children's educational achievements are tested and evaluated, to further categorize the Japanese child in an educationally stratified meritocratic society (see Sugimoto [1997: 107–35] for a description and critique of this system, which he calls 'Educational Credentialism'). This kind of evaluation (medical, behavioural and educational) is experienced widely in the mainstream. Yet professional evaluation takes on extra meaning for children with disabilities, and their families. Marks observes that 'Children have far less control over their lives than adults. This relative powerlessness is further exacerbated for many disabled children, who are subject to extra restrictions that are imposed as a result of various forms of care to which they are subjected' (1999: 91).

No child is fully independent, so in many ways the child with a disability is cared for in much the same way as any other child, and thus should be considered a child first, with a disability second, as the Japan Down Syndrome Network states. Still, the diagnosis of disability (either confirmed or suspected) changes the child from being 'just a child' to being instead a 'watched child' (Gill 1993: 40), and the family too becomes an object of professional and amateur scrutiny. At the prenatal and infancy stage, diagnosis and prognosis experiences can dominate the life of a child with disability. The child is tested repeatedly for function and aptitude, often to the bewilderment of the little girl who does not understand why twice-annual audiology tests are required, or why this little boy with a cough must be hospitalized for observation while other toddlers with chest infections are treated at home. Parents of young children with disabilities are often concerned with milestones, as they can be used diagnostically, but such use is problematic, as variation amongst children, both those with the same disability and those with different issues, makes it difficult to evaluate progress. Furthermore, these families are not infrequently isolated from each other and thus have no comparative viewpoint (Quinn 1998: 40), making it more difficult for them to judge their children's potential outside the external, 'professional' gaze of doctors and therapists.

A child with a disability is most frequently 'watched' for *progress*; these outcomes are then evaluated for disability categorization, which in turn become determinants in educational decisions. The parents are primarily 'watched' to evaluate their parenting skills: are they coping? Do they need extra support? Are the child's needs being met? Is their relationship under too much stress? This 'watching' occurs on some level with all new parents, but the public gaze is more intense on a family of a child with a disability. Some have argued that this 'gaze' creates an expectation of conformity on the part of the child and that this has lifelong consequences on the socialization of the adult with a disability:

> [c]hildren who have disabilities are taught to behave appropriately as a disabled child from early on. They are taught a pattern of socially acceptable behaviors known to sociologists and disability theorists as the impaired role. [The 'i]mpaired role' is a set of scripts that people with disabilities are expected to stick to in exchange for the non-disabled society to tolerate their presence. The primary feature of this role is that a disabled person must act as the passive mirror of other people's affection and good will, so that non-disabled people can affirm their own goodness. The forced lifelong immersion in this role makes it extremely difficult to question or to challenge potentially self-serving or manipulative motives behind others' presumably altruistic actions.
>
> (Koyama 2006)

In Japan, the Ministry of Health, Labour and Welfare recorded that 49.5 per cent of all queries to the public 'child guidance centre' (*jidōsōdanjo*) refer to 'counselling on mental and physical disabilities' (Statistics and Information Department – Minister's Secretariat 2009). Abe also observes this common scenario, especially with regard to children whose disabilities are undiagnosed, and cites committees associated with these centres that specifically offer these families advice on school enrolments (1998: 92).

From Table 5.1 we can see that the total number of children with physical disabilities has dropped during the postwar period described above; this can be accounted for in the first place by the use of high-quality medical intervention, but we must also note that the falling birth rate in Japan means that fewer children are born overall, with the result that at the same time, the births of fewer children with disabilities will also be recorded. With reference to children with

Table 5.1 Children with physical disabilities in Japan, 1965–2006

Year	Total number[a]	Visual impairment	Hearing/ communication impairment	Mobility impairment	*Internal* (naibu) disability
1965	116,600	14,400	26,000	76,200	–
1970	93,800	7,000	23,700	57,500	5,600
1987	92,500	5,800	13,600	53,300	19,800
1991	81,000	3,900	11,200	48,500	17,500
1998	81,600	5,600	16,400	41,400	18,200
2001	81,900	4,800	15,200	47,700	14,200
2006	93,100	4,900	17,300	50,100	20,700

Source: adapted from e-Stat (Seifu Tōkei no Sōgo Madoguchi) 2007.

Note
a The total may differ from the sum of all columns owing to instances of multiple disabilities, e.g. a child having both a visual and mobility impairment.

physical disabilities, birth trauma was noted as a significant cause of mobility problems (28.3 per cent of children) (Naikakufu 2009).

Comparable statistics over the same time frame as that of Table 5.1 were not available for numbers of individuals with intellectual disabilities, and this is most likely due to difficulties in diagnosis and lack of awareness about intellectual disability in earlier decades. With regard to recent developments, Table 5.2 gives us some idea about how intellectual disability can be understood using the lifecycle approach. It shows that in terms of intellectual disability, diagnosis is primarily a childhood occurrence, with the majority of all surveyed individuals being diagnosed either after birth or between the ages of three and six, suggesting that while physical disability is diagnosed at all times during an individual life (illness and accidents have the potential to occur randomly throughout one's life), intellectual disability, when not immediately apparent at birth, appears to be firmly connected to childhood milestones such as toddler development and entrance to primary school. Table 5.3 shows that, while the hospital remains a significant site for diagnosis of intellectual disability, in both the general category and the two age-related categories, intellectual disability is most commonly diagnosed at an early childhood clinic when the child is quite young.

Table 5.4, interestingly, suggests intellectual disability in older people tends to be interpreted as 'other than severe' more often than in children under the age of eighteen, with 54.6 per cent of children being considered 'severe' but only 39.3 per cent of the adults (this is assuming those not in possession of the handbook would also not be categorized as 'severe'). One reading of this data could be that doctors are now more adroit at diagnosing disability, and are able to do so with greater accuracy, resulting in more detail in diagnoses; another contributing factor may be the implementation of early intervention therapies, sometimes not available in the past, that have helped some children achieve categorizations above the 'severe' mark who would have fallen into that group if they had not received the therapy. Whatever the reason, it appears that for today's young people, there is more variation in the degree of intellectual disability across the population.

In 2010, the Japanese government reported that there were 121,815 students enrolled in 1,039 public and private special schools (*tokubetsu shien gakkō*) across the country, slightly up from previous years (e-Stat 2012). These schools were established under the 1948 School Education Law which calls for segregation in special education. Article 72 states:

> The aim of special needs schools is to provide children who are blind, deaf, intellectually disabled, physically handicapped [*shidaifujiyūsha*], as well as physically weak [*shintaikyojakusha*], with education appropriate to their needs at kindergartens, primary schools, junior high schools and high schools, together with the necessary intellectual skills to plan for independence and to overcome their difficulties with education and lifestyle resulting from their disability.
>
> (Gakkō Kyōiku Hō 1948, my translation)

Table 5.2 Age of diagnosis of intellectual disability, general age statistics and children's statistics

	Total number	Directly after birth (%)	During an infant health check (%)	At the 18 month health check (%)	At the 3 year health check (%)	Upon enrolling in primary school (%)	While enrolled in primary school (%)	Upon enrolling in junior/senior high school (%)	While enrolled in junior/senior high school (%)	Don't know/ unclear (%)
All respondants	329,200 (100%)	10.7	6.5	7.4	13.7	13.3	2.8	8.5	12.4	24.7
Respondants under 18	93,600 (100%)	18.2	13.5	13.5	18.8	15.2	1.5	5.4	6.2	7.7
Respondants over 18	221,200 (100%)	8.1	3.8	5.3	12.0	12.5	3.4	10.5	15.5	29.2
Age unclear	14,400 (100%)	2.8	1.4	1.4	6.9	12.5	1.4	5.6	4.2	63.9

Source: adapted from e-Stat (Seifu Tōkei no Sōgo Madoguchi) 2000.

Table 5.3 Place of diagnosis of intellectual disability, general age statistics and children's statistics

	Total number	Public infant consultation centre[a] (%)	Public rehabilitation centre for people with intellectual disabilities[b] (%)	Public health care centre[c] (%)	Hospital (%)	Other (%)	Unclear (%)
All respondants	329,200 (100%)	40.9	14.2	5.6	28.0	–	11.3
Respondants under 18	93,600 (100%)	48.2	1.5	9.6	34.0	–	6.6
Respondants over 18	221,200 (100%)	38.5	19.9	26.7	26.7	–	10.7
Unclear	14,400 (100%)	29.2	9.7	–	9.7	–	51.4

Source: adapted from e-Stat (Seifu Tōkei no Sōgo Madoguchi) 2000.

Notes
a These centres were established under article 12 of the Child Welfare Law (Jidōfukushi Hō).
b These centres were established under article 12 of the Law for the Welfare of People with Intellectual Disabilities (Chitekishōgaisha Fukushi Hō).
c As per the Regional Public Health Order (Chiiki Hoken Hō Jikkō), most recent revision 1997.

Table 5.4 Severity of intellectual disability, general age statistics and children's statistics

	Total number	In possession of a 'rehabilitation handbook'				Not in possession of 'rehabilitation handbook' (% of total)	Unclear (% of total)
		Number (% of total)	Severe ID (%)	Other than severe (%)	Severity unclear (%)		
All respondants	329,200 (100%)	289,100 (87.8)	43.5	47.5	9.0	7.9	4.3
Respondants under 18	93,600 (100%)	84,400 (90.1)	54.6	40.4	5.0	9.0	0.09
Respondants over 18	221,200 (100%)	195,500 (88.4)	39.3	50.6	10.2	7.3	4.4
Unclear	14,400 (100%)	9,200 (63.9)	30.4	47.8	21.7	9.7	26.4

Source: adapted from e-Stat (Seifu Tōkei no Sōgō Madoguchi) 2000.

110 *Disability and the lifecycle*

The seven categories of special education as recognized by the Ministry of Education are schools for the 'blind and partially sighted, deaf and hard of hearing, mentally retarded [sic], physically disabled, health impaired and physically weak, speech impaired and emotionally disturbed' (Abe 1998: 92). These schools are administered by the Ministry of Education and must include grades one to nine (primary to junior high) (Gakkō Kyōiku Hō 1948). Primary and junior high school education was compulsory for blind and deaf children, and while the 1948 law allowed for children with other kinds of disabilities to be 'delayed' in starting school (Abe 1998: 88; Heyer 1999: 8–9), in 1956 the law was revised to make education of young children compulsory regardless of disability (Abe 1998: 89).

In terms of nomenclature, institutes of education for children with disabilities all come under the broad term *tokubetsushiengakkō* (special needs education), and are then further distinguished as schools for the blind (*mōgakkō*), schools for the deaf (*rōgakkō*) and special developmental schools (*yōgo gakkō*). Not all special education classes are segregated; regulations provide that 'small classes for children with comparatively mild disabilities ... may be established in regular elementary and lower secondary schools' (MEXT 2009), though Heyer notes that the 'mainstreaming of children in special classes is the exception', and is not funded (1999: 8). In 1997, there were 800 special schools in Japan and 89 per cent of those students who finished junior high went to high school (Iwakuma 2003: 126). In 2003, there were 995 schools, more than half of which were dedicated to teaching children with intellectual disabilities (National Institute of Special Education 2004: 6), and as we saw above, in 2010 there were 1,039 (e-stat 2012). In line with Japan's decreasing birth rate, the number of schools in general, from primary to tertiary levels, is not growing as there are fewer children to fill the students' seats, and schools as well as universities are merging rather than expanding. Special education in Japan, however, with numbers holding steady and even slightly increasing, can be seen as the one sector in the industry that is growing. Not all students with special educational needs attend special schools, however; in 2003 there were 30,921 'special classes' programmes (which are integrated in local mainstream schools, where some classes and other activities are performed together); there are also *tsūkyū* (special classes) offered to students at mainstream schools (e-stat 2012). These *tsūkyū* classes are mostly attended by students with language and learning disorders.

In 2009, there were approximately 306,000 children attending some kind of special education class at the primary and junior high school levels (Naikakufu 2010b: 42). The government states that '0.001% of children are allowed postponement of or exception from school because of their disabilities' (National Institute of Special Education 2004: 6). For those who attend 'special schools', class sizes are accordingly adjusted to needs: three students in a class with multiple disabilities; six in a class for special developmental schools; and eight in a special class embedded in a mainstream school (Abe 1998: 91). Regarding educational reform, Abe states that new directives in special education have been effective for those with moderate to profound disabilities, but that students with mild disabilities have been less fortunate up to the late 1990s in attracting funding from the Ministry of Education for their needs (1998: 96).

What are some of the specific experiences of Japanese families with children with disabilities? Eyal Ben-Ari writes about the discovery, and the maintenance, of difference in Japanese preschool. In these first public arenas for social interaction, families of children with disabilities learn where their children are 'ranked' against the 'normate' child. Ben-Ari describes a preschool in Japan that kept careful records of its enrolees with disabilities (including cerebral palsy, Down Syndrome, hyperactivity and autism), because these records:

> form a corps of texts that (at once) documents a child's behaviour, allows systematic comparison with the child's past actions and with those of other children, and facilitates teachers' proper handling of these behaviours...
>
> In these bureaucratic texts, it is relatively difficult to report, let alone formulate, explicit statements about intangibles like moods, anxieties or temperament. [I]n filling out forms, teachers ... simply follow organisational rules, they receive little invitation to reflect upon the notions embodied in the texts.
>
> (2002: 125)

In this life stage, of interest is the emphasis on the family in all aspects of decision-making. While this is not unusual – the age of consent in Japan is twenty years, so it is necessary for parents to make decisions for children, disability or no disability – the retention of responsibility for decision-making by the parent of a child with a disability leaves the 'child' under the control of the 'parent' for a disproportionately long time, an experience which colours the individual's experience at later life stages as well. Control over these children – first by the parent, and then by the state – replaces the ability of children to learn to take control over their own life choices as they grow older and this has dire consequences for their futures.

Young adults

> [G]ranting exemption from work due to a 'physical disability' is in one sense viewed as a proper act of mercy ... – the simultaneous recognition of human limitation and human obligation. Although the very young and the very old are released from official labor by similar logic, the disabled social category is harder to escape and far more stigmatizing than youth or age, which are seen more as stages in the lives of productive people than as immutable identities.
>
> (Thomson 1997: 50–1)

Only 1 per cent of high school students with a disability go on to attend tertiary education, and more than half 'stay at medical/welfare institutions' after graduation (Iwakuma 2003: 126). Sakamoto confirms this: 55 per cent of Japanese students who graduate from special developmental schools in Japan enter welfare

112 *Disability and the lifecycle*

facilities (*fukushi shisetsu*) (2006: 6). This is most likely because, as Oliver notes in the case of the United Kingdom, special education

> has neither equipped [children with disabilities] to exercise their rights as citizens nor to accept their responsibilities ... [T]he special education system has functioned to exclude disabled people not just from the education process but from mainstream social life ...
>
> It ... sociali[ses] disabled people into accepting a life without work and ... fail[s] to give disabled people the necessary skills to enter into the labour market in the first place.
>
> (Oliver 1996: 79, 91)

This section looks at some of the issues confronted by young adults with disabilities who wish to enter the labour market, after having graduated from secondary school, the last life stage associated with childhood. Japanese students leave school at age eighteen; at that juncture all individuals are confronted with the question, 'what shall I do with my life? Job? College? What kind of college? If not, what kind of job?' While the previous chapter included a synopsis of the laws encouraging the employment of people with disabilities, how these are experienced is discussed in more detail here, as an example of the most enduring and definitive characteristics of adulthood in Japan: as a *shakaijin* (literally 'a person of society'; in practice, a person with independent means and responsibilities), one assumes the identity of worker or employee rather than that of child or student.

The lingering recession of the 1990s (which deepened again after the global financial crisis in 2008; the national economy was put further under strain after the 11 March 2011 triple disaster) has put a special burden on employment seekers with disabilities (Iwakuma 2003: 126); admittedly, youth unemployment is a continuing problem in general. Sato noted well into Japan's post-bubble economy that while approximately 36 per cent of high school leavers in Japan enter tertiary education, the national rate of employment of high school graduates is only 16.7 per cent (2005: 12). As noted in Chapter 4, the Law for the Promotion of Employing People with a Disability (Shōgaisha no Koyō no Sokushin nado ni kansuru Hōritsu) posits a quota for middle-sized to large companies, yet, as we have seen, these theoretical targets remain just that. The 2005 census found that 61.5 per cent of the Japanese population aged fifteen or over participated in the labour force (MIAC 2005c). The Japanese Organization for the Employment of the Elderly and People with Disabilities (JEED) was formally established in 2003, after an amalgamation of several separate associations which supported the employment of people with disabilities and those supporting elder workers (JEED 2010: 3); it provides support and training to people with disabilities as well as working with employers.

Despite these difficulties, some businesses in Japan are making strides in addressing inequity for job seekers with disabilities. A pathbreaker in this field is the clothing retailer UNIQLO, whose 2010 achievement of approximately

90 per cent of UNIQLO stores with an employee with a disability, exceeding the 1.8 per cent minimum with an 8.04 per cent employment rate (Fast Retail Co. 2010), is unmatched by any other large-scale employer in Japan. How does it integrate its employees in these almost seven hundred stores? In 2009 UNIQLO published a volume in its 'e-book' series, called *Fuku no Chikara* vol. 1: *Shōgaisha to hataraku to iu koto* (*The Power of Clothing*, vol. 1: *Working with People with Disabilities*). It featured on its cover Yamada Tetsuyoshi, a young male UNIQLO employee with a physical disability from Osaka, riding a bicycle. Individuals working in stores in Okinawa, Osaka, Yamaguchi Prefecture and Tokyo tell their stories, with interviews with employees with and without disabilities. Each story features a different disability: deafness, physical disability, intellectual disability and acquired brain injury. Their working lives are detailed in each profile; for example, Yamada starts the day by sorting change in each cash register, puts clothing on hangers, participates in the morning company assembly (*chōrei*) before the shop opens, serves customers and checks inventory (UNIQLO 2009: 9). His story notes that he started out 'mostly working in the back room' (*bakkuyādo chūshin no shigoto*) but 'gradually' worked his way up to serving customers and operating the register (8).

While some of the stories include somewhat inexplicable (even condescending?) phrases from non-disabled people ('I don't know the pain of disability, but we understand each other's feelings about the pain of living' [6]), at the same time the anecdotes reveal that employees with disabilities are not treated with kid gloves: the Okinawan manager tells us how she has argued with Uehara Rieko, her deaf employee, and Yamada tells how his boss became '*mecha mecha*' ('really') angry at him after a mishap (6, 8). This is in contrast to a perception that people with disabilities are *kawaisō* (pitiful, or in other words, inspiring pity in others) and the normate person should not criticize them. Another example of a mundane situation shows Miura Chieko, who has an intellectual disability, taking clothing out of shipping boxes and sorting them by colour and size (11). This publication, though at times sentimental, highlights the ordinariness of the extraordinary situation that these people occupy in its accounts of day-to-day work at UNIQLO. The final essay in the e-book, written by the president of a company called Fukushi (Welfare) Venture Partners, states that the greatest impediment to growth in the employment rate of people with disabilities is 'not knowing'; that the visibility of working people with disabilities is low, so instead the general image of them is one of receiving services rather than providing them (14). If the economic contribution of people with disabilities is not at least imagined, it is all the more difficult for the individual to actualize his or her potential in mainstream society.

After one has established oneself as an employed *shakaijin*, the logical next step in Japan's hetero-normative society is to continue and maintain the *ie* (stem family) as described in Chapter 2. Reproductive partnership in Japan is most frequently recognized as legal marriage, making sexuality another issue for young adults with a disability, because they are 'often seen as asexual' (Marks 1999: 92). Charlton explains this as an 'epiphenomenon of disability oppression';

that the mainstream social conflation of the body and sexuality in many aspects of private (and increasingly public) life means that people who don't possess a 'body beautiful' are thus seen as non-sexual (1998: 58). The film *Babel* (2006) contained a sub-story about a Japanese high school girl who is deaf, and struggling to come to terms with her mother's death. In several scenes, the character behaves in sexually provocative ways – to boys her own age, as well as an older man – to express the frustration she feels, presumably not just because of her own transitional age as a student, but also because of her disability identity, which has caused her to live what she sees as a sheltered and oppressed life. While some of the student's actions in the film would be considered inappropriate at any time or place, the fact that the character is profoundly deaf cannot be disregarded; her interest in sex cannot be merely written off as 'normal' curiosity, but instead is bound up in her feelings of isolation due to her disability and the loss of her mother. Her desire for sexual activity makes the adults around her, as well as the audience, uncomfortable because of the complications arising from her disability identity. If she cannot communicate with a hearing person, how can she have a sexual relationship with one?

The infantilization of people with disabilities with regards to their sexuality is, with respect to heterosexuality, formalized in the Koseki Hō, or Family Registration Law. This is a law that affects every Japanese citizen through birth, marriage and death as these must all be recorded in the family (or household) registration (*koseki*) system. The *koseki* is an official document authorized by the Koseki Hō. The current Koseki Hō is the 1947 postwar version, replacing the 1871 law. As part of the Civil Code, the 1947 Koseki Hō was seen as the last legal remnants of the *ie seido*, or family system, where the stem family (rather than the individual) was the basic legal unit. The Meiji Civil Code (enacted in 1898), which preceded this set of laws, was 'modelled after European codes' (Oda and Stickings 1997: 21) and adopted as part of Japan's attempt to emulate a 'modern' legal system in keeping with its global place in the late nineteenth century.

In the Japanese Civil Code, marriage, divorce and succession or inheritance laws ('Book Four: Relatives' and 'Book Five: Succession') were 'totally replaced' in the postwar era (Oda and Stickings 1997: 21), giving individuals some legal standing outside their family unit, but the registration system kept this corporate unit part of Japan's national identity. Seen as a legacy of Japan's 'feudal' past, the family system privileged males in a hierarchically structured system with respect to legal rights and inheritance, and also privileged heterosexual unions, as these were the only kinds of marriages that were legally recognized. This shift resulted in an uneasy compromise between the enduring importance of the family and the desire to promote individual rights: in the Koseki Hō, an individual may have his or her own *koseki*, but it is linked to others through its representation as a two-generation household. Each *koseki* contains the individual's gender, date and place of birth, parents' names and marital status, the father's place of registration (*honseki*), 'sibling position' and any marriages or divorces. *Koseki* can contain only two generations; if a third generation enters the scene, a new *koseki* must be created. This reinforces the idea that not only marriage but also parenthood is an important part of asserting 'adult' status. The *koseki* is normally patriarchal and patrilineal: in the case of two Japanese spouses, the couple is registered under the man's name, and to be legally registered, the woman must change her name to her husband's (in the case of 'adopting' a son-in-law, the man will take the wife's family name). A marriage only 'becomes effective by notification thereof in accordance with the provisions of the Family Registration Law' (Article 739.1 of the Civil Code, cited in Oda and Stickings 1997: 151). In fact, in Japanese, the word for 'marriage' (*kekkon*) is one based on social, and even ritual, expectations, but the term for the legal recognition of a heterosexual conjugal relationship is the more prosaic compound 'entry to the register' (*nyūseki*).

Why is the Koseki Hō relevant to people with disabilities? A male, upon marriage, becomes the head of a household, legitimized through his status in the *koseki*. Associated with this position are ideas of independence, responsibility and (re)productivity. One of the prime characteristics of the family is reproduction and generational continuity, as seen through *koseki*, and these documents are always linked back to previous generations through the listing (in the corner of the document) of the *honseki*, or permanent domicile. Independence, responsibility and (re)productivity are not concepts normally associated with adults living with disability. Rather, they are dependent (on carers – either the family or the government); they may not be able to take responsibility for earning an income to support an entire family; and they are often discouraged by their families and friends from reproducing. The usual reason for such discouragement is twofold: the perception that disability is biological and thus genetic and could be passed down; and/or because they are considered unable – physically or intellectually – to cater to the needs of a child. With respect to women with disabilities, Tsutsumi writes: 'Most women with disabilities are raised without a presumption of femininity, or even of femaleness. Normally people expect girls will, as women, become brides, but when there's a disability it's the opposite: marriage is [assumed to be] out of the question' (1996: 142). Nakanishi notes that '[e]specially' women with disabilities 'often struggle with their family's protectiveness' (cited in Heyer 1999: 12). It seems the reproductive potential in women's bodies makes them more vulnerable, and thus requiring closer monitoring.

People with disabilities are expected to remain as the children of a household head, never to head the household themselves. They are, in effect, frozen in time on their parents' *koseki* and considered unable to progress through social and legally recognized life stages. This infantilization of people with disabilities is reminiscent of traditional Japanese society, where '[d]isabled citizens ... were still assumed to be dependents of their parents and siblings and no public policies existed to support them' (Hayashi and Okuhira 2001: 856). A 'child' at any age, a person with a disability who is unmarried is considered less than a full human being in terms of their rights and expectations according to these laws. Whoever does not cross over into the legally and socially expected categories of adulthood through marriage and employment will remain forever a child under these policies. Of course, the rebuttal to this is 'what is independence, then?' If a Japanese person is not married, and not reproductive, can he or she be considered '*ichininmae*' (a term translated as 'to become independent', or 'to come of age')? If disability prevents the individual from attaining these socially expected roles, are they forever children? Interestingly, the Koseki Hō discriminates against not just people with disabilities who do not marry, but a variety of people such as gay, lesbian and transgender people, as well as those who choose for whatever reason an unmarried life. Japanese law recognizes them as children until they choose to create a new *koseki* or until the death of their parents.

Older adults

According to a recent national census, there are 17.2 million households with a member aged sixty-five or over; 3.86 million of these are 'aged single person households', and this latter category is on the increase (MIAC 2005b). As noted in the introduction to this book, Japan's low fertility rate, combined with high-quality medical care and longevity rates, has contributed to a rapidly ageing society. In fact, some believe the Japanese population is decreasing (Okita *et al.* 2011: 20); even though politicians and some demographers have optimistically predicted that trends in the falling birth rate were 'cyclical' and were likely to pick up again over time, trends since 1970 show that the Japanese fertility rate is consistently falling, and is likely to continue to fall (21, 42).[8]

The process of ageing is often concomitant with the development of medical conditions that can cause impairment, or increased risk of incidents that can be disabling (e.g. stroke, or even a fall resulting in broken bones). Yet we must take care not to conflate the two processes, for not every individual over the age of sixty-five can be classified as 'disabled'; nor does every single individual in an assisted living environment score as having a disability based on the ADL ('activities of daily life') scale. What is interesting about discussions of disability at this life stage is the distinction that is often made between a disability and ageing: when is an individual considered 'disabled' rather than merely elderly? The answer to this question lies in the expectations of older people in society; if the elderly person can function in acceptable anticipated ways, theoretically no disability is present. This distinction is not necessarily novel, but what may be variable is where the line is drawn. In a society that is ageing at a brisk pace, Japanese policymakers are constantly reviewing where that line should lie.

As noted in the introduction, considerable scholarly literature has been published on ageing in Japan. Research monographs in English abound, starting with David Plath's *Long Engagements: Maturity in Modern Japan* (1980) through to the recent edited collection by Yoshiko Matsumoto entitled *Faces of Aging: The Lived Experience of the Elderly in Japan* (2011); other notable scholars publishing such books, book chapters and scholarly journal articles include John Creighton Campbell (especially his 1992 monograph *How Policies Change: The Japanese Government and the Aging Society*), Susan Orpett Long, John W. Traphagan and Leng Leng Thang (see bibliography for specific titles). Thang, for example, problematizes the notion of elderly people in Japan as passively looking back at their lives, and instead suggests that many of today's Japanese aged sixty and over are '[l]eading an active "second life" (*dai-ni no jinsei*) in retirement' (2011: 183), and while they may no longer be in the job market, many are still 'contribut[ing] to society' through part-time work, volunteer work and other community activities (ibid.), although she notes that this capacity depends on the individual 'enter[ing] later life with good health, both physically and financially' (183–4).

The periodic Nakakufu surveys on people with disabilities gives us some idea of how many people over the age of eighteen in Japan have been categorized as having a disability (see Table 2.1), but they do not release specific age grade data within the category. Some regional governments, however, do report on the proportion of elderly people amongst the total number of residents registered for the *shōgaisha techō* (disability passbook). The Chiba Prefectural Government reports that in a survey conducted in 2010, 107,595 of 170,780 physical disability passbook holders (or 63 per cent) were aged over sixty-five (Chiba-ken 2010).[9] With reference to physical disability, the rate of impairment increases with age: for example, a 2006 survey conducted by the MHLW found that of a sample of 3,483 individuals with a physical disability (including visual, hearing and mobility impairments), 63.5 per cent were over the age of sixty-five, and 51 per cent were over the age of seventy (Kōseirōdōshō Shakai Enjokyoku 2008: 11).

These statistics are important to Japanese lawmakers because of the costs they imply; if significant numbers of people over the age of sixty-five are considered 'disabled', and this sector of the population is growing, then the balance between contributing members of society and those drawing on the labour of others through pensions is thrown out of equilibrium. Oliver writes that disability and ageing are inevitably linked because they are both products of the 'economic and social forces of capitalism itself' (1996: 131). In other words, elderly people (who do not work, and have not amassed a comfortable savings nest-egg to draw upon) and people with disabilities both constitute an 'economic problem' (ibid.), as neither group contributes actively to the labour market; both are thereby 'forced into situations of dependency' (132). Oliver observes that ageing is in general seen through the lens of a 'disengagement theory', which has people going through stages of old age and further 'disengaging' from society as they become older (135). He rejects the inexorable logic of disengagement theory, arguing that it was not age but good health and stable income that made rates of social engagement stable over time (ibid.), echoing Thang's description of the '*dai-ni no jinsei*' (2011: 183).

Japan's concern for the welfare of its ageing society mirrors other developments abroad. The World Health Organization forecasts ageing around the world, with 690 million people over the age of sixty-five by 2020, and the majority of them living in developing nations (Davis 2002: 24). In Japan, as elsewhere, elderly people with disabilities are often categorized as 'disabled', but Davis asks (regarding America), if the majority of the population is elderly with some impairment – that is, if late-acquired disability edges out congenital or early acquired disability as the dominant mode of disability – will the 'disability' badge criteria require redefinition? (Davis 2002: 24) As Japanese society ages, more and more of the total population will move into the high-risk categories for disability and chronic illness. Forecasting for this future, and subsequently budgeting for its cost, is a key policy concern for Japanese lawmakers. While any person of advanced age runs the risk of developing a disability, the Japanese government is particularly watching the population of elderly living alone, and considering how support can be provided to elderly people with disabilities at home.

While I have argued that elder disability should not crowd out discussions of other kinds of disability through the lifecycle, statistics show that it is still a significant concern, and there has been much handwringing in the popular press about meeting the medical and livelihood costs of Japan's ageing population. Campbell and Ikegami, however, believe that the ageing of Japanese society is not the 'main cause' of Japan's recent economic stagnation; in fact, the country spends less proportionately on health care than the USA does (2003: 12), so the future organization and management of the health-care system in Japan is a more important issue for discussion than merely trying to rein in net costs of elderly clients. Thang is also similarly suspicious of 'gloomy' forecasts: an emerging culture of 'vitality' for retirees, along with improved geriatric care and medical and caregiving technology, mean that the needs of an ageing Japanese society can be met (2011: 183–4).

Conclusion

This chapter has highlighted some of the age-specific issues that affect disability. In particular, prenatal diagnosis, special education, employment and independence (both personal and financial), and the conflation of disability with life stages (the infantilization of adults, for example) have been selected as flashpoints for different discussions about disability. Disability too has its own lifecycle: theoretically, it proceeds along the path of diagnosis – prognosis – categorization of disability (grade) – 'appropriate' education – 'appropriate' employment or other financial support – long-term care.

While unborn children and the elderly are at the opposite ends of the age spectrum, prenatal and end-of-life issues can be seen as linked because they both raise the matter of right to life. Mirroring the eugenics debate at the start of life, there is significant discussion regarding the withholding of medical treatment and euthanasia/assisted suicide for elderly people with significant impairments, where

> the termination of fetuses with disabilities and the potential use of euthanasia/assisted suicide on persons with disabilities ... could redefine the social position of persons with disabilities. Both of these notions are premised on the eradication of disability, and thereby persons with disabilities, through medical science. Raising the spectre of a new eugenics movement, these issues indicate that persons with disabilities may have a very tenuous place in society.
>
> (Jaeger and Bowman 2005: 126)

The unborn, the very young and the frail elderly with dementia all have to rely on family members or other appointed guardians to make decisions on their behalf. In this sense we can perceive an individual's life course path as one where agency increases during childhood, peaks at middle age and then recedes in old age. The presence of disability complicates this expected trajectory.

Once a baby is born, the struggle for development begins as the child is observed, evaluated and ranked according to 'normal' features. Marks observes that 'Children have far less control over their lives than adults. This relative powerlessness is further exacerbated for many disabled children, who are subject to extra restrictions that are imposed as a result of various forms of care to which they are subjected' (1999: 91).

Adults with disabilities – both young, middle-aged and older individuals – have similar issues with control over their lives. They are viewed as having the same social status as children, as noted not just in this chapter but also previously in Chapter 4 on policy and law; this is demonstrated in the welfare laws of Chapter 4 and in the family registration laws described here. Such laws make it difficult for the individual with a disability to be seen as separate from his/her caregiving family, particularly in a society where being independent is part of the definition of adulthood, as per the *shakaijin* and *ichninmae* discourse. Elderly people too experience the loss of control that Marks detects in children; it is possible that the desire for Japanese elderly not to be a burden to their family (as explicated in the next chapter on caregiving) is connected to this fear of losing control, either to an institution or to adult children.

Because the ability of an individual varies at each life stage, the meaning of disability is very different for an infant who is diagnosed at birth than it is for an elderly person who has acquired a significant physical or neurological impairment due to a fall or a stroke. Yet much of the generic disability policy and welfare law, as discussed in Chapter 4, treats disability as an age-independent issue. This is despite the fact that the life trajectory of disability in an individual is not always constant: 'disabled children grow up to be non-disabled adults, non-disabled people become impaired through accident or in old age' (Shakespeare 2006: 65). While there is certainly bound to be some overlap in concerns associated with different life stages, we can also identify aspects of each life stage that are distinct and thus make the conflation of disability experiences undesirable. Expectation about what disability is, and therefore what people with disabilities can or should do with their lives, changes as their age-related roles shift. As Japan is one of the most quickly ageing nations in the world, many of its disability policies are legitimately aimed at supporting a burgeoning population of frail elderly people. But will these same laws address the needs of children with disabilities in Japan and young adults as well as aged people? It is only with a close look at the different age stages of disability that we can meet specific needs throughout the lifecycle.

In this chapter, we have considered disability using a lifecycle approach, yet the converse – looking at the lifecycle through disability – also has important ramifications. Disability has the potential to throw what we expect as 'normal' life sequences into disarray; childhood is prolonged, and independence through marriage and/or employment is discouraged. The 'normal' sequence of events is also subverted: the child with a disability may pre-decease the parents; if not, the practical worry of who will continue caring for the adult child often crowds out the psychological mourning of the parent by the child and other family members. While the social oppression associated with disability is often spoken of in political and economic terms, this disruption of the simplest of routines – the journey travelled by all individuals – needs further attention.

6 Caregiving and the family

> Economists configure caregiving as 'burden.' Psychologists talk about 'coping', health-services researchers describe social resources and healthcare costs, and physicians conceive it as a clinical skill. Each of these perspectives represents part of the picture. For the medical humanities and interpretive social sciences, caregiving is a foundational component of moral experience. By this I mean that we envision caregiving as an existential quality of *what it is to be a human being*. We give care as part of the flow of everyday lived values and emotions that make up moral experience.
>
> (Kleinman 2010: 27)

The family's interactive role in disability is significant for many reasons, the first of which is the hours of unpaid care and therapy provided to people with disabilities by family members. Families are always important to some extent, but the close familial bonds that keep people together can be intensified and become more long-lasting when a disability is present; one might argue that such families provide a level of care, financial support and sociality that is seldom matched in the dynamics of families with unimpaired members only. Laura Mauldin, a sociologist, writes that 'Disability and families are so intertwined ... How we expect families to respond to disability reveals not just how much or little our culture values persons with disabilities, but also our expectations of medicine, mothers, fathers, and siblings' (2008: n.p.).

Disability throws these values into clear relief and tests the boundaries of social and ideological expectations about family roles and relationships. The onerous aspects of the caring responsibility are often highlighted, as in the professional opinions mentioned above: it is costly, personally stressful and often requires specialized knowledge. Academics can be similarly pessimistic in their assessment of disability and caregiving: for example, the abstract of an English-language article on aged disability in Japan published in a demographic studies scholarly journal begins with the blunt sentence: 'Disability is a burden to individuals and society' (Schoeni *et al.* 2006: 39). Yet, as Kleinman rightly points out, ideally caregiving should be viewed not as the response to a rare or a tragic event, but as part of everyday life – disability only affects *the extent* of care an individual receives, not whether or not s/he will require it. Caregiving should be not just part of the 'personal tragedy theory of disability' (Oliver 1996: 31) but an aspect of every person's life. While disability intensifies care needs, it is oversimplifying, and often incorrect, to think of able-bodied people as wholly 'unencumbered, physically and cognitively intact' beings (ibid.). At some stage in their lives, *all* people require some kind of care; Shakespeare reminds us that '[g]iving and receiving care is something which no individual can escape from at some points in the life cycle' (2006: 135). It is undeniable, though, that people with disabilities frequently need more care, and for lengthier periods. This is, of course, closely related to their intrinsic impairment or medical condition, but it is important to remember that disability can also isolate them from economic and social opportunities that would assist independent living. In other words, the social (as distinct from medical) fact that people with disabilities are more vulnerable to social oppression and financial hardship is a separate and cumulative source of their intensified care needs.

Caregiving in Japan is frequently seen as synonymous with eldercare; this is understandable, as the number of people aged over sixty-five and registered as having a disability is much larger than the number of those under the age of twenty. Still, there are more than 335,000 young people in Japan who may require some kind of long-term care for disability (Naikakufu 2010b). Furthermore, the potential for any person in Japan to acquire a disability means that there is no precise way to predict how many people in a given society will require care, and for how long. Therefore, viewing disability care as something that must meet the needs of all people with disabilities, regardless of age, is important for planning purposes.

The family unit has been considered 'the only [reliable] system available for safeguarding the lives of its family members' (Yōda 2002: 7); this cultural ideal of family as main caregiver persists today. While Japan is not the only society where families play a major role in the lives of people with disabilities, distinctive characteristics of the *ie seido* (or stem family system), and the way it works with the country's welfare system, offer us some insight into caregiving in the country, which is, arguably, a concept in flux owing to changes in attitudes and practical considerations surrounding caregiving and disability. Whether as eldercare, childcare or at any time in between, caregiving is inextricably connected to family relationships; this is because in Japan, as elsewhere, children are ideally looked after by their parents, and this care is presumed to be reciprocated subsequently in old age. Disability complicates this progression, especially in the case of families who may have caregiving responsibilities at both ends of the generational spectrum: elderly parents and an adult child with a disability.

Another aspect of caregiving is the relegation of care recipients to childlike status: they are dependent on caregivers who make decisions on their behalf. Whether the care is family based or institution based, caregiving is often marked by extending – or reverting to – 'childhood' roles within the family structure after the onset of impairment. This refers back to some of the arguments presented in Chapter 5 on the different lifecycle stages of people with disability. On the one hand, it is 'normal' to give intensive care to an infant, even when there is no impairment or illness present; yet, as these children emerge as young adults, their family role as care recipients can 'freeze' their social development within the family, and other personal attributes of a maturing individual, such as financial and social independence as well as sexual identity, are muted.

The term 'care' is usually discussed in tandem with the term 'needs'; ideally, care should be matched to needs (Marks 1999: 93–113). These two terms give us two different but interrelated perspectives by which to understand caregiving and disability. The term 'needs' tends be seen as objective, or as a professional assessment, which is more neutral than the more emotional term 'care'. If care is something that grows out of 'needs', activists claim that it should be seen not as a privilege, but as a right, or an entitlement. Yet it is often impossible to remove the emotional aspect of the expectations and responses experienced by caregivers and recipients. The relationship between people who need assistance and those who provide it varies widely from distant and professional to very personal and intimate, and all shades in between, and this can complicate the lines drawn between professional and personal relationships between the carers and the cared for.

The terms 'needs' and 'care' are always socially constructed and their content determined by ideological expectations of what an individual is capable of, to what extent people rely on others for assistance in 'normal' situations, and how these two will or should interact. To demonstrate how expectations determine the definition of caregiving, let us consider the stereotypical married man who cannot cook, clean or do his own laundry; yet he is not considered 'disabled', merely fortunate to have a wife to perform these tasks for him (Orbach cited in Marks 1999: 97). This is very true in Japan, where Japanese gendered roles are considered complementary, allowing each role mastery as part of its social status both at home and in the community; in fact, Edwards calls this the 'gender as complementary incompetence' model (1989: 120–3): 'Men are not able to live by themselves, it is often said, and if they do, they will not live properly...' (121). It is the family that steps in and supplies the conditions for the man to live 'properly', first in the form of the mother, later in that of the wife (and perhaps even later in the form of the daughter-in-law, according to Japanese patrilineal customs). Nevertheless, we do not consider these cared-for men as 'disabled' because of their ability to support their caregivers with an earned wage. This example is given to show the constructed nature of 'needs' and 'care' (and the value placed on capital generation and independence in mainstream society, at least for those deemed capable).

Practically speaking, however, in Japan as in other countries, 'needs' and 'care' are determined based on the 'activities of daily life' (ADL) scale (see Chapter 4), which is inextricably connected to the evaluation of a person's ability to perform self-care versus dependent care; its base definition is: does the person need assistance to 'maintain physical well-being, personal appearance, hygiene, safety and general functioning in [their] home and community?' (Sotnik and Jezewski 2005: 29). Results of the ADL are used to estimate levels of assistance, as either financial contributions (to replace or supplement income, or to purchase specialized aids and equipment) or access to services such as therapies or other

124 *Caregiving and the family*

facility-based programmes. The economics of care are important but financial assistance is only part of the picture; it pays for the required personal assistance (help with dressing, bathing, assistance going out and so on), or other practices of caring, that is at the centre of caregiving. However, rather than focusing on the actual performance of care itself, this chapter is concerned with the socially constructed and reproduced ideas and beliefs about care.

This chapter first explores the characteristics of family-based caregiving in Japan, including a focus on gendered caregiving, which includes gendered roles in the family as well as in the public sphere; I would argue that the strong association of caregiving within the family with gender has come to be projected publicly, given that the majority of professional caregivers in Japan are female. Secondly, I survey the published work of Japan's most celebrated caregiver, winner of the Nobel Prize in Literature Ōe Kenzaburō, as an example of how one family sees its relationship to disability through caregiving. Lastly, the discussion turns to changes in ideas about caregiving in Japan, with a focus on the implications of a sense of gradual commodification of care through the Long-Term Care (LTC) insurance programme. LTC was initially conceived of as a solution to the 'graying crisis' (Thang 2011: 185) Japan confronts with its ageing population, but this programme does more than just find financial solutions. It also offers the possibility to transform care from a moral obligation to another consumer choice.

The Japanese family and caregiving

How do we approach the idea of Japanese families and their role in disability caregiving? A comparative perspective can be instructive. Here, as one example, is a passage from a textbook for North American disability workers on how to understand and work with cultural variation – in this case, how 'Western' social workers should deal with Asian American caregivers (grouping together Chinese Americans and Japanese Americans). This external perspective asserts that 'the Asian' carer should seen as 'different', and so it recommends that American social workers:

1   Use a formal, professional mode of interaction; avoid personalism.
2   Do not pressure or encourage family members to reveal problems.
3   Do not emphasize the independence of children in front of the family.
4   Offer concrete assistance rather than counselling or psychotherapy.
5   Be cautious about using family-centered, partnership approaches ... because the family is likely to be passive and respectful toward the professional.

(Seligman and Darling, 2007: 83)

This passage sets up an image of an archetypal 'Asian' family: emotionally distant (1); secretive, or at least highly private (2); controlling (3); suspicious of psychological therapies (4); and showing deference to professionalism and specialist knowledge (5).

While some of these stereotypes may sound familiar, a look at the anthropological as well as fictional and non-fictional writings about the Japanese family demonstrates the existence of a much more complex situation. Family studies in Japan are far from few, as the institution of 'family' in Japan has long fascinated both scholarly and lay audiences for many of the reasons that compelled these American social workers to write their handbook: how can an apparently universal institution appear to differ so starkly from our own? Some of the seminal works in anthropology (a discipline that has traditionally given priority to the study of kinship) that address these 'differences' are Ruth Benedict's *The Chrysanthemum and the Sword: Patterns of Japanese Culture* (first published in 1946 and often critiqued, but still in print); Takeo Doi's *The Anatomy of Dependence* (1981); Merry White's *Perfectly Japanese: Making Families in an Era of Upheaval* (2002); and Joy Hendry's *Marriage in Changing Japan: Community and Society* (2010). The parent–child relationship in Japan has been much discussed, criticized and re-analysed by academics in both Japanese and other languages, while eldercare and its impact on the family have been much researched (see especially the work of Susan Orpett Long, 2000 and 2008). In these and other books, scholars have considered notions of parental love, duty and honour the psychological 'glue' that holds family relationships together, and which in turn helps to reproduce the institution in the future. One of the primary functions of the family is to provide care to those who require it, first through childcare, and later through eldercare. In both these cases, the care providers occupy the middle stratum of the generational structure: as parents (not children, not grandparents or great grandparents). This precedent has imparted to caregiving in general a paternalistic tone, against which many Japanese disability activists have protested (see Aoi Shiba no Kai's declaration in Chapter 2).

Family-based care is a form of affective labour, which is a cross-cultural phenomenon: most cultures view '[c]are [a]s affective as well as effective' (Kohn and McKechnie 1999: 1). Cultural attributes are thus only part of the story, and arise not just from the affective ties between people but also from the ways these ties are interpreted, and how they are challenged over time. Disability caregiving provides one of those challenges to emotional ties by complicating and intensifying the caregiving relationship. These challenges are played out in the Japanese kinship system and the Japanese Civil Code. Japanese kinship can be described in a number of ways: the *ie seido*, as introduced in Chapter 2, refers to the structure of kinship organization (the extended, or stem, family). *Ie* technically means 'house', but it also means the family line (as in the 'House of Windsor') as much as the structural home; other relevant terms are *kazoku* (also translated as family, but refers to people related by blood, and also includes spouses) and *setai* ('household', referring to people who physically live together, and therefore may or may not be related by blood). The *ie* functions as an economic unit as well as a social, emotional and spiritual one. There is no single 'type' of *ie* in Japan; along with geographical variation (e.g. there are differences in inheritance patterns between north-eastern regions and southern regions [Hendry 2003:28]), a family is flexible because of the evolving nature of family organization through time. Members

126 *Caregiving and the family*

move out of the home, and start new families; it may adopt new members or take back former members. Fluidity of family shape and organization is a common occurrence; it is interesting, however, to look at how disability changes the 'normal' flow from one family shape to another.

The trope of gendered caregiving can be seen reflected in welfare legislation as well. The Six Laws of Welfare, primarily concerned with minors, the elderly and those with disabilities, were until 2005 the standard legal programmes defining the role of the state in providing care for these groups. In a sense, this set of laws conflates three vulnerable groups of society, all requiring care, into one category; and all three of these groups are associated with feminine care, for women are the primary caregivers to children and young adults with disabilities as well as to the elderly, in their role as daughters or daughters-in-law, because their husbands are usually in external employment.[1] Caring for family members with a disability, either children or elderly relatives, frequently falls into the category of the 'domestic', and is thus a woman's domain: 'Originally, in Japan, responsibility for the welfare of people with disabilities was a private matter, assigned entirely to "family love"…, a euphemism for the physical labour of female relatives' (Yōda cited in Stibbe 2004: 21).

Stibbe argues that gendered identification in caregiving and disability are closely interrelated. Many of the psychological qualities given to people with disabilities in fictional media portrayals can also be seen as feminized: 'All the disabled characters … display *gaman* [silent, passive patience in adverse circumstances] to some extent but it is particularly clear in the portrayal of female characters' (2004: 28). Lastly, because women live longer than men, it is they who will more frequently occupy the role within a family, and present to wider society, as a frail aged person needing part-time or full-time care. Disability identity is thus blurred with gender identity, as an ageing society that gradually presents more and more members of its population as 'disabled' through ageing may further associate disability with gender as it is likely that aged women will fill these ranks. Theoretically speaking, it is possible to imagine an 'aged' Japanese society, according to current trends, where women are engaged, both privately and professionally, in caring for large numbers of frail aged women.

The gender ratio among caregivers in Japan is 1.3, or one man for every three women (Takahashi *et al.* 2005: 478). In reality, family care in Japan often means female care: this is a kind of 'invisible labour' which 'affects gender relations at work and at home' and, perhaps unfairly, places much of the responsibility for caring for people with disabilities on women (Mackie 2003:189–90). Shakespeare agrees that there has 'develop[ed] an almost essentialist idea of women as carers' (2006:144), but given the changing role of women in Japanese society as in other developed countries, we must question the practicality of expecting a female 'natural' affinity with caregiving roles (Kohn and McKechnie 1999: 3). Not all women in varying family situations will have the practical capacity to provide consistent home care to family members. The option to outsource disability care in the family is seen as a fraught choice, as caregiving is often categorized as a moral act (rather than neutral work). Despite its high moral status, professional caregiving is not a high paying job, and is cut off from the higher-status occupations associated with highly technical medical care (ibid.: 4). Japan's family and professional roles have always been deeply gendered; it is no surprise, then, that the role of primary caregiver in Japan is strongly gendered, and mothers are often seen as indistinguishable from their child with a disability. With respect to care for children with disabilities, Yōda writes

> a disabled member of the family, who is viewed as non-productive and in need of support, is denied the chance for independent living, and the mother, regarded as the natural caretaker under the principle of self-help on the part of the family, is obliged to assume all the burden of caring for the disabled person. This is why disability issues in Japan manifest themselves not only as problems affecting people with disabilities themselves, but also, and with no less intensity, as problems involving their mothers.
>
> (2002: 8)

This is reflected in eldercare as well; in a 2009 survey of middle-aged people conducted by the Ministry of Health, Labour and Welfare, while men did participate in 'long-term care', the length of their hours spent in caregiving per week compared with that of women was less in all categories, but the gap was most dramatic in those who spent more than 20 hours per week providing care: in this upper category, the number of women providing significant care was double or more that of men (MHLW 2009a: n.p., fig. 3).

The gendering of caregiving is seen not only at home but also in the professional sphere: women are over-represented in nursing, welfare and other care-providing occupations in Japan, as well as in volunteer activities and domestic work caring for family members. The 2004 census figures show that more than 76 per cent of the 5,310,000 individuals registered as employed in 'Medical, Health Care, and Welfare' jobs are female (MIAC 2005a). Policies that support the gendered dignity of people with disabilities to choose their caregivers are not yet in place, and the limited capacity to meet this need demonstrates how notions of femininity associated with caregiving within the home are projected into the public and professional spheres. The gendering of caregiving in the professional sphere has caused some problems; for example, male clients felt they should be able choose a male worker if they wished, but this was often not an option because of the over-representation of women in such occupations. The disability rights movement in Japan, with respect to care provided by non-family members, has fought for the clients' right to choose their workers, supporting the concept of 'same-sex workers' (Hayashi and Okuhira 2001: 863).

The blurred boundaries between gendered caregiving and disability identity are also implicitly expressed in social welfare policy. As described in Chapter 4, children with disabilities were not a focus in early postwar welfare programmes because these children were seen as the sole responsibility of a stay-at-home mother, while public funds for rehabilitation were primarily directed towards

128 *Caregiving and the family*

replacing lost income to disabled breadwinners, in other words, adult men who had returned from the war. There were some programmes supporting women during and right after Japan's wartime period, when the welfare focus necessarily shifted to include the widows of soldiers and their children, who were without a male breadwinner (Endō 1999: 123, 127, 130). As noted earlier, priorities in welfare benefits were first designed to benefit men with physical disabilities incurred during military service; this masculine and workforce bias disadvantaged females with disabilities and female carers who were not independent wage earners; again, this group of people could not be compensated for the productivity they never had.

The family as caregiver: the writings of Ōe Kenzaburō

As mentioned in Chapter 5, the Japanese Civil Code (the Koseki Hō, or Family Registration Law) explicitly recognizes the familial roles of father, mother and children. As I argued in that chapter, notions of independence are connected to a fully fledged adult status, so people with disabilities who are not deemed capable of caring for themselves (or others) have been discouraged from marriage, leaving them legally 'children' on their parents' register. This 'frozen in time' phenomenon, reinforced by the Civil Code, reinforces the family's role in caregiving in the case of disability. In pre-modern Japan, family members were primarily responsible for care, and Chapter 2 described how, in the spiritual realm, disability was seen as an affront on two levels: it represented embodied impurity in the Shinto religious worldview, and was read as 'bad karma' according to Buddhist beliefs. Familial caregiving, therefore, was often thought of as an outcome of spiritual imbalance, and thus association with destiny and retribution. A related sense of parental dismay and dread at the birth of a child with a disability is poignantly recounted in the context of postwar Japan in the novel *Kojinteki na Jiken* (*A Personal Matter*) by Ōe Kenzaburō, who was later awarded a Nobel Prize for Literature in 1994. Taylor and Kassai write that in this novel (and in the many other fictional works by Ōe on this topic), parents 'alternate between a mixture of guilt, fear, and shame, and are afraid to accept their babies' (1998: 643). This novel, first published in 1964, was groundbreaking for the brutal honesty with which Ōe describes the birth of his first child and his own and others' reactions to the event (including doctors, nurses, family and friends); his own initial instinct to flee from his caregiving responsibilities; and the emotional moment when he realizes that he can become a father to this child. This process is similarly sketched out through the longer novel *Mannen Gannen no Futtobōru* (*The Silent Cry*, first published in 1967), while the relationship between father and son is described in a number of ways in the short story 'Warera no kyōki o ikinobiru michi wo oshieyo' ('Teach us to Outgrow our Madness', first published in Japanese in 1969) and the novel *Pinchi Rannā Chōsho* (*The Pinch Runner Memorandum*, first published in Japanese in 1976). Even in works that primarily focus on other aspects of Japanese society, such as 1999's *Chūgaeri* (*Somersault*, which takes up issues arising from the 1995 Aum Shinrikyō incident), Ōe almost always includes in his cast of characters a family that contains a child with a disability (in *Chūgaeri*, it is a woman whose brother has a disability, rather than the typical father/son pairing of the other novels).

The family features in Ōe's non-fiction writing as well. *Kaifuku Suru Kazoku* (translated as *A Healing Family*, 1996) includes a vignette that illustrates how caregiving is difficult but is also an integral aspect of his family's life. In the book, Ōe describes his son's view of his family's caregiving responsibilities (at the time, Ōe's elderly mother-in-law was living with them):

> Eventually, though, at five o'clock, which is still too early for the rest of us to eat, my wife takes her mother's dinner to her room. As a rule, though there are exceptions, the end of her final meal of the day means the end of her trips to the gate – and the end of Hikari's worrying on her behalf, at least for another day. [Hikari writes:] 'I like the evening every day. You bring dinner. It's the same in every family. By "evening" I mean five o'clock.' ... I think the thing that struck us most in Hikari's message, however, was his idea that 'it's the same in every family.'
>
> (Ōe 1996: 68)

Hikari, despite his cognitive disability, can articulate clearly how extra tasks create extra stress on his mother, yet he sees it as a 'normal' part of everyday life. Hikari's consciousness of his grandmother's needs helps Ōe to 'normalize' the caregiving experience, and this in turn suggests that the family can be considered an organic entity that has the potential to 'heal' itself (as per the book's title) along the often difficult path of caregiving. Ōe, his wife and his son all come to perceive that caregiving (in this case, both eldercare and adult childcare) makes demands on the family, but after his years of experience, Ōe can now describe the caregiving dynamic in this way:

> Still, though it may seem at times that something is always being lost or broken as our family rattles along day by day, it is just as certain that things also somehow get mended and rehabilitated ... [T]aking the long view of things [my mother-in-law] has made periodic improvements over the years; and don't all of us live in those moments, those periodic respites and recoveries with which we are blessed?
>
> (Ōe 1996: 71)

Ōe does not, however, romanticize caregiving as something it is not; he says 'each phase of our lives passes, and we can't linger over memories. Frankly, we're just too busy to do so' (ibid.). He warns readers not to be too idealistic about caregiving in the family, overestimating the benefits as well as the difficulties:

> It is sentimental, however, and inaccurate to think that the lives of the mothers of handicapped children are just a constant struggle ... The truth is

that their children give them real joy ... I can attest to it too, from my own experience at home. And yet I also know that both my wife and I have said to ourselves on any number of occasions those too familiar words: 'We've got no choice. Let's just get on it with it.'

(Ōe 1996: 59)

Ōe's body of work, which has been acclaimed by both Japanese and overseas critics for its honesty, demonstrates the personal struggle family caregivers must confront. It is particularly interesting to look at his writings because his observations do challenge some of the stereotypes about Japanese families (e.g. emotionally distant, acquiescent to professionals, focused on the mother's role as caregiver rather than the father, and so on). Ōe's accounts speak to a variety of experience. He writes of Dr Moriyasu, the surgeon who treated Hikari as an infant, in warm terms (1996: 17), yet in his fictional work on the birth of his son, the paediatricians seem distant (1964). In another account, he reflects on his nervousness before the operation, feeling foolish because 'All we could do was rely on Doctor M.' (2002: 45). Yet he is an actively involved father, who participates in much of the everyday routine of his son (1996, 2002). Varied as they are, Ōe's representations of his experiences are each neither 'true' nor 'false'; instead they communicate the vast range of responses individuals have to a similar situation. The long-term care of a child with a significant disability can be daunting, expensive and exhausting, but it is an integral part of what it means in Ōe's world to be human, for his son 'has illuminated the dark, deep folds of my consciousness as well as its bright sides' (Taylor and Kassai 1998: 643). Ōe's work is especially striking in that he writes as a father in a world where most caregivers, private and professional, are female, but this does not make his observations ring any less true for carers; in fact, his work is all the more expressive because it crosses these gender boundaries. Its expressiveness further challenges the stereotype that Japanese families are private and secretive about disability. While some of the more dramatic episodes of his caregiving experience are narrated in fictional works (the scene where Eeyore, a name he often uses for Hikari in his fiction, confronts his family holding a kitchen knife in *Rouse Up O Young Men of the New Age!* [2002: 7], for example), his interviews and non fiction also contain many moments of confession. In an interview, Ōe states

My son has been extremely important to me. Having a handicapped child has had an important influence on my way of thinking about culture, and on my way of thinking about politics ... I have written about extremely isolated, independent individuals, I've written about my son. By writing about those extremely personal things, I have gone down a tunnel of personal affairs, which perhaps eventually connects with universal affairs. Maybe my writing about personal things could be taken as a hint about the nature of universality.

(Kinsella 2000: 237)

Ōe's attitude towards caring is striking: while he is a Japanese father caring for a son with a disability in Japanese society, he feels that his experience is one that can be shared cross-culturally, and that unites him with others through his writing.

While Ōe is probably Japan's most famous family caregiver, there are others who have made their role as caregivers public; when this is a public figure, these announcements are often paired with a celebrity endorsement of a charity, awareness-raising or even political campaign. Imai Eriko, member of the very successful 1990s group Speed, announced in 2008 that her son (born in 2004) has a hearing impairment, and soon thereafter she began a television appearance campaign promoting sign language (Elly 2011). Imai has made her views available on her official website: 'Disability is individual (*kosei*). It is merely inconvenient, but it is not misfortune (*fukō*)' (ibid.). Several celebrities have revealed publicly that they have children with Down Syndrome: Matsuno Akemi (originally a long-distance runner), Kaneko Emi (model) and Mizukoshi Keiko (singer/songwriter) have all acknowledged their caregiving roles. Most politically active is the athlete-turned-*tarento*-turned-politician Matsuno, who was quoted as running for local office because she wanted 'make this town easier to live in for people and children with disabilities' (*Asahi Shimbun* 2010: 30). In many cases, the mass media plays up these announcements in a positive light, portraying the parents as positive in outlook and capable caregivers.

Changing care: long-term care insurance

Changes in caregiving should always be seen as embedded in the social context; this context can be defined including gender issues, patient 'diversity' and the expectations of people receiving care. Meanwhile, other factors can influence the way care is given and received, such as changes in medical technology and intervention in care, and established codes of care ethics (Kohn and McKechnie 1999: 3–10). Furthermore, the severity and the type of disability inevitably affect the individual's capacity for autonomous decision-making about care. All of these factors are relevant, but here I focus on the social expectations of care in Japan. Webb notes a growing acceptance by 2000 among older Japanese that 'we cannot expect family care anymore' (2002: 119), based on the changing values of those who would have been the providers of such care, the '*shinjinrui*' generation, born into a peaceful and affluent postwar society and with different and more individually oriented values (120). Where 65 per cent of survey respondents in 1950 expected support in their old age from their children, only 13 per cent expressed this view in 1996 (Ogawa and Retherford cited in Webb 2002: 120). Elderly people envisioned themselves living alone (*hitorigurashi*) as long as possible, or finding a place in a residential institution. In a white paper published by the Prime Minister's Office in 2010, researchers found that independence for the elderly is rising: in 1980, 11 per cent of elderly women and 4.3 per cent of elderly men lived alone, but these rates steadily rise over the decades and the government expects that by 2030 almost 21 per cent of elderly women and about 18 per cent of men will be living alone (Naikakufu 2010a).

Mirroring this trend of lowered expectations regarding family care and increased desire for independence, caregiving, as a profession providing services in institutions as well as private homes, is growing. In the 2005 census, the Ministry of Internal Affairs and Communication notes that the major industrial group which recorded the 'largest increases [in employment] both in number and rate of increase' over the preceding five years was 'medical, health care and welfare', which reached 5,353,000 registered employees or 8.7 per cent of the entire workforce (2005a). Manufacturing and retail are the only two named sectors that outnumber employees in the medical, health-care and welfare category (ibid.). Yōda notes that the few progressive changes in the social welfare policy have aimed to 'relieve the family of its burden' (2002: 8) and encourage a reliance on professional carers to provide long-term care for people with intellectual and physical disabilities.

These concerns have been debated in government circles for some time. In 1997, the long-term care insurance system (*kaigo hoken seido*) was created by means of a law that came into force in 2000. Under this law, those covered will receive 'personal assistance for bathing, toileting, eating, occupational and physical therapy, nursing care, medical supervision and other treatment for physical conditions ... brought about by advanced age, such as being bedridden or having dementia ...' (JSRPD 2007–9).

This social insurance system supplements other national insurance schemes for pensions, health and unemployment, but focuses on the financial costs of caring for someone with a disability. Those enrolled in the programme can receive 90 per cent of the cost of private home care for an insured family member through public funds (split between local and national government funds). As stated in the law, it is aimed at families who care for (or envision future care for) the elderly, but there are also provisions to be made for those with appropriate medical issues over the age of forty (these would be, most likely, people with long-term disabilities whose own parents/carers were ageing). The law defines participation in this scheme through contractual payments, which vary for levels of disability. It is not income tested, which takes away some of the social stigma that is associated with applications for social welfare in Japan (Izuhara 2003: 398). The Ministry of Health, Labour and Welfare explicitly states that one of its goals is to

> separate long-term care services from medical care insurance ... [and to r]e-examine the inequalities of users' costs associated with the separation of welfare for the elderly and medical care services for the elderly, and do away with long-term so-called social hospitalization in ordinary hospitals, etc., when long-term care is the overriding need.
> (MHLW 2002)

The ministry further states that the elderly should be the 'policyholders, and ... [they should] bear the cost of premiums where possible', at a fixed rate percentage charge (ibid.). This policy reflects some of the neoliberal language and values in the Supports and Services for People with Disabilities Act described in

Chapter 4, where independence is valued (here, to 'do away with' disempowering, 'ordinary hospitals') and a user-pays system is introduced.[2] When an individual takes out this insurance, they are paying into a fund that will eventually be drawn upon for their own long-term care. The programme was groundbreaking in other areas of caregiving as well because it 'introduced a different concept to the public that ... care was no longer to be "expected" from the family or "allocated" by the state. It has become part of a social contract based upon a system of mandatory contributions and consumer choice' (Izuhara 2003: 396).

The new programme was implemented with the goal of reducing the burden on families with elderly relatives with disabilities and theoretically lowering demand for institutional care. As women's roles in the family are still skewed towards nurturing and caregiving, with three caregiving women for every single caregiving man in Japan, as mentioned above, it is fair to say that caregivers' insurance could not only impact on the quality of life for the person with the disability (improving his or her access to professional services) but can also transform attitudes towards family life of female family members. In fact, Arai *et al.*'s preliminary study of families of relatives enrolled in the long-term care insurance system found that

> The LTC system has demonstrably changed the attitudes of caregivers. It was found that more caregivers came to believe that society must look after the elderly ... in the short space of a year, there was an obvious shift from the idea that the care of the elderly falls to the family to the virtually unheard of notion that society must shoulder the problems of the world's fastest-graying population.
>
> (Arai, Kumamoto and Washio 2004: S54)

The distinct departure from paying cash allowances to the family (which often further ties female members closely to the care) to a social contract with the state frees traditional caregivers from their role as 'unpaid' workers (Izuhara 2003: 405), even though most of the professional workers in the system are middle-aged women (407). The LTC insurance system has had an impact in the way that people view their role as caregivers, but it seems as if more time for integrating these ideas is needed before the quality of life of caregivers of the elderly with disabilities will improve. Takahashi *et al.* found that this group of informal caregivers (in nearly all cases, family members) showed higher scores in depression rating tests than professional carers, even though the hours spent caring were similar and the levels of utilization of social services were uneven (2005: 477, 478).[3] The Ministry of Health, Labour and Welfare found that middle-aged people who provide long-term care were more likely to feel negative emotions (e.g. 'jittery', 'hopeless', 'depressed' and so on) the longer they were involved in caregiving (MHLW 2009a: n.p., fig. 4).

Society (and policy, which reflects its mainstream values) has begun to consider the individual with a disability independently from the family, but the extent to which the emotional separation of family members has occurred appears in question. Arai *et al.* state that there seems to be a 'demonstrable change' in attitudes, yet also found that there were no significant differences in the results of caregiver surveys before the commencement of the LTC insurance programme and after its implementation; in other words, carers were feeling just as 'burdened' as before (2004: S54). Even though people's concept of caregiving has changed from one that is solely private to one that includes the public, their psychological attachment to the task is still strong. One can argue that the programme was meant to empower the individual, rather than leaving decisions to family members who might be unprepared emotionally and financially for the task. Despite Japanese welfare policy shifts, detaching from their caring duties seems to be difficult for caregivers.. Regarding LTC for the elderly, Harris and Long call for a mix of family and service provider care as the next developmental step (2000: 34). In both eldercare and childcare, the break between the family and caregiving is far from complete.

LTC is primarily utilized by carers of the frail elderly; nevertheless, considering the outcomes and implementation of the LTC insurance system is important because it explicitly addresses the family as caregiver to all kinds of people in the context of disability. There are provisions for the LTC to be made available for those with appropriate medical issues over the age of forty (in other words, adults with long-term disabilities who are being cared for by ageing parents). The refocusing of LTC towards ageing carers rather than aged clients is an interesting take to this relatively new approach to the family as caregiver.

Caregiving, however, cannot be bluntly categorized via a simple dichotomy between the family and the state; Hayo and Ono's survey suggests that while families still play a major role as caregivers for the elderly, other aspects of care are firmly in the public sphere. For example, when asked 'Who do you think should be responsible for the ... (a) livelihood of the elderly, and (b) health and long-term care of the elderly?' the clear majority of respondents felt that funding and care should be shared between families and the government, but more people felt that the government should be responsible for these two aspects of eldercare than those who felt the family was solely responsible for eldercare. (2011: 79)

Conclusion

Japanese family structures have always been conceptualized as both encompassing an unchanging 'tradition' that preserves identity through generations (as evidenced by the *ie seido* and its attendant Buddhist beliefs, symbolized by the family gravesite), and being adaptable to specific situations both internal and external to the family (as evidenced by the *ie*'s fluid boundaries to include residential members, and to adopt members to sustain the lineage). The *ie seido*'s generational structure thus provides ideological precedence and approval for family-based care of elderly family members with disabilities; this, however, is not tenable for many contemporary Japanese families whose home environment and individual situations do not provide a good fit with the practicalities of full-time home care. Similarly, the multi-generational structure of the *ie* could disperse responsibility to family caregivers of children and young adults with disabilities, but as the number of nuclear families increased in the second half of the twentieth century, caregiving became more of an individual than a communal pursuit, resulting in calls for the government to step in and provide support. This support does not mean a return to institutionalization, however; the Cabinet Office's statistics from 1999 to 2009 (see Table 2.1) demonstrate that while the total number of people registered with a disability is rising, the number of institutionalized cases (this can be interpreted as the number of people requiring a high level of care) is decreasing, which suggests that home care is meeting the needs of people with disabilities. On the other hand, there is the question of the extent to which this care is better care, or merely another funding model, for caregivers who utilize government programmes still attest to higher levels of stress.

There have been several changes to the way care is given and received in Japan in recent years. As listed in Figure 2.1, the numbers of people registered with their local government offices to receive disability passbooks rose in all disability categories (physical disability, intellectual disability and psychiatric disability) and in all age groups in the period 1999–2009 (Naikakufu 2003, 2006, 2009), yet the only grouping which shows a decline is those who are institutionalized. This means that despite the overall increases (likely due to more nuanced diagnoses and the overall ageing of Japanese society), a smaller proportion of the disability community is receiving institutional rather than home-based care. This does not necessarily mean that they are all being cared for by family members (e.g. young adults are being cared for by middle-aged or elderly parents, or the elderly being cared for by their adult children); it suggests that individuals are increasingly using a combination of home-care patterns including independent living and local council-supported home help as well as family care. Still, the family will always be at the centre of these debates. Even when family care is the individual's preferred option, the ageing of Japanese society means that carers are ageing as well. Medical advances mean that more and more children with disabilities are living longer, and potentially outliving their parent caregivers. So while eldercare fronts public discourse in Japan, the ideological shift in caregiving from family to serviced-based care is likely to occur at many levels – not merely at the end of life. The JIL movement has been successful in supporting adults making choices to live at home, but in general the movement assumes that the consumer is capable of making autonomous decisions. For those with severe intellectual impairment, this is not an option. The family, or a state-appointed guardian, will always be responsible for this decision-making, and no matter how much 'independence' new structures allow for, for some people with disabilities, the family will always play a central role in decision-making about care and its delivery.

As noted in the introduction to this chapter, every person experiences 'conventional dependency' at some stage during their lifetime (during childhood and periods of illness, for example), but 'extensive dependency' (Shakespeare 2006: 146), as experienced by people with disabilities, tests these familial bonds. Every child with a disability begins with a 'normal' family experience of dependency; yet they are often 'frozen' in that childhood stage. Ōe Kenzaburō writes of a

136 *Caregiving and the family*

realization he experienced while his son was ill with a cold. He had recently overheard a conversation between doctors while visiting a hospital and felt helpless and angry for not speaking up; he recalls this later at home:

> As I looked at his bright red face and watery, staring eyes, I was struck by the realization that my son, whom we so often treat as a child or even a baby, was in fact an independent adult – a young man absorbed at the moment in his own discomfort ... I remembered my experience in the hospital cafeteria, the smoldering anger I'd felt then now flaring back to life. Anyone watching me might have seen my face turn as red as my son's, heard my breathing become as ragged as his. Yet as I continued to watch him lying there suffering like that, my anger subsided; and a short while later, after merely refilling the cup of water by his bed and adjusting his blankets, I switched off the light and returned to my room. This little episode had somehow succeeded in unravelling the knot in my heart from the week before and I went back to bed feeling at peace.
>
> (1996: 17)

The realization that his son's cold causes the same discomfort to him as it does to any individual allows Ōe to care for him as a 'normal' child, and let the righteous anger as a special needs parent and caregiver go. This episode most eloquently encapsulates the 'normalization' of caregiving in the family context, as called for by Kleinman at the start of this chapter.

In the introduction to this chapter, we read how Schoeni and colleagues began their article abstract with the term 'burden' because of their consciousness of the costs associated with increasing levels of caregiving for growing sectors of a population. But cost is not the only issue; more pressing is the limited time that parents can spend with their adult children. Ōe Kenzaburō and his wife, Yukari, assisted by their children, have cared for their son in their home for many years, but Ōe, now in his mid-seventies, and his wife cannot care for Hikari indefinitely. Disability care does come at a cost, but as Kleinman writes, caregiving should not be seen as exceptional but rather as part of the normal 'flow' of life (2010), despite the fact that most societies, especially those which value capital production and individual free will over other attributes and relationships, will always view caregiving as a negative activity that limits the productivity and autonomy of the caregiver. Nevertheless, there have been shifts in the way Japanese lawmakers, care professionals and family caregivers are responding to caregiving needs. The new LTC system does not eliminate all of the stresses that come with the caregiving role, but it does offer options for both caregiver and recipient. Still, this directive needs to be carefully implemented to ensure that the professional care encourages independent living where appropriate.

While society must provide financial and social support to caregivers who are experiencing hardship, caregiving must not be glossed entirely as 'tragedy' but seen as an omnipresent part of social life, as Ōe and others have argued. In fact, we might say that one of the reasons why caregivers experience such strong feelings of depression and hopelessness is not only because of the efforts required but also because of the low esteem in which their activities are held. If caregiving were a terrible sacrifice and burden, why wouldn't caregivers feel depressed? If it were thought of as the norm, rather than the exception, caregiving as a valued activity could give insight into all kinds of human relationships, and our understanding of where and how the individual – all kinds of individuals – fits into a collective society. One way that we can envision caregiving as 'normal' is as a kind of ongoing and ever present responsibility of a society that pledges a minimum standard of living and human rights to its members.

7 Accessibility and the built environment in Japan

> At every turn, at every stair, at every missing handrail ... the environment declares, 'Disabled [people], we weren't expecting you to show up.'
> (Titchkosky 2003: 120)

> The watchword of dismodernism could be: Form follows dysfunction.
> (Davis 2002: 27)

This chapter explores the uneasy juxtaposition between the user access and user reality of 'barrier-free design' (*bariafurii desain*) in urban Japan. I argue that the growing number of accessibility features in Japanese public spaces has not necessarily resulted in a 'barrier-free' society. While these visible reminders raise public awareness about the difficulties physical and intellectual disabilities pose to individuals, many people with disabilities (and often their carers) still live in social isolation, primarily because of the reality of the urban landscape and pressure from the number of users. The 'environment brings out *who* disabled people *are* and disabilities bring out *what* an environment *is*' (Titchkosky 2003: 112). These two entities – people with disabilities and the environment – are often separated, and seen in conflict; there is no 'natural' flow between them.

Gaps between idealism and practical reality inform our understanding of disability and how it colours the relationship between individual and society. Making public places accessible is quietly seen as a moral imperative, relying on the 'kindness of strangers', rather than as an entitlement or an expression of basic human rights. This ambivalence leads to many people with disabilities experiencing compromised access to public life, which has a far-reaching effect on the creation and maintenance of concepts of citizenship. With a specific concern for disability, Mike Oliver defines citizenship as 'a shorthand device for talking about the relationship between individuals and their societies' (1996: 44). Another important aspect of citizenship is the 'possibility of participating in public discourse on political issues' (Mackie 2002: 201). The potential to participate in social and economic life should also be included in this definition. Accessibility allows people with disabilities full participation in political, social and economic spheres, bringing the rights, responsibilities and benefits of their citizenship, complete with its accompanying exercise of human rights, into full play – but this can only happen when their participation is feasible; otherwise, there is no potential. The absence of accessible features in public places means that people with disabilities (and, in many cases, their long-term care providers as well) are excluded from important activities that give individuals a voice in the way decisions are made in business, politics, education and social life.

In the international context, 'accessibility', 'usability' and 'universal design' are terms that are used to describe various relationships between people, activities, the environment, ideology and policy. Accessibility is the 'possibility to take part in something desirable' and is closely related to the 'parameters that influence human functioning in the environment, thus defining accessibility as an environmental quantity' (Iwarsson and Ståhl 2003: 58). 'Universal design' implies that the design of buildings, vehicles or the environment, for example, takes into account the needs of a diverse population rather than just an able-bodied one, and includes the interests of not just those with physical and/or intellectual impairments but also those who are elderly, children as well as adults, and people of diverse ethnic and national backgrounds (61). Universal design 'upholds the democratic ideals of social equality and personal empowerment ... [Its] first principle ... "Equitable Use", mandates that no one be segregated, stigmatized or disadvantaged by design' (Weisman 2000: 158). Also important to its definition is the fact that it is 'dynamic, not static, changeable, adaptable and recyclable over time in response to the changing needs of the people who use [it]' (166).

In cases of 'impairment' and/or 'disability', accessibility is crucial because it addresses the 'handicap', or the 'activity limitations' and 'participation limitations' (World Health Organization and World Bank 2011: 5) that result from impairment. Within the disability context, the accessibility debate arises from where the stakeholders draw these lines between ideology, policy and implementation: to what extent should the individual be able to function 'independently' with these features, and carry out these desirable actions with a minimum of difficulty (Iwarsson and Ståhl 2003: 58)? What is considered a 'minimum' of difficulty? Who decides what are 'reasonable' steps that should be taken to remedy inaccessibility? As we will see, in the Japanese context, accessibility is relatively well established. What needs monitoring is the 'reasonable use' of accessibility features, and how this is ensured.

The definition of accessibility can be widened to include issues of barriers in many other contexts: '[disabled people's] scope for social participation was limited either by segregation in medically managed spaces or by problems of access to the public domain, most notably, mainstream education, transport and the labour market' (Barnes cited in Hughes 2000: 556). Without access to education, which leads to more prestigious and higher paying waged labour in urban Japan, people with disabilities are limited in their participation in the wider economy and political life. Education and employment are important contributing factors to any individual's ability to succeed, but in the case of people with disabilities, the examination of 'barrier-free' design is crucial because this underpins the 'accessibility' of education and the job market to those who could appropriately participate in and contribute to them. Another aspect of accessibility involves information flow: just as a stairway presents a barrier to a person with a physical disability, a standard telephone creates issues for a person who is deaf. Whether the barrier is physical, informational or even psychological, I posit that barrier-free design is the first step to understanding the practical levels of social and economic integration experienced by people with disabilities in Japan.

Accessibility is also used to describe intellectual access, not just physical access, and refers to '"access to information" contained in physical documents, electronic documents, or other conduits for information' (Svenonius cited in Jaeger and Bowman 2005: 66). Examples of intellectual accessibility include the provision of Braille or sign language, or a TDD (telecommunication device for the deaf) option; it could also mean different ways of presenting information to people with learning disabilities, especially on the internet, as hypertext mark-up tends to use a very different layout style and requires different kinds of reading skills to those associated with the more linear modes of books or other physical documents. This chapter, while mindful of the importance of information access, focuses on the built environment because of its immediacy and impact on daily life. My conclusions are drawn from the combination of two methods: textual analysis of documents (publications authored by government and corporate institutions as well as private individuals) and seven trips over six years to the Tokyo Metropolitan area, accompanied by my daughter who uses a wheelchair during outings.[1] The accessibility data presented in this chapter are primarily situated in Yokohama and Tokyo, 20006.

Japan as a barrier-free society

In Japan, as elsewhere, 'barrier-free' means the inclusion of design features to increase accessibility to public areas. In 1994 lawmakers passed legislation to set

Figure 7.1 Shopping mall in Nippa, Yokohama

recommended standards in accessibility features in public buildings, which is colloquially called the Hāto Biru Hō ('Heart Building Law') because of the heart-shaped logo buildings receive if they meet its criteria.

In 2000, the Ministry of Health and Welfare established the *bariafurii no machizukuri no katsudōjigyō* (Project for Building Barrier-free Cities) to fund these projects. '*Bariafurii*' as a catchphrase was not only a government initiative but also soon became a part of the mainstream discourse after the success of a 2000 drama, *Beautiful Life* (TBS), which featured a heroine in a wheelchair. Many scenes of this love story between an able-bodied man (played by Kimura Takuya) and a woman with a degenerative illness (played by the able-bodied actress Tokiwa Takako) brought the issue of accessibility to living rooms throughout Japan. This drama eloquently demonstrated the many inaccessible features of metropolitan Tokyo, from the difficulties of finding parking wide enough to accommodate a wheelchair to finding an accessible restaurant for their first date. Another major accomplishment of this drama was that it demonstrated that disability, so often associated with Japan's ageing population, affects people of all ages, including young people who face a lifetime of limited access to public life.

The 2009 White Paper on Disability, in describing the government's recent efforts, prioritizes the provision of public housing that is accessible to people with disabilities (Naikakufu 2009). Other examples of barrier-free projects in Japan include the provision of lifts, slopes and kerb cuts, 'no-step' buses, and specially equipped public toilets. Barrier-free projects are undertaken in public government offices, hospitals and clinics, train and subway stations, and shopping and leisure districts. To encourage use of these facilities, the government proposed and has implemented a '*raku raku odekake netto*' (the 'easy going out' network) where users can log in and obtain accessibility information regarding lifts, toilets and ramps at national rail stations, bus terminals and airports, a service which can be accessed not only by computer but also by mobile phone (ibid.).

The safety of these features is important, especially considering Japan experiences not infrequent natural disasters such as earthquakes and typhoons. Evacuation of the urban population during a disaster is a public responsibility, so the government established a need for disaster prevention policy in 2004, and in the following year created a plan that focused on the evacuation of the elderly and people with disabilities in the case of a natural disaster, which included 'a policy aimed at the provision of information, evacuation assistance, and the management of evacuation camps in the event of an emergency due to natural disaster' (Naikakufu 2009). Other emergency situations that require accessibility include emergency email addresses and fax numbers and modifications to police stations (ibid.). Accessibility is not just about convenience, but can at times become the difference between life and death during a catastrophe. Nakamura describes the aftermath of the 1995 Hanshin earthquake as disproportionately hard on people with disabilities, who tended to live in low-income (cheap and/or old) housing which did not contain the latest anti-earthquake or fire technology, and notes that residents with disabilities, unlike able-bodied people, were unable to flee to relatives' home in safer areas (2009: 83).

Architectural and attitudinal impediments

While it has raised public awareness, the barrier-free movement has not proceeded without some hiccups. In 2006 the *Japan Times* published a critical series on disability in Japan. In an article titled 'Is "Disability" Still a Dirty Word in Japan?', a journalist reported that there are

> around 6.5 million individuals [with disabilities in Japan]. But where are they? Granted, we see more ... elevators, ... accessible toilets and buses with passenger lifts nowadays ... [But we] hardly ever encounter those who use them – let alone anyone with non-physical disabilities. In fact, apart from people with disabled family members or friends, most Japanese quite likely live their whole lives without ever interacting with their disabled fellow citizens.
>
> (Otake 2006)

The newspaper article amply demonstrates the limitations of the implementation of barrier-free design in Japan's major cities. Japan is by no means the only society struggling to implement universal design. The Americans with Disabilities Act (ADA) only requires compliance with technical norms and standards, while it states nothing about performance: how a building or setting actually works for a range of users, for example (Iwarsson and Ståhl 2003: 59). Societies all over the world are struggling to implement the ideals set forth in international agreements and domestic legislation in practical terms.

Regardless of whether the need is urgent or everyday, Japan's urban areas confront many specific practical issues with implementation.[2] Japanese cities are amongst the most densely populated in the world. Thus the utilization of the scarce resource of space is problematic owing to competition among varied interests and a high rate of usage. For example, single-storey buildings are not as common in urban Japan as they are in other less-populated areas because they do not represent the most efficient use of space. Thus, wheelchair users in urban Japan are constantly confronted with stairways. If a building is already equipped with a lift, it is considered 'accessible' (and not in need of modification), but in many older buildings, these lifts were constructed for able-bodied users (narrowly designed for 'standing room only') and they can rarely accommodate a wheelchair and a carer unless almost empty. Japan's seismic instability is also a major issue. Even minor tremors mean that lifts are shut down until an aftershock 'all-clear' is given from the Japan Meteorological Agency.

Some slopes are too steep; some road surfaces have uneven paving for decorative purposes that can catch wheels. Ramps help but footpaths are non-existent in many small streets, and even when they are available, they must share the space with bicycle traffic and bicycle parking, so it is often difficult to push a wheelchair through the narrow maze that once was a smooth ramp to a railway station. There are gaps of varying width between trains and station platforms; some can be quite difficult to cross, depending on the size of the wheelchair's wheels. Tokyo lawyer Murata Minoru, in his book *The City as Seen from a Wheelchair* (1994, 2000), describes being stranded. He poignantly writes of his reluctance to ask for help because of the embarrassment his requests cause, because many Japanese people have never touched a wheelchair and do not know how to handle them. Murata gives instructions on how to move a wheelchair over a curb without dislodging the occupant (33–4). He provides maps of large Tokyo railway and subway stations such as Shinjuku and Shibuya – not just as a guide for those with disabilities but also to make the able-bodied person aware of the detailed planning that must go into even such a mundane trip.

The provision of public toilets for people with disabilities allows them to participate in public life for longer periods of time. The '*minna no toire*' (the toilet anyone can use) has caught on as it eschews the 'disabled' tag. Yet disabled toilet users complain frequently that their doors are too heavy, disabled toilets are located on an upper floor with no lift and toilets marked as disabled are not wide enough to accommodate a wheelchair and caregiver (Connell, 2006). Murata writes of his childhood experience of refraining from urinating from morning until evening. Even now, he writes that he carries a plastic bag and limits his fluid intake while away from home (1994, 2000: 39–40).

Accessibility theory versus reality: empirical examples

The high-speed *shinkansen* 'Bullet Train' symbolizes the pinnacle of Japanese transport technology; I tried a short trip with my family to test the overall accessibility of this system. We took the local *shinkansen* from Shin-Yokohama to Odawara and found that the train itself was equipped for wheelchairs, but only in one of the total sixteen carriages. Wheelchair users are unable to access the first class 'green' cars. The main problem was not the train itself but the stations where the super-express trains stop. We had to carry the wheelchair up and down stairs at two *shinkansen* station platforms.[3] This also proved to be the case on the Tokyo Metropolitan Subway: on the Hibiya line, we discovered neither Kamiyachô nor Ebisu Station was equipped with lifts. The Kamiyachô station instructed disabled users to notify the station staff through an intercom on the platform. We could not imagine what the staff would do if notified, so we chose to carry the wheelchair up the stairs ourselves – luckily our group included two able-bodied adults.

Once above ground, we encountered a variety of situations as we visited department stores, shopping areas and leisure districts. Most memorable was the new shopping complex on Tokyo's famous boulevard, Omotesandō. Omotesandō Hills' universal design was remarkable in that it contained six floors of commercial space above ground, all connected by a gentle slope (there were lifts, but they were provided as an option, not as a necessity, allowing all users the freedom to move within the flow). This building, designed by architect Andô Tadao and the Mori Building Company, was completed in 2006. It was near-perfect, in my opinion, in terms of accessibility; yet the design group's website states that its sloping design was chosen to reflect the gentle angles of the natural environment, and omits to mention that it also functions as a universal design feature (Mori Biru Kabushikigaisha 2006).

We visited Tokyo Tower, built in 1958 and located in Tokyo's central Minato Ward. Its lifts were wide and fully accessible when travelling up to the observation deck, but we had to use a short set of stairs to access the downward lifts. A Tokyo taxi driver in Roppongi quickly and cheerfully opened the boot for our wheelchair and gave us the disabled discount (about 10 per cent of the fare), even though my daughter does not carry the official Japanese *shōgaisha techō* (disability passbook). We also found a wheelchair-only pathway in a Tokyo neighbourhood located in front of a day surgery clinic. For those traversing narrow city streets, fighting both cars, pedestrians and bicycles for space, this was a real help to wheelchair users. This lane, however, was soon blocked by a car, which was trying to inch around another car waiting to turn right at a nearby intersection. The accessibility feature was there, but the practicality of the feature was negated by inappropriate use.

Barrier-free features and their 'proper' use in public places

The wheelchair-only pathway example demonstrates an important problem: even when the kinks in the design are ironed out (such as gaps in access to lifts in Tokyo Tower), the feature's use-in-practice must be considered. The dense population of urban centres makes their appropriation by the able-bodied a constant issue. Access to the accessible features must be managed. This in turn raises questions: should the facility managers allow free access to the accessibility features, which gives users with disabilities freedom to move but in competition with other users? Or should the managers restrict access, giving people with disabilities priority but impinging on their ability to move freely with the ebb and flow of the mainstream population? If they do manage the access, how should it be done? The following section debates the 'pros' and 'cons' of managing the 'access to the access'.

In the 'free access to the access' scenario, accessible features are open to anyone who chooses to use them for whatever reason. For example, 'priority lifts' at Narita Airport and large train stations such as Shibuya and Yokohama are self-activated, but the long lines in front of these lifts (especially in the user-heavy environment of public transport in Japanese train stations) eloquently demonstrate their inability to meet demand. During my many trips to Japan, I noticed these lines consist of many different kinds of people: those with heavy bags, mothers with children in strollers, people with disabilities, the elderly and anyone else who does not wish to take the stairs or escalator. Our experience was that waiting for a lift was the norm in large train stations. To address this bottleneck of use, in Yokohama Station's lift for the Tôyoko line, visual and audio cues are repeatedly presented to users. (See Figure 7.2.)

Of note is the multi-sensory approach: the repeated nature of the audio cues on top of the visual signage gives some of those who hear it a sense of urgency.

Accessibility and the built environment 145

Figure 7.2 Notice on a lift in Yokohama Station

Others appear to treat the audio cue as background noise. From my experience, however, the system was ineffective. We always waited for several lifts before we were able to board, and users without a disability never gave us 'preference'. In the particular case of Yokohama's Tôyoko line, the lift was quite small; it accommodated a manual wheelchair and four or five ambulant people. It would have been quite difficult to accommodate two wheelchairs, especially a power wheelchair.

The second scenario – restricting assess to accessibility features – cuts down on overuse but has its own drawbacks. While the Tôyoko line's entrance from Yokohama Station was open and overcrowded, the station managers at the Hiyoshi Station in Yokohama had locked the lift from the station entrance to the lower platforms. People with disabilities were advised to summon the stationmaster from the lift by pressing a button; they would then speak into an intercom, presenting their disability or explaining the situation. I used this lift frequently, and the dialogue often went like this:

    [I press the button]
    'Yes?'

146   *Accessibility and the built environment*

'I have a child in a wheelchair ...' [I am not sure if the station manager can see me or only hear me. I speak into the intercom speaker and look in vain for a closed circuit camera.]

'Uh, okay. Just a minute, please.'

[I wait a few minutes and someone comes out of the ticket sales office with a key that opens the lift door; they enter the lift with us and accompany us in silence to the lower floor that adjoins the train platform.]

The time the station employee took to arrive was anywhere from two to five minutes, depending on how busy the station workers were with other business. I encountered a further problem when I attempted to use this lift on 23 July 2006, the day of a strong earthquake in the Tōkai region (magnitude 6 on the Japanese scale). I could see from outside the station that the trains were running, so I attempted to take this lift to the platform. When I summoned the station employee, she informed me that although the trains had been given the all clear, the station lifts had not. Another silence followed, and then on my suggestion, we descended the stairs. I carried my daughter (who was five at the time) and the employee carried her chair. In sum, restricting access means that people with disabilities do not move freely but must stop and wait for accessible features to be made accessible to them. It represents another layer of inaccessibility in barrier-free design.

Visibility or invisibility? Accessibility through displacement

Another strategy to prevent overuse is what I call displacement. When an accessible feature (most commonly, a lift) is built in an area with low use and low visibility, it tends to experience low use. Mainstream users utilize accessibility features out of convenience rather than necessity. A person with a wheelchair cannot make do with stairs, so he or she must seek out inconveniently located features. For example: unlocked and empty, a 'priority lift' (*yūsen erebētā*) in Yokohama's Sogō Department Store was hidden away in a relatively unused corner of the showroom. We found it, wandering around the first floor after being unable to board the crowded central front lift. I was pleased, but I could not help but wonder if its location made a statement – although displacement protected the access to the access, people with disabilities were also necessarily relegated to the recesses of the public arena. We encountered a different mode of displacement at Narita Airport where we were given priority check-in, security check and immigration check. While we welcomed the convenience, we were, once again, separated from the 'normal' flow of traffic. Features such as these take people with differently functioning bodies and minds out of the public's gaze. They are not seen as part of the everyday landscape. This strategy can be attributed to what Marks calls 'rationalization', a common psychological response of non-disabled people:

The suggestion that wheelchair users might find the back entrance to a building more convenient to use than coming in through the front door may express not just the material self-interest of the owners wishing to avoid the expense of building an accessible entrance, but also serve as a psychic rationalisation for the wish to keep disabled people out of sight and mind.

(1999: 24)

Another variation of the displacement strategy was found in large train stations that serve as hubs or connectors for several train and/or subway lines. Often these connections are made through underground shopping areas with entrances and exits that almost always have steps. Signs in Yokohama Station stated that if a user with a disability wanted access to the train line on the other side of the flat, central JR station, they could do so by taking a lift above ground, and then circling the station out of doors, then re-entering the station to get to the adjoining private line platforms. Besides taking considerably more time, this 'redirection' meant that users with a disability did not pass through the crowded shopping areas that linked the transportation lines, missing out on the local economy that these areas support, and the public visibility that accompanies them. Accessibility features in public transport, like the *shinkansen*, direct them away from the luxury offered in the 'green car'. Not only are they invisible, they are also expected to make do with what is made available to them, with fewer choices than the able-bodied consumer.

Barrier-free design is meant to integrate people with disabilities into mainstream life, yet as we have seen, in some cases the outcome is directing users away from the public gaze; in others, poor planning and misuse mean that the special ramps and lifts blend into the 'everyday' landscape. In such situations, the only visible reminder that people with disabilities exist, ironically, is the signboards that mark these often unused or misused features. (See Figures 7.3–7.5.) These signs were of particular interest to me because their wording suggested a mild but persistent ethical dilemma. Because of their focus on behavioural 'norms', these signboards reminded the public of things they might not necessarily *want* to do, or might forget to do when in a hurry, but *should*.

Accessibility, if observed properly, can lead to restriction and inconvenience for the mainstream, but to entice them to conform, praise is offered in return. 'Giving up for the greater good' demonstrates the psychological divide between the two cultures, highlighting the individual desire versus the collective good.

This tension between the able-bodied and the disability community is all about identity and communication, clearly articulated by Titchkosky:

> [It is] ... elicited by a non-disabled person's opening a door for a blind person in absolute silence, and then watching while the blind person gropes for the door ... [T]he sighted person who silently opens the door for a blind person is somehow unable to address a person as a disabled person, or is addressing that person with an un-workable concept of disability.
>
> (2003: 110)

A barrier-free society arises from an environment that conforms to the 'intentions and interests' of mainstream society, which is suddenly confronted with an

148 *Accessibility and the built environment*

Figure 7.3 'Manner' notice at Yokohama Station (Tōyoko Line)

Figure 7.4 'Manner' notice in the car park of a shopping mall, northern Yokohama

'unexpected minority' (Titchkosky 2003: 113–14). Barrier-free design, while 'fixing' the problem, also highlights the fact that some public places (in Titchkosky's case, the university; in our case, the Japanese train station, footpath or shopping mall) were never meant to host such participants. They were designed without the expectation that people with disabilities would use them. In that sense, accessibility serves to highlight the differences between these two 'worlds'.

What does this ongoing tension between the two 'worlds' of users tell us about the individual in society? In the culture of ability, individuals make independent choices from a wider range of options. This contributes to a sense of agency and power. In the culture of disability, people with disabilities have a narrower range

Figure 7.5 'Manner' notice inside a train carriage on the Tōyoko Line

of options available. Even when the choice exists for the person with a disability, often the user must ask for 'help' or for 'permission'. In sum, the catchphrase 'barrier-free' is recognition without empowerment. There is reduced agency; the user must not only ask permission but also be judged worthy of its use. This judgement is most easily made if the user has a 'badge' of disability such as the universally recognized wheelchair, but the request for permission is more difficult if this is not the case – an unseen intellectual disability, for example. The need to obtain permission recalls the infantilization of people with disabilities by mainstream society and is reminiscent of the controlling atmosphere of institutions in the early postwar era, where 'permission' had to be gained for even the slightest of human actions (Hayashi and Okuhira 2001: 858).

Not all people with disabilities are disempowered, but a look at those who have succeeded brings up another critical intersection between disability and the environment; in this case, one that is mediated by socioeconomic class. Ototake Hirotada, a graduate of Waseda University, worked as a broadcaster for the news programme *Nyūsu no Mori*, and from there launched a successful media career. Born in 1976 without hands or legs, Ototake captured the hearts of the Japanese through his intelligence and positive outlook. When Ototake's mother embraces her infant in joy despite his dysmorphic features, we are moved (Ototake 2001, 2004: 3). When Ototake refuses to use disability as an excuse for failure we are deeply impressed with his faith in himself. His memoir has sold almost five million copies, and although it is an inspiring view of personal strength in the face of diverse obstacles, it also presents a view more aligned with 'normalization' than one that demands radical social change. Still, his self-proclaimed nickname, 'The Wheelchair King' (*kurumaisu no ōsama*) (2001, 2004: 11), is an unusually positive and proactive take on this individual's struggle to integrate into mainstream school, despite the difficulties he would have experienced as a minority member of the class.

The socioeconomic status of the broadcaster Ototake and the lawyer Murata (the wheelchair user mentioned earlier), important contributors to the barrier-free movement, must also be considered when investigating the extent to which people with any kind of disability are able to enjoy a full public life, with or without accessibility features. Iwakuma interviewed people with disabilities, asking them what they thought of Ototake's success, and found that many said things like 'Ototake is in no way a part of the world in which we [the disabled] are living'; that the book had a 'peeping-Tom effect vis-à-vis the voyeuristic curiosity of the nondisabled public'; and 'he does not have a clue' (2003: 131).

Ototake's media visibility calls attention to one of the most important barriers to public participation by people with disabilities: educational segregation. Education is closely associated with financial success in Japan, and even though the Japanese government encourages people with disabilities to work, the educational sector's unwillingness to integrate children with disabilities in mainstream schools even where appropriate represents one of the main mechanisms of their long-term disempowerment. Onoue Koji, spokesperson for DPI-Japan, says that this segregation makes it difficult for most people with disabilities to find mainstream work and salaries (Otake 2006), which would give them a stronger voice in society. Murata and Ototake, as university-educated individuals, were able to conquer this discrimination, but we must note that this is because their physical disabilities were not accompanied by intellectual impairments. This allowed them to act as effective symbols of the barrier-free movement.

Public and private space/public and private citizens

Any discussion of accessibility returns to its definitive function, its attempt to bridge the differences between ability and disability, the people who 'can' versus people who 'cannot'. Rosemarie Garland Thomson refers to the former group as 'normate' society, explaining that '[n]ormate ... is the constructed identity of those who, by way of the bodily configurations and cultural capital they assume, can step into a position of authority and wield the power it grants them' (1997: 8). When one's bodily configuration does not match the requirements of the public arena (and it prevents the individual from accruing cultural and/or financial capital) the disabled body is then relegated to a private sphere, outside the 'power lines' of education, business and government.

In many ways, 'citizenship', as an abstract noun, captures many aspects of 'public life' that are distinguished from 'private life' and at the same time are dependent on the individual's ability (both intellectual and physical) to interact with others, and to exercise their human rights as per the Japanese Constitution's Article 25. This states that 'All people shall have the right to maintain the minimum standards of wholesome and cultured living. In all spheres of life, the State shall use its endeavors for the promotion and extension of social welfare and security, and of public health' (Constitution of Japan 1946, 2012). The right to support oneself economically, where possible, requires some kind of accessibility: physical accessibility as in the universal design features described in this

Accessibility and the built environment 151

chapter, and/or 'virtual' accessibility such as the communicative ability to perform waged labour in other contexts, using the internet and other technologies. As we have seen, both can be problematic. The act of voting, which is prescribed by law and involves specific procedures and spaces, is infrequently geared towards people with disabilities. Participation in religious ceremonies is often difficult as many older temples and shrines do not have accessibility features (Mackie 2002: 209). Shopping and leisure activities, as we have seen, are frequently compromised. When exercising one's political power through democratic procedure is compromised, and individuals find it difficult to participate in community rituals that confer social status on their participants – and this is compounded by a fraught relationship with the local economy and educational system – then surely their 'minimum standards of wholesome and cultured living' are more 'minimal' than those of able-bodied compatriots. In sum, their status as full-fledged citizens of the nation is reduced as compared with those who find no obstacle to the performance of such duties. Thomson reiterates this: 'In other words, people deemed disabled are barred from full citizenship because their bodies do not conform with architectural, attitudinal, education, occupational, and legal conventions based on assumptions that bodies appear and perform in certain ways' (1997: 46).

This relegation to the private sphere means that, in many cases, the family becomes the primary, and sometimes sole, expression of agency of a person with a disability. Nobel Laureate Ōe Kenzaburō, arguably Japan's most famous carer, speaks from an intensely personal position about his son's interaction with wider society. While he writes most often on wider issues, he does touch on accessibility when he notes his own, as well as his son's, discomfort regarding their ability to cross a busy Tokyo street in the short time allotted by the signal (1996: 36). Clearly, accessibility impacts not only the individual, but also the carer. Ōe observes

> how closely integrated the problem of private and public acceptance of a disability is. It all became rather easier to grasp, I felt, when one thought of society as a family writ large; the trick, as it were, was to model a society's actions – all its best efforts – on those of a family that has actively welcomed a handicapped child into its midst.
>
> (ibid.: 96)

Here Ōe tries to overcome this division by merging the 'private' family with 'public' life. It is through these families' public face and active participation that larger society learns about the diversity of human experience, supporting the barrier-free movement both literally and ideologically. Until people with disabilities can cross the street comfortably, attend social and political functions without undue stress and difficulty, and earn a living where appropriate, we cannot say that they are truly 'public' individuals. Instead, their identity and their lives are privatized, away from the public eye, and their existence made invisible to wider society.

Accessibility features help to provide public visibility for people with disabilities, but there are other venues that allow this group to be seen in mainstream society. As previously noted, disability has made some inroads in popular culture, but the idealized representation of disability in serial dramas such as *Beautiful Life*, while representing physical barriers, stops short of some of the more critical aspects of life with a disability. The female protagonist is wheelchair bound, but she is also well educated (she is a librarian), attractive and well spoken. While I applaud TBS for making this drama series, I also wonder to what extent this character's life is truly illustrative of the lives of people with disabilities in urban Japan.

More provocative is the children's show *Stretchman2*, a show broadcast twice a week on NHK's educational channel. *Stretchman2* is specifically created for children with intellectual disabilities, but because it is shown embedded within the regular children's programming timeslot on weekday mornings, it can also be seen as an attempt to break free from some of the conceptual barriers between mainstream and disabled society. In each episode, the character 'Stretchman' travels to a different special developmental school (*yōgo gakkō*) where he runs through a series of simple physical exercises ('stretches'), which can be seen as a game incorporating physiotherapeutic techniques. The show features students at these schools in their physical and intellectual fullness; there are no actresses pretending to be disabled, no celebrity journalists or elite lawyers in sight. The students, often in wheelchairs or propped up by teachers' aides, try their utmost to follow Stretchman's motions, and there are no camera techniques, costumes or cosmetics used to reduce the visual impact of these children's moderate to severe disabilities. The students are encouraged in a typically cartoonish way to try hard (*gambaru*) in their exercises, but I do not interpret this tone as condescending as much as it is in line with many mainstream children's shows that rely on exaggerated super hero dialogue for dramatic effect. Conversely, one could argue this style embeds their experience in a 'normate' cultural landscape. NHK's official website claims that the show is aimed at 'giving children with intellectual disabilities the chance to move physically' (Nippon Hōsō Kyōkai 2006). I believe, however, its position within the mainstream programming is an even more important outcome, because it allows 'normate' children to see inside *yōgo gakkō*, without apology or romanticizing, and it represents a rare opportunity for the sheltered world of special schooling to be broadcast to the mainstream public. After countless trips pushing a wheelchair through crowded train stations, *Stretchman2* to me was a breath of fresh air, and held out a much more powerful representation of 'barrier-free' society than the long lines in front of the department store lifts.

The invisibility of people with disabilities – in part due to accessibility problems, in part due to the ongoing discouragement and discrimination which arises from barriers both physical and emotional – forms the backdrop against which the journalist quoted earlier in this chapter asks: where are all the people with disabilities in Japan? It has proved tempting for scholars to rely on an Orientalist vision of 'Asian family values' or 'Culture and Personality' driven notions of 'shame' for answers in the context of disability. While the legend of Hiruko/Ebisu, as described in Chapter 2, conveys a dual nature of disability (Hiruko's disability arises from bad luck, but his transformation to Ebisu, the god of fortune, is a result of persistence and patience in the light of misfortune), some acknowledge only the negative aspects of this myth. For example,

> The first child ever born in Japan, according to its mythology, was abandoned because he was born deformed. This was not an auspicious start for the new nation. Ever since, the disabled person in Japan has been considered not only imperfect, an embodiment of ugliness, but at a deeper socio-spiritual level – and especially if they are actually born disabled – a sort of a curse.
> (Henshall 1999: 99)

Following this line of thinking, we could assume that barrier-free features gather dust (or are used by normate individuals without a second thought) because Japanese people with disabilities do not want public lives. Families do not bring out their children because they are 'ashamed'. To what extent this was empirically accurate in the past is now conjecture. Contemporary stories of Ototake's mother's joy at her son's birth and Ōe's ongoing commitment to his adult son Hikaru's care tell us that today's Japanese families work hard to participate as much as possible in the 'normate' world. Can we posit, instead, that it is not necessarily 'shame' but perhaps frustration with 'normate' attitudes that keeps Japanese people with disabilities at home today? This frustration arises despite the best of intentions: consider the irony of the fact that many of the attitudinal barrier examples given in this chapter come from my experience riding the Tōyoko line, owned by the Tōkyū Private Railroad, which was lauded by the Ministry of Health, Labour and Welfare as one of the top ten large employers of people with disabilities, exceeding the minimum employment quota of 1.8 per cent with a score of 2.43 per cent (*Yomiuri Shimbun* 2007).

The study of accessibility helps us to identify the real problems and at the same time consider new, empowering possibilities when considering the reality for people with disabilities in Japan. This study must include not just observations of physical features but also a recognition of the use of these features as symbolic of a wider attitude towards integration, for '[a]rchitectural and communications barrier removal is often easier than the removal of social and economic barriers' (Shakespeare 2006: 45). Shakespeare has a point when he says the barrier-free movement has limits, for it is just about impossible to make society truly barrier-free for each according to their needs (48–9). In light of this and my experiences in Japan, I would say that what would be more liberating is not the continued introduction of more features that would cater to ever more individual needs, but a serious examination of the attitudes surrounding the usage of current features which, compared with other countries, appear to be more than adequate.

Attitudes are powerful. Why, despite the ramps and special lifts, do Japanese people with disabilities tend to stay out of the public gaze? I hope this chapter has argued strongly against resorting to a handy explanation of a culture of shame or hardship. Let us discard these pre-conceived notions of Japan as a 'traditional' society, and instead look at more pressing issues: poor planning, demographic pressure, and segregated education and employment, all of which result in reduced human agency. As Oliver puts it,

> If you're kept in seclusion by State or family, if little of society's public spaces are accessible to you, then it is small wonder that disabled people find it difficult to organise collectively ... Precisely because disability in all parts of the world is an isolating experience, most disabled people only experience their disabilities in individual terms. Thus, they may internalise the ideology of personal tragedy, they may come to see themselves as a burden and feel that their problems are their own fault.
>
> (Oliver 1996:122)

Isolation does not empower people with disabilities. But in looking at causes for this isolation, we need to undertake a careful review of the Japanese 'disablement heritage': to what extent is it mired in a static historical tradition (Miles 2000: 616)? Or are there elements of contemporary Japanese daily life, such as the gentle lines of the Omotesandô Hills Project and the honesty of the television show *Stretchman2*, that more eloquently demonstrate the hollowness of the traditional Japanese disablement mythology? Considering the rapid ageing of Japanese society, the increasing need for accessible features means that future developments could challenge the hegemonic Western model of social progressiveness. I believe this is a possibility, but until the widespread recognition of barrier-free features for the purpose of accessibility (and some agreement on their function and use) is achieved, the voices of Japanese people with disabilities will continue to be muted.

8 Conclusion

> Disabled people remain the unintended and unexpected minority, even though this minority may not be so minor.
>
> (Titchkosky 2003: 121)

My first aim in writing this book was to integrate ideas from the interdisciplinary field of disability studies, which is a marginalized area in many universities, into Japanese studies; it has been part critical literature review, part ethnography and part autoethnography. To highlight and question social and cultural attitudes about disability in Japan and elsewhere, I have examined demographic statistics, legal documents, discussions in the public sphere, and environmental and architectural infrastructure, and analysed them from an anthropological perspective as well as from the point of view of a primary carer of a family member with a significant disability.

This book has devoted much space to interrogating the meaning of the term disability, vis-à-vis related terms such as impairment and handicap. Disability is problematic in both English and Japanese. Disability is difficult to define because of its 'instability'. This is because

> [d]isability, unlike most other characteristics, is not a static, unchanging or immutable condition. Most people who have a disability were not born with it ... Disability can manifest as a physical or cognitive issue, coming from a range of factors – genetics, accident, external circumstances, or advancing age ... Some people who have disabilities argue that they do not have one ... In short, it can be very difficult to establish a comprehensive definition of disability that accounts for the full range of conditions and impacts.
>
> (Jaeger and Bowman 2005: 6)

Yet scholars and activists are still committed to defining disability because of its potential for putting into words the experience of disability. Any explication of these terms, however, must be embedded in the larger intellectual frameworks that influence how we identify, manage and experience disability; they will generally fall within either the medical (or individual) model or the social model, or somewhere in between. The most vocal critic of the medical model is Michael

Oliver, and his motivation for doing so is not just an intellectual one but a political one: he wishes to take the authority to speak about disability away from medical professionals exclusively and share it with people with disabilities. This authority is created when disability is conflated with an illness that must be 'cured'.

> Justification for this criticism rests upon the distinction between illness and disability and the fact that they are not the same thing; some illnesses may have disabling consequences and many disabled people have illnesses at various points in their lives. Further, it may be entirely appropriate for doctors to treat illnesses of all kinds ... doctors can have a role to play in the lives of disabled people: stabilising their initial condition, treating any illnesses which may arise and which may or may not be disability related.
>
> The problem arises when doctors try to use their knowledge and skills to treat disability rather than illness. Disability as a long-term social state is not treatable and is certainly not curable.
>
> (Oliver 1990a)

Scholars in general have felt that the Japanese system still clings to the medical model, and I would concur, as evidenced by some of the language used in disability discourse in Japan (e.g. the focus on 'rehabilitation' in Japan's national research centre, the Kokuritsu Shōgaisha Rihabiritēshon Sentā). Disability scholars in Japan such as Nagase, Ishikawa, Tateiwa and Yōda have targeted this tendency explicitly in their writings, calling for change along the lines of US and UK disability activism, while noting that Japanese society in general struggles between valuing assertiveness (through the act of reclaiming power) and deferring to others (Ishikawa 2004). Despite the fact that no scholar openly identifies him- or herself with the medical model (Shakespeare 2006: 15), influential organizations such as the UN and the World Health Organization (16) still rely on medical model definitions in their policy papers. Yet there is no social model utopia, as Shakespeare claims, because disability is too often a condition that requires medical intervention for so many individuals. He reminds us that certain aspects of disability are not entirely socially generated, and distinguishing between the pain an individual experiences arising from the impairment and that arising from social discrimination is often very difficult, if not impossible (Shakespeare 2006: 36). My experience as a carer has made me sympathetic to many of Shakespeare's criticisms. I find, however, that the experience of disability as social oppression is only partially explained by the social model. The social model, at its most simplistic, externalizes problems surrounding disability (e.g. if only *other* people didn't feel that way). While the widespread acceptance of this model has done much to empower people with disabilities, it still doesn't offer solutions to every problem that a person with a disability confronts. Sometimes the disability *itself* is the battle. Often a person with a disability must fight both kinds of oppression.

Conclusion 157

The first kind of oppression is recognized by the social model. For example, here is an account of the experience of dehumanization that results from disability. This episode occurred on a commuter train between Yokohama and Tokyo in 2007. Because my daughter was in a wheelchair, we often rode in the section of the car closest to the door, as there is more open space near the exit than in the centre of the train. One day during a non-rush hour period, we were standing around my daughter's wheelchair when the train pulled into a station. A young Japanese man who had been reading or dozing in his seat bolted upright, realizing the train had reached his destination. He was seated near my daughter's wheelchair, and fearing he might miss his stop, he jumped up and moved the wheelchair so he would not have to walk around it to reach the exit. He then bolted out of the carriage and on to the platform. We were speechless; it seemed that the wheelchair had objectified my daughter to the point that she became a 'thing' that he could move without asking permission, even something as small as a quickly uttered '*sumimasen*' (in Japanese, this phrase is used as an apology as well as a request for attention – 'excuse me') which would have caused us to move out of the way in an instant. We could not imagine a stranger silently picking up an able-bodied child in this manner in order to pass. While train 'manners' are often contested in Japan given the demographic pressures of a large metropolitan space, I believe that disability made my daughter occupy a specific social role that did not require even the minimum standards of etiquette. Another similar example of this kind of interaction in urban public spaces was when I was sitting in a coffee shop attached to a train station in Yokohama, which was rather narrow. My daughter's wheelchair was well tucked out of the way of any pedestrian pathway, but another female customer saw an empty table at the other side of the small seating area. Concerned that she might miss the chance to claim that table, she decided that rather than walking around our table to reach her target, she would step directly over my daughter's wheelchair footrest (and her feet) as a short cut to the open table. This was done without eye contact, gesturing or any verbal recognition of these actions. These kinds of actions are taken not only because the wheelchair objectifies the human seated in it, but his/her disability status obviates any need on the part of the other person to ask permission or to apologize for any imposed convenience. In other words, there was no fear on the part of the woman (or the young man in the train) that my daughter would speak out against this behaviour; thus, action could be taken without the need of pleasantries or mutual respect.

While this is not the only kind of social oppression we experience, it does seem to occur not infrequently, and it supports the validity of much that has been written about the social model. The reason why this is a social and not a medical issue is that her specific condition or impairment was not relevant. If she had had no disability, or an 'unseen' disability, she could just as easily have been standing in the way of that young man. The social model argues that it is precisely because of the external expression of her social disability (e.g. she is immobile and nonverbal; not that she has a duplication of the short arm of the fourth chromosome) that the man did not treat her as an equal human being.

158 *Conclusion*

On the other hand, over the years of experiencing relational disability, I have to admit that not all forms of social oppression arise from this kind of objectification resulting from physical or mental difference. Often we battle with the disability itself. This is demonstrated in the many confrontations we have in our home when my daughter clearly expresses frustration regarding our 'oppression' of particular behaviours. This confrontation is seen as oppression from her perspective; from our perspective, we are 'managing her sensory needs'. She experiences this intervention as oppression, yet no one responsible for her safety can argue that allowing her to freely express herself through chewing on plastic bags is a viable option. This kind of oppression is very real to her, but I do not think it can qualify as discrimination under the social model of disability. Rather, it is a disconnect between her specific 'wiring' which requires certain sensory input and the objective reality of environmental safety as we, her carers, understand it. Chewing on plastic wrapping is physically and objectively dangerous, and we cannot allow this to happen. In this case, it is the mental wiring that pushes her to this behaviour that is the issue, not whether or not we are depriving her of agency as an individual. In this sense, the medical model cannot be entirely dismissed, because this sensory need is associated with the general dyspraxia that impairs her understanding of actions, outcomes and safety. This kind of oppression seems to affect our daughter more vividly than the kind described in the previous paragraph; she takes the stares and other kinds of exclusion in public places in her stride. Her expectations are different, perhaps, although this is not to say that she does not understand when someone is treating her with disdain or discomfort. When she senses a person recoiling from her either physically or emotionally, her behaviour deteriorates rapidly.

To complicate matters further, another kind of oppressive act arising from my daughter's disability status is, somewhat perversely, a result of people trying to understand or accept her (and our family). In both Australia and Japan, when discussing our family life with people without disabilities, we often hear phrases such as 'I just don't know how you do it', '*Kyarorin san wa erai wa ne*' ('Carolyn, you are so admirable'), and 'but she's so cute!' (*kawaii!*) or 'at least she's healthy!' (*genki de yokatta*). While these statements are meant to be compliments and/or to acknowledge the hardship that may accompany disability (or in my case, relational disability), they also serve as a socially distancing tool: I am not like other mothers because of my daughter's disability; she is not judged quite the same way as other children. At the beginning of my caring experience, I often responded cynically to these kinds of statements. In Australia, I replied to 'I just don't know how you do it' with 'Well, actually, I think it's against the law if I don't ... what's the jail time for child abandonment?' Needless to say this kind of sarcasm did not go over well, and I soon stopped even trying to reply. Equally, irony is not generally well received in Japanese humour, so in the Japanese context, I would merely bob my head in acknowledgement to these claims of being '*erai*' or my daughter being '*genki*' or '*kawaii*'. This interaction is reflected in Kohama's comment regarding disability in Japan: 'the majority often put the minority on a pedestal to balance their "superiority" complex in relation to the minority' (cited in

Iwakuma 2003: 130). I too realized that these compliments are often given as compensation for the discomfort people felt when they were confronted with my daughter's limitations; in other words, while it is unsettling to speak of a future for a child who will never learn to speak, or live independently, at least (for now) she is 'cute'.

Any experiences of oppression – whether they are dehumanizing, frustrating or isolating experiences – are often connected to disability activism, accompanied by changes in individual consciousness and personal identification. Activism, however, may have 'little to do with defining who is disabled'; instead activism is generally about 'rais[ing] consciousness and empowerment' (Charlton 1998: 82) in relation to these moments of frustration and isolation. Social change is the main goal of nearly every disability movement: in terms of both better concrete benefits and also an improved social atmosphere, where people with disabilities feel more accepted and equal in wider society. Activism achieves this latter goal incrementally, but importantly through espousing what Marks calls 'impairment literacy' (1999: 131), where a non-disabled person is able to become 'more sensitive and educated' about impairments. Education about disability has been hampered by the general ideology of segregation (or even pity, as per the exchanges described above), which means that non-disabled people are shielded from knowing about people with disabilities, or allow their knowledge about people with disabilities to be dominated by unhelpful stereotypes. Activist movements, even if they are ineffective in achieving concrete benefits, cannot be considered failures if they have contributed to raising impairment literacy, or awareness about disability. Rather than focusing on individual impairments, knowledge about a 'disabling environment' (Marks 1999: 133) results in a better understanding of the real effects disability has on people's lives. Activism in Japan has been accorded more muted praise: 'Japan's approach to disability rights has never been as pro-active or as progressive as its activists might wish' (Gottlieb 2001: 993). This activist movement shares some attributes with other social movements in Japan, such as the desire to empower the person with the disability in contrast to the medical and bureaucratic profession which had previously held most of the social, economic and political control over the lives of people with disabilities. Unfortunately most of the empowerment has been ideological rather than practical, considering that the Supports and Services for Persons with a Disability Act has worked to limit benefits rather than expand them (as per Chapter 4). Changes in ideology affect not just the disability community but the entire society: '[w]ho needs a spokesperson more, the group they represent, or the audience?' (Iwakuma 2003: 131). It is not enough to rest on the victories of awareness-raising if people with disabilities are still systematically disadvantaged, but it is an achievement nonetheless.

Disability policy and law is an area of disability discourse where scholars can clearly see concrete change: there are annual White Papers published on disability policy, periodic enactments or repeals of laws, occasional referendums and so on, all of which mark what I would call concrete declarations of change in the public sphere. Despite many legal changes, there are some constants throughout policy and law. In Japan, as elsewhere, disability policy and law primarily focus on the individual's capacity to undertake recompensed labour. While the laws were written in the spirit of social equity, often they result in 'moral' inequity because 'to be officially or sympathetically relieved of the obligation of productive labor – cast out of the public economic realm into the private sphere of charity – is also to be excluded from the privilege of laboring in a society that affirms work as ... "the core of moral life"' (Thomson 1997: 51).

Welfare recipients are generally recognized as individuals who are unable to work as 'normal' employees, yet the receipt of benefits can still quickly arouse suspicions in Japan that they are unearned (Nakamura 2005), and result in resentment towards people receiving disability pensions. This negative association is linked to the prevailing attitudes of neoliberalism and normalization, as discussed in Chapter 4. The 2005 Supports and Services for People with Disabilities Act, we might argue, incorporates the Japanese word *jiritsu* (independence) precisely because it satisfies the desire of disability activists both to promote the social agency of people with disabilities and to confront the lingering criticism that people with disabilities need to be less 'dependent' on hand-outs.

Yet the law, for all its clarity in expressing change and the potential for progress, also reveals inequity. All disabilities are not seen as equivalent in Japan; there are different laws for different kinds of disabilities which are not necessarily equal, and even when one law exists for all (e.g. the 1960 Law for the Promotion of Employing People with a Disability), exceptions are made for cases of intellectual and psychiatric disabilities. This means that disability is still interpreted according to individual disability (as per the medical model) rather than the surrounding society (the social model). Take, for example, this statement made in a scholarly journal by Japanese academics: 'in Japan, adults with mental disability tend to be less adaptive to the community than those with physical disability' (Suzuki 2009: 229). The article goes on to claim that the reason for this is that there is a higher rate of institutionalization for people with intellectual disabilities than for those with physical disabilities (ibid.). This is truly a medical model interpretation of the data, in which the interactive relationship between the minority and the majority is not recognized; the social model would argue that the institutionalization of people with intellectual disabilities could also mean that mainstream society cannot cope with them.

While much has been made of the need to look more closely at disability definitions, this book has also argued for an increased awareness of disability as related to age stages across the life course. For many, views of disability in Japan are often focused on the needs of the elderly, who do constitute the largest group, but this does not mean we should not give proper attention to the needs of people with disabilities at other stages of the lifecycle. Furthermore, a sensitivity to what age stages mean in the disability lifecycle is also crucial. Disability in Japan should not be cornered into the *rōjin mondai* ('problems of an ageing society') basket, because '[a]nyone at anytime and anywhere may become disabled ... [it is] a social category whose membership is always open' (Gadacz cited in Titchkosky 2003: 121). This is problematic because in Japan the government – and society in general – often recognizes the individual with a disability as someone 'frozen in time', unable to achieve socially recognized milestones such as marriage, employment and parenthood. As long as Japanese society values productivity and reproduction in the ways it currently does, people with disabilities (as others who do not contribute in these ways) will never be seen as fully fledged adults (*ichininmae*).

The conflation of people with disabilities at any age with childhood is undoubtedly related to attitudes about caregiving. The more care an individual requires, the more likely society is to infantilize that person. Davis points out that there are differences between 'care *of* the body, care *for* the body and car[e] *about* the body' (2002: 27–8, original emphasis), and it is in these prepositions that our views on what care is can change from something that is an 'expected' part of life or even a pastime, and something that generates income, to something that affects one's personal identity to the point that it requires action:

> Care of the body is now a requirement for existence in consumer society ... involv[ing] the purchase of a vast number of products for personal care and grooming, products necessary to having a body in our society ... [C]are *for* the body ... [includes] the healthcare industry and the dependent care industry ... In most countries, this industry makes up the largest sector of the economy. There are obviously huge economic advantages to the creation and maintenance of the disability industry ... [C]aring *about* the body ... [is about the] attention paid to human rights and civil rights that have to be achieved to bring people with disabilities to the awareness of other identity groups.
>
> (Davis 2002: 27–8, emphasis original)

What needs to be added to this discussion relates to who does the caring, who pays for it, and whether it defines the individual. In care of the body, the care is generally self-conducted and almost always paid for privately. Care for the body is a for-profit industry that both benefits and exploits people with high care needs, including people with disabilities. Caring about the body is an entirely different issue: it is when the needs of the body (and I would include in this the mind) become a part of that person's social identity and have the potential to limit their human rights. In Japan, care of the body is a popular consumer pastime; in these contemporary beauty practices, transformation of the body is seen as a form of personal improvement (Miller 2006). Yet these actions are all conducted in a competitive but private beauty industry in Japan. Care for the body is both private and public, as we saw in Chapters 4 and 6. For example, the medical system in Japan operates using both public funds (through the Six Laws of Welfare) and private (through employer-sponsored or self-paid insurance programmes). The long-term care insurance programme demonstrates how care for people with disabilities can be stitched together from a combination of public and private funds. Activists, like those involved in the independent living movement, ask us to care about the body, to be concerned with how care for the body represents a political and human right. The Japanese Constitution guarantees this right through its statement in Article 25, that 'All people shall have the right to maintain the minimum standards of wholesome and cultured living.' Caring about the body is about making that statement a reality for people with disabilities without stretching those minimum standards so low that it means they are degraded.

In writing this book I have hoped to challenge some of the set notions about disability in Japan. These challenges, presented as academic discourse, have the potential to create a vision of a future(s) where '[i]mpairment is the rule, and normalcy is the fantasy. Dependence is the reality, and independence grandiose thinking. Barrier-free access is the goal, and the right to pursue happiness the false consciousness that obscures it' (Davis 2002: 31). This is perhaps an overestimate of the role disability might play in some future (dys)topia, but it is a provoking statement on what most people currently hold now as 'true' about human society. I hope that it has inspired people who do not have much contact with disability in their day-to-day lives to reflect on how it should be a part of their lives, and how they might think of new interpretations of 'ability' and 'disability' in Japan as well as in their own culture.

Notes

1 Introduction: thinking about anthropology, disability and Japan

1 In this book, I will use the term 'person with a disability' rather than 'disabled person', but accept there are many arguments for and against this choice (e.g. 'person with a disability' puts the person first and the disability second; conversely, this choice of terminology separates the disability from the personal identity of the individual, which is incongruous with many individuals' experiences). I prefer to refer to my daughter as a child with a disability rather than a disabled child, because I feel this expression suggests the unbalanced translocation is something that 'disabled' her, making her subject of an active verb ('disabling'). There are, however, many important scholars in disability studies who disagree and prefer the term 'disabled person' (see Shakespeare 2006: 32 for a discussion on 'disability correctness' in this context). I have thus respectfully kept quotes in their original terminology.
2 I did have cultural baggage from my years of living in New York City, but these carried different connotations, and experience in the Japanese context made me look at homelessness in the United States differently.
3 Within this line of thinking there is even the call for an explicit feminist disability studies discipline: Wendell argues for this, noting that 'more than half of disabled people are women and approximately 16 per cent of women are disabled' (1997: 261).
4 Oliver states, however, that the individual model encompasses the medical model: there is no such thing as the medical model of disability; there is instead an individual model of disability of which medicalization is one significant component (cited in Priestly 1998: 75).
5 Details of the work of UPIAS in creating the foundations for the social model can be found in Shakespeare (2006: 10–14), who goes so far as to call this the 'UPIAS/Oliver social model' in his history of the theory (13).
6 Oliver rejects the randomness of disability across populations, however, noting that 'you are far more likely to be disabled if you are a young or old black working-class woman living in the third world than a white middle-class man living in Britain or the United States' (1996: 120).
7 Shakespeare points out the circularity of this argument using 'contextual essentialism', claiming that this predetermines our understanding of people with disabilities as all oppressed, and that few or none experience positive reactions with non-disabled people (2006: 57).
8 In Japan, the legal age of adulthood is twenty; however, this particular set of statistics defines children as aged fourteen and younger (MIAC 2005d: 16), mostly likely because fourteen is the age at which compulsory education ends.
9 While a variety of medical and behavioural health scientists have long researched ageing in this region, social anthropologists of Japan have particularly contributed to this area: for example, see recent work by Susan Orpett Long, John W. Traphagan and Leng Leng Thang given in the references.

164 *Notes*

10 Shakespeare states that his own approach to disability studies is similarly interdisciplinary, uniting strands of thought from feminism, Foucauldian thought, post-structuralism and postmodernism (2006: 54).
11 Goodey believes that the medical manipulation of disability through prenatal diagnosis and pre-implantation genetic diagnosis will result in fewer people with disabilities being born, further limiting medical and therapeutic professionals' ability to state that they have a deep understanding of disability (2003: 552).

2 Disability in the Japanese context

1 Illnesses that are today preventable, or at least treatable, were often considered disabling in pre-modern and early modern Japan. Hansen's disease (leprosy), first observed in Japan in AD 700, is an example. Even earlier was the occurrence of tuberculosis, which was present in Japan from prehistoric times (Johnston 1995: 41).
2 See Stibbe (2004) for this and other discussions of disability on Japanese television drama shows.
3 The ministry lists facilities granted under the new Supports and Services for People with Disabilities Act and the former Law for the Welfare of People with Physical Disabilities separately.
4 In fact, the JSRPD's current website demonstrates an implicit compliance with a paternalist social paradigm; the group has a 'Royal Patron' who, at the time of writing, was 'His Imperial Highness Hitachi' (JSRPD 2004).
5 A significant number of protests in Japan have been targeted at the media and government regarding language usage, especially in the mass media – this will be detailed in the next chapter.
6 In the UK we see a shift away from 'single-impairment organisations' (Shakespeare 2006: 32) as a response to the overarching aims of the social model to create a disability collective against social oppression.
7 Kwok *et al.* also found this to be the case in disability self-help organizations in mainland China, Thailand and Vietnam (2002: 72, 117, 123), but not so in Hong Kong (83) or Taiwan (109).
8 One of the earliest indicators of a congenital defect apart from visible malformations is an abnormality in the nuchal region. Nuchal fold measurement – the thickness of an area behind the neck of the foetus due to an accumulation of fluid – via ultrasound, is one of the 'earliest and the most sensitive and specific markers' related to a range of trisomies (Geipel *et al.* 2010: 537).

3 Disability, language and meaning

1 Interestingly, pre-war Japanese documents show that the kanji compound 障碍 was in use already then; the current compound 障害, now being phased out in favour of the former combination, is actually a postwar coinage (Niji Zaitaku Kanwa Kea Sentā 2003).
2 The adoption of foreign terms to express ideas that are not easily communicated in Japanese is neither new nor value neutral; pre-war campaigns to rid Japan of English not only demonstrated the soured relationship with America but also sought to underscore the belief that changes to the national language could constitute a threat: a threat not just to Japan's cultural tradition but also to its sense of political power.
3 Gottlieb writes that Japanese disability activists entered the debate in the 1970s, but similarly notes this occurred after other social movements such as the Burakumin Liberation League set an example by protesting against the way they were portrayed (2005: 106).
4 Much has been written about the relationship between the mass media and the government and private industry (see Freeman 2000), but for the purposes of this argument I am not so concerned with the self-censorship that arises from a too-close relationship

Notes   165

between the media and figures of economic and political power – all of which are said to exist to the detriment of the media's efficacy in communicating in the public sphere and creating an environment of transparency. Instead, I am concerned with the relationship between the media, the perceived expectations of an imagined 'mainstream' audience, and the statements of dissatisfaction (or approval) from people with disabilities and their supporters.

5 Self-censorship is not a uniquely Japanese press phenomenon: see Sedler (2011) for instances in the US media.
6 In reports archived on their home page, as late as 2006 NHK is using the 害 character but by mid-2011 this has changed to the phonetic *hiragana* rendition, as in the UNIQLO publication.
7 Some internet publications seem to object to the demonization of terms (for example, the website Hōsōjiko [Broadcast Accidents] in 2007).

4 Disability policy and law in modern Japan

1 This chapter has been informed by ongoing discussions with colleagues at the Asian Law Centre, University of Melbourne, especially Associate Director Stacey L. Steele. I am also indebted to Professor Kazuhiro Nishida, specialist in social law at Okayama University, who offered important insights into the Japanese legal system.
2 The Japanese legal system is made up of six kinds of laws; thus the basic legal system is called *Roppō* or the 'Six Laws', or Codes. These include the Japanese Constitution (*Nihonkoku Kempō*), the Civil Code (*Minpō*), the Commercial Code (*Shōhō*), the Criminal Code (*Keihō*), the Code of Civil Procedure (*Minjisoshōhō*) and the Code of Criminal Procedure (*Keijisoshōhō*).
3 I thank Stacey Steele for this interpretation of how constitutional amendments can be made in principle but not practice.
4 English translations in this chapter are drawn from three main sources, ranging from the specific to the general: the Disability INFormation Resources English translation webpage (JSRPD, 2007–9); Oda and Stickings (1997); and the Japanese government website, www.japaneselawtranslation.go.jp. The Japanese title Shōgaisha Jiritsu Shien Hō means 'a law to support the independence of people with disabilities'; it is interesting to note that the term 'independence' is absent from the official translation into English.
5 For example, this would include individuals caring for family members with disabilities but who were not associated with the military in some way (e.g. without an absent, deceased or disabled *father*).
6 The government now realizes that its programmes need to change, noting that 'compared with other kinds of disabilities, the history of people with intellectual disabilities is very thin', as demonstrated by the insufficient numbers of facilities that are purpose built for this group (Naikakufu 2003).
7 See Oda and Stickings (1997) and Oda (2009) for an overview of Japanese law in English.
8 This perspective arises from discussions with my colleagues at the Asian Law Centre; see Steele and Ueno (2010).
9 This information comes from a discussion with Professor Nishida Kazunori on 21 March 2011.
10 Until September 1998, this law was called the Seishinhakujaku Fukushi Hō, which implies mental 'feebleness' rather than intellectual disability.
11 Despite my choice not to use 'disabled', I do use the phrase 'abled economy' as I believe mainstream society still does presuppose certain physical and intellectual abilities.
12 The law was revised in 1984 to include the phrase 'independent living and provision of opportunities' in a variety of passages (Heyer 1999: 11).

13 In general, I have preferred to use the plural 'people with disabilities' to express the multiple experiences of different disabilities, and the possibility of multiple disabilities, but here I present the 'official translation' by the Japanese government in the singular.
14 Historically speaking, it would be erroneous to say that the Japanese had no expectation of employment for people with disabilities. In the pre-war era, employment training was, at some special schools, offered to visually impaired students in the area of music performance and physical therapy (massage and acupuncture), but as Ogawa notes, these professions were highly unstable (1999: 30) and did not guarantee a secure livelihood.
15 The company also has stores in the UK, the USA, France, China, Hong Kong, Singapore and Russia.
16 While UNIQLO is regarded as far and away the top employer of people with disabilities, other large corporations also were recognized for hiring practices that were above the minimum quota, including the fast food chain McDonalds (2.94 per cent), the clothing store Shimura (2.83 per cent), the family restaurant Skylark (2.82 per cent) and others (*Yomiuri Shimbun* 2007).
17 This information comes from a discussion with Professor Nishida Kazunori on 21 March 2011
18 I again thank Professor Nishida for conceptualizing the relationship to me in this way.
19 This translation comes from Dr Kodate Naonori, public policy researcher.
20 I am indebted to Jeremy Breaden for this clarification.

5 Disability and the lifecycle

1 Goldfarb and Frankel, in a study of more than six hundred people with intellectual disabilities, found that '61.4% were undiagnosed as to etiology [a known cause]' (2007: n.p.).
2 Selective abortion can include procedures such as the reduction of embryos in a multi-foetal pregnancy following fertility treatments, but here I am solely using it to refer to a termination after an abnormal prenatal testing result.
3 Pre-implantation genetic diagnosis can also be defined as a prenatal test but is much less common than other sorts of tests as it is used exclusively in cases of known genetic disorders. It is 'performed in Japan under much stricter regulations than ... in the UK or the US' due to disability protests (Kato 2009: n.p.).
4 The Eugenic Protection Law was promulgated in 1947; it replaced the Kokumin Yūsei Hō (Mackie 2003: 165) which had been in effect since 1940. The change of name was part of a group of amendments to the Eugenic Protection Law passed in 1996.
5 Japan was not the only nation-state that embraced eugenic philosophy; from the late 1800s to the early twentieth century, the USA, UK, Australia and some European countries had eugenic policies in place (Jaeger and Bowman 2005: 13), including the 'prohibition of marriage', 'institutionalization or banishment' and 'involuntary sterilization' (35).
6 'Perinatal mortality' in Japan is higher than 'infant mortality' as the former includes miscarriages and stillbirths (MHLW 2009c: 29).
7 Shakespeare and colleagues have created a comprehensive support website entitled 'AnSWeR' (Antenatal Screening Website Resource) for people who are considering prenatal testing, undergoing it or deciding whether or not to continue the pregnancy (Shakespeare *et al.* 2003–6).
8 Okita *et al.* note some variation in the overall fertility rate: while births to women aged thirty-five and younger are clearly decreasing, there has been some increase in births to older Japanese mothers, reflecting a desire to delay childbearing (2011: 32).
9 Chiba Prefectural records of the age of intellectual disability passbook holders reflect the Prime Minister's Cabinet Office figures, with only two categories – under eighteen and over eighteen (Chiba-ken 2011).

6 Caregiving and the family

1 Izuhara writes that in 1998, 240,000 women in Japan were caring for elderly family members (2003: 403).
2 This is a familiar story, but Thang notes a certain irony in its implementation: while government policy and the wording of this law encourage supported care as the ideal, in reality waiting lists for institutional care for the elderly continue to increase (2011: 182). She suggests that this is because of a number of factors, such as economic incentives that work against home care and a decreasing resistance to institutional care (ibid).
3 Takahashi *et.al.* also found that professional caregivers, although scoring about the same as the control group for depression, had lower responses with regard to their perception of their own quality of life, suggesting that environmental factors affect professional caregivers' mental health (2005: 477).

7 Accessibility and the built environment in Japan

1 The earlier trips were made using a Maclaren Buggy Major (purpose-built stroller; made in the UK), but in 2006 we used a CUBE Grand Satsuki (aluminium-frame manual wheelchair; made in Japan).
2 Disability as experienced in Japanese rural areas will differ, and this must be addressed in further research. My sense is that owing to lower levels of population density, competition for space when creating accessible features is less intense, but precisely because of the lower numbers it is likely there are fewer community and social supports for people with disabilities, and thus the potential for psychological isolation is comparable overall. Obviously, there is no 'ideal' environment for a community that includes persons with disabilities.
3 Because of safety issues regarding these high-speed trains, at Shin-Yokohama there were separate platforms for embarking and disembarking from the trains. Shin-Yokohama, the more central station, was unexpectedly inaccessible with no lifts to these platforms, while Odawara had lifts on both sets of platforms.

Bibliography

Abe, Y. (1998) 'Special Education Reform in Japan', *European Journal of Special Needs Education*, 13: 86–97.
Albrecht, G. L., K. D. Seelman and M. Bury. (2001) 'The Formation of Disability Studies', in G. L. Albrecht, K. D. Seelman and M. Bury (eds) *Handbook of Disability Studies*. Thousand Oaks, CA: Sage, pp. 1–8.
Alexander, L. (2010) 'Romance with Disabled Girls: How (and Maybe Why) an Unusual Video Game Came to Be', *Kotaku*. Online magazine. Available at http://kotaku.com/5461619/romance-with-disabled-girls-how-and-maybe-why-an-unusual-video-game-came-to-be?skyline=true&s=i (accessed 16 March 2012).
Americans with Disabilities Act (ADA). (1990; amended 2009). Available at www.ada.gov/pubs/adastatute08.htm (accessed 10 May 2010).
Arai, Y., K. Kumamoto and M. Washio. (2004) 'Assessment of Family Caregiver Burden in the Context of the LTC Insurance System: J-ZBI', *Geriatrics and Gerontology International*, 4: S53–S55.
arsvi.com. (2010a) 'arsvi.com', Ritsumeikan University and MEXT. Available at www.arsvi.com/index.htm (accessed 16 April 2010).
———. (2010b) 'Shōgaigaku to Seisaku [People with Disabilities and Policy]', Ritsumeikan University and MEXT. Available at www.arsvi.com/d/dpp.htm (accessed 16 April 2010).
Asahi Shimbun (Tokyo). (2010) 'Matsuno san Kumamotoshigi ni [Ms. Matsuno [elected] to Kumamoto City Council]', morning edition, p. 30.
———. (2011) 'Daunshōji ga Rendora Shutsuen – Kyakuhonka "Arino Mama no Sugata o" [A Child with Down Syndrome to Appear on a Serialized Television Drama [says] the Scriptwriters of "The Way You Are"]'. Available at www.asahi.com/culture/update/0511/TKY201105110493.html (accessed 12 May 2011).
Asaka, J., M. Okahara, F. Onaka and S. Tateiwa. (1990, 1995) *Sei no Gihō: Ie to Shisetsu wo Detekurasu Shōgaisha no Shakaigaku [Ars Vivendi: A Sociology of the Lives of People with Disabilities who Have Left the Family Home and Institutions]*. Tokyo: Fujiwara Shoten.
Australian Human Rights Commission. (n.d.) 'A Brief Guide to the Disability Discrimination Act'. Available at www.hreoc.gov.au/disability_rights/dda_guide/dda_guide.htm (accessed 7 May 2010).
Avenell, S. (2006) 'Regional Egoism as the Public Good: Residents' Movements in Japan during the 1960s and 1970s', *Japan Forum*, 18(1): 89–113.
———. (2008) 'From the "People" to the "Citizen": Tsurumi Shunsuke and the Roots of Civic Mythology in Postwar Japan', *Positions*, 16(3): 711–42.

Ben-Ari, E. (2002) 'State, Standardisation and "Normal" Children', in R. Goodman (ed.), *Family and Social Policy in Japan: Anthropological Approaches*. Cambridge: Cambridge University Press, pp. 111–30.
Benedict, R. (1946, 1974) *The Chrysanthemum and the Sword: Patterns of Japanese Culture*. New York: Houghton and Mifflin.
Bestor, V. L., T. C. Bestor and A. Yamagata. (2011) 'Introduction', in V. L. Bestor, T. C. Bestor and A. Yamagata (eds) *Routledge Handbook of Japanese Culture and Society*. New York: Routledge, pp. 1–10.
Boeltzig, H., and M. Suzuki. (2008) 'English Language Resources Related to Disability and Disability Studies in Japan', *Disability Studies Quarterly* 28(3). Available at www.dsq-sds.org/DPubS?service=Repository&version=1.0&verb=Disseminate&view=body&content-type=html_1&handle=osul.dsq/1217618496# (accessed 12 May 2010).
Botai Hogo Hō [Law for Maternal Protection]. (1948; renamed in 1996; latest revision 2006). Available at http://law.e-gov.go.jp/cgi-bin/strsearch.cgi (accessed 23 September 2011).
Brown, I. (2009) *The Boy in the Moon: A Father's Search for his Disabled Son*. Melbourne: Scribe.
Campbell, F. A. K. (2008) 'Exploring Internalized Ableism Using Critical Race Theory', *Disability and Society*, 23(2): 151–62.
Campbell, J., and N. Ikegami. (1999) *Long Term Care for Frail Older People: Reaching for the Ideal System*. Tokyo and New York: Springer.
———. (2003) 'Japan's Radical Reform of Long-term Care', *Social Policy and Administration*, 31(1): 21–34.
Campbell, J. C. (1992) *How Policies Change: The Japanese Government and the Aging Society*. Princeton, NJ: Princeton University Press.
———. (2003) 'The Demographic Dilemma: Japan's Aging Society', *Asia Program Special Report*, 107: 10–15. Woodrow Wilson International Center for Scholars.
Caprio, M., and Y. Sugita. (2007) 'Introduction: The US Occupation of Japan – Innovation, Continuity and Compromise', in M. Caprio and Y. Sugita (eds) *Democracy in Occupied Japan: The US Occupation and Japanese Politics and Society*. London: Routledge, pp. 1–25.
Carpenter, B. (ed.) (1997) *Families in Context: Emerging Trends in Family Support and Early Intervention*. London: David Fulton Publishers.
Charlton, J. I. (1998) *Nothing about Us without Us: Disability Oppression and Empowerment*. Berkeley: University of California Press.
Chiba-ken (Chiba Prefectural Government) (2010) 'Shintai Shōgaisha Techō shojishazū [Numbers of Possessors of the Physical Disability Passbook]'. Available at www.pref.chiba.lg.jp/shoufuku/toukeijouhou (accessed 4 January 2012).
———. (2011) 'Chiteki Shōgaisha Meibō Tōsaishazū oyobi Techō Shojishasū [The Number of Registered People with Intellectual Disabilities and the Number of Possessors of Passbooks]'. Available at www.pref.chiba.lg.jp/shoufuku/documents/230331chiteki.xls (accessed 4 January 2012).
Chiteki Shōgaisha Fukushi Hō [The Law for the Welfare of People with Intellectual Disabilities]. (1960; renamed 1998). Available at http://law.e-gov.go.jp/htmldata/S35/S35HO037.html (accessed 22 March 2011).
Chomsky, N. (1999) *Profit over People: Neoliberalism and Global Order*. New York: Seven Stories Press.
Coffey, A. (1999) *The Ethnographic Self: Fieldwork and the Representation of Identity*. London: Sage.

Bibliography

Coleman, L. M. (1997) 'Stigma: An Enigma Demystified', in L. J. Davis (ed.) *The Disability Studies Reader*. New York: Routledge, pp. 216–31.

Commonwealth Consolidated Acts [Australia]. (1992) Disability Discrimination Act 1992. Available at www.austlii.edu.au/au/legis/cth/consol_act/dda1992264/ (accessed 21 May 2012).

Connell, R. (2006) 'Japan's Handicapped Facilities – Ready, Willing but Disabled', *Mainichi Daily News*. Available at http://mdn.mainichi-msn.co.jp/waiwai/archive/news/2006/02/20060224p2g00m0dm021000c.html (accessed 28 August 2006).

Constitution of Japan. (1946, 2012). Available at www.sangiin.go.jp/eng/law/tcoj/index.htm (accessed 11 May 2010).

Daihonzan Nakayamadera (Nakayama Temple Headquarters). (2011) 'Kosazuke Kigan Anzan Kigan [Prayers for Fertility and Safe Delivery]'. Available at www.nakayamadera.or.jp/top.html (accessed 29 August 2011).

Davies, C. A. (1999, 2008) *Reflexive Ethnography: A Guide to Researching Selves and Others*. London: Routledge.

Davis, L. J. (2002) *Bending over Backwards: Disability, Dismodernism and Other Difficult Positions*. New York and London: New York University Press.

de Ferranti, H. (2009) *The Last Biwa Singer: A Blind Musician in History, Imagination and Performance*. Ithaca: Cornell University, East Asia Program.

Disabled People's International (DPI). (2010) Official website. Available at http://v1.dpi.org/lang-en/index (accessed 4 May 2010).

Doi, T. (1981) *The Anatomy of Dependence*. Tokyo: Kodansha International.

Douzinas, C. (1999) 'Human Rights at the End of History', *Angelaki: Journal of Theoretical Humanities*, 4: 99–114.

DPI-Japan (Shōgaisha intānashonaru Nihon Kaigi [Japan National Assembly of Disabled People's International or DPI-Japan]). (2008) Official website. Available at www.dpi-japan.org/english/e-japan.html (accessed 4 May 2010).

Duncan, M. (2004) 'Autoethnography: Critical Appreciation of an Emerging Art', *International Journal of Qualitative Methods*, 3(4): 2–14.

Edwards, S. D. (2003) 'Prenatal Genetic Screening for Intellectual Disability', *Journal of Intellectual Disability Research*, 47: 526–32.

Edwards, W. (1989) *Modern Japan through its Weddings: Gender, Person and Society in Ritual Portrayal*. Stanford, CA: Stanford University Press.

Elly (Imai Eriko). (2011) 'Profile'. Available at http://ellymusic.com/profile/ (accessed 13 January 2012).

Endō, K. (ed.) (1999) *Shashin Kaiga Shūsei Nihon no Fukushi [A Photographic and Pictorial History of Japanese Welfare] – Daiichimaki: Ishizue o Kizuku [Volume 1: Laying the Foundations]*. Tokyo: Nihon Tosho Sentā.

e-Stat (Seifu Tōkei no Sōgo Madoguchi). (2001) 'Chitekishōgaiji/sha Jittai Chōsa 2000 [Survey of Persons with an Intellectual Disability in 2000]'. Available at www.e-stat.go.jp/SG1/estat/List.do?lid=000001047564 (accessed 4 June 2010).

———. (2007) 'Shintaishōgaiji/sha Jittai Chōsa 2006 [Survey on Persons with a Physical Disability in 2006]'. Available at www.e-stat.go.jp/SG1/estat/List.do?lid=000001059905 (accessed 4 June 2010).

———. (2012) 'Gakkō Kihon Chōsa Nenjitōkei – Tokubetsu Shien Gakkō [Basic School Survey; Statistics by Year – Special Education Schools]'. Available at www.e-stat.go.jp/SG1/toukeidb/GH07010201Forward.do (accessed 8 January 2012).

Fairman, C. M. (2010) 'The Case against Banning the Word "Retard"', *Washington Post*. Available at www.washingtonpost.com/wp-dyn/content/article/2010/02/11/AR2010021103896.html (accessed 7 April 2010).

Fast Retailing Co. (2010) 'Daibāshitei no Suishin [Promoting Diversity]'. Available at www.fastretailing.com/jp/csr/employee/ (accessed 4 May 2010).
Four Leaf Studios (2007–12) 'Katawa Shōjo – Sakuhin Gaiyō [Cripple Girl: Outline]'. Available at http://katawa-shoujo.com/about.php (accessed 16 March 2012).
———. (2008) 'The Name of the Game'. Available at http://katawashoujo.blogspot.com.au/2008/11/name-of-game.html (accessed 16 March 2012).
Freeman, L. A. (2000) *Closing the Shop: Information Cartels and Japan's Mass Media*. Princeton, NJ: Princeton University Press.
Gakkō Kyōiku Hō (School Education Law). (1948; most recent revision 2007). Available at http://law.e-gov.go.jp/cgi-bin/strsearch.cgi (accessed 23 September 2011).
Geipel, A., A. Willruth, J. Vieten, U. Gembruch and C. Berg. (2010) 'Nuchal Fold Thickness, Nasal Bone Absence or Hypoplasia, Ductus Venosus Reversed Flow and Tricuspid Valve Regurgitation in Screening for Trisomies 21, 18 and 13 in the Early Second Trimester', *Ultrasound in Obstetrics and Gynecology*, 35(5): 535–9.
Gill, B. (1993) *Changed by a Child: Companion Notes for Parents of a Child with a Disability*. New York: Doubleday.
Goffman, E. (1997) 'Selections from *Stigma*', in L. J. Davis (ed.) *The Disability Studies Reader*. New York: Routledge, pp. 203–15.
Goldfarb, D. L., and A. E. Frankel. (2007) 'Intellectual Disability Etiologies and Associated Psychiatric Disorders', *Mental Health Aspects of Developmental Disabilities*, January–March. Available at http://findarticles.com/p/articles/mi_6883/is_1_10/ai_n28437067/ (accessed 10 May 2010).
Goodey, C. F. (2003) 'On Certainty, Reflexivity and the Ethics of Genetic Research into Intellectual Disability', *Journal of Intellectual Disability Research*, 47: 548–54.
Goto, Y. (2008) 'Cultural Commentary: Critical Understanding of the Special Support Education in Social Contexts', *Disability Studies Quarterly*, 28(3). Available at www.dsq-sds.org/DPubS?service=Repository&version=1.0&verb=Disseminate&view=body&content-type=html_1&handle=osul.dsq/1217618493# (accessed 12 May 2010).
Gottlieb, N. (2001) 'Language and Disability in Japan', *Disability and Society*, 16(7): 981–95.
———. (2005) *Language and Society in Japan*. Cambridge: Cambridge University Press.
———. (2006) *Linguistic Stereotyping and Minority Groups in Japan*. London: Routledge.
Hall, J. W. (1983) *Japan: From Prehistory to Modern Times*. Tokyo: Charles E. Tuttle.
Hanagoyomi (a pseudonym). (2002) 'Shuyō Masukomi "Iikae" Yōgoshū [Principal Media Paraphrasing Vocabulary List]'. Available at http://kan-chan.stbbs.net/word/pc/list.txt (accessed 6 December 2011).
Harris, P. B., and S. O. Long. (2000) 'Recognizing the Need for Gender-Responsive Family Caregiving Policy', in S. O. Long (ed.) *Caring for the Elderly in Japan and the US: Practices and Policies*. London: Routledge, pp. 248–72.
Hasegawa, T. (2007) 'Equality of Opportunity or Employment Quotas? A Comparison of Japanese and American Employment Policies for the Disabled', *Social Science Japan Journal* 10(1): 41–57.
Hashimoto, W. (2007) 'Gairaigo no Tsūjiteki Suii: [The Diachronic Transition of Loan Words]', *Gengo*, 36(6) (special issue on loanwords): 30–6.
Hayashi, R., and M. Okuhira. (2001) 'The Disability Rights Movement in Japan: Past, Present, and Future', *Disability and Society*, 16(6): 855–69.
———. (2008) 'The Independent Living Movement in Asia: Solidarity from Japan', *Disability and Society*, 23(5): 417–429.
Hayo, B., and H. Ono. (2011) 'Livelihood and Care of the Elderly: Determinants of Public Attitudes in Japan', *Journal of the Japanese and International Economies*, 25: 76–98.

172 Bibliography

Hendry, J. (1981, 2011) *Marriage in Changing Japan: Community and Society*. London: Routledge.

———. (1993) *Wrapping Culture: Politeness, Presentation and Power in Japan and Other Cultures*. Oxford: Oxford University Press.

———. (2003) *Understanding Japanese Society*, 3rd edition. London: Routledge.

Henshall, K. (1999) *Dimensions of Japanese Society: Gender, Margins and Mainstream*. New York: St Martins Press.

Herzog, P. J. (1993) *Japan's Pseudo-democracy*. New York: New York University Press.

Heyer, K. (1999) 'From Special Needs to Equal Rights: Japanese Disability Law', *Asian-Pacific Law and Policy Journal*, 1(1): 1–21.

Hirunuma, T. (2012) 'Heroin Zen'in ga Shōgaisha no Ren'ai Gēmu "Katawa Shōjo" Kaihatsu Chīmu Intābyu [An Interview with the Developers of Katawa Shōjo, a Love Game Where All the Heroines Have Disabilities]', *Nikkan Cyzo*. Available at www.cyzo.com/2012/02/post_9880.html (accessed 16 March 2012).

Hoshika, R. (2007) *Shōgai to wa Nani ka: Disabiriti no Shakai Riron ni Mukete [What is Disability? Toward a Social Theory of Disability]*. Tokyo: Seikatsu Shoin.

House of Councillors. (2001) The Constitution of Japan, The National Diet of Japan. Available at www.sangiin.go.jp/eng/law/tcoj/index.htm (accessed 20 July 2012).

Hughes, B. (2000) 'Medicine and the Aesthetic Invalidation of Disabled People', *Disability and Society*, 15(4): 555–68.

Hugman, R. (1991) *Power in Caring Professions*. Basingstoke: Macmillan.

Ichibangase, Y., and S. Hanada (eds). (1999) *Shashin Kaiga Shūsei Nihon no Fukushi [A Photographic and Pictorial History of Japanese Welfare] – Daigomaki: Bunka ni Ikuzuku [Volume 5: Living Culture]*. Tokyo: Nihon Tosho Sentâ.

Ikeda, S. (2004) 'Japan and the Changing Regime of Accumulation: A World-System Study of Japan's Trajectory from Miracle to Debacle', *Journal of World-Systems Research*, 10(2): 363–94.

Ikeda, T. (2010) 'Shūsanki no Gai o Fusegu [Preventing Brain Injury in the Perinatal Period]', *Gakujutsu no Dōkō*, April: 8–14.

Inoue, N. (2003) 'Introduction: What is Shinto?', in N. Inoue, S. Itō, J. Endō and M. Mori (eds) *A Short History of Shinto*. Abingdon: RoutledgeCurzon, pp. 1–11.

Irwin, S. (2001) 'Repositioning Disability and the Life Course: A Social Claiming Perspective', in M. Priestly (ed.) *Disability and the Life Course: Global Perspectives*. Cambridge: Cambridge University Press, pp. 15–25.

Ishikawa, J. (2004) 'Japan: The Dawning of a Society for Disability Studies', *Disability World*, 23. Available at www.disabilityworld.org/04-05_04/news/japansds.shtml (accessed 12 May 2010).

Ishikawa, J., and O. Nagase (eds). (1999) *Shōgaigaku e no Shōtai: Shakai Bunka Disabiriti [An Invitation to Disability Studies: Socio-cultural Disability]*. Tokyo: Akashi Shoten.

Ivry, T. (2006) 'At the Back Stage of Prenatal Care: Japanese Ob-Gyns Negotiating Prenatal Diagnosis', *Medical Anthropology Quarterly*, 20: 441–68.

———. (2010) *Embodying Culture: Pregnancy in Japan and Israel*. Piscataway, NJ: Rutgers University Press.

Iwakuma, M. (2001) 'Ageing with Disability in Japan', in M. Priestly (ed.) *Disability and the Life Course: Global Perspectives*. Cambridge: Cambridge University Press, pp. 219–30.

———. (2003) 'Being Disabled in Modern Japan: A Minority Perspective', in E. M. Kramer (ed.) *The Emerging Monoculture: Assimilation and the 'Model Minority'*. Westport, CT: Praeger, pp. 124–38.

Iwarsson, S., and A. Ståhl. (2003) 'Accessibility, Usability and Universal Design – Positioning and Definition of Concepts Describing Person–Environment Relationships', *Disability and Rehabilitation*, 25(2): 57–66.

Izuhara, M. (2003) 'Social Inequality under a New Social Contract: Long-term Care in Japan', *Social Policy and Administration*, 37(4): 395–410.

Jaeger, P. T., and C. A. Bowman. (2005) *Understanding Disability: Inclusion, Access, Diversity, and Civil Rights*. Westport, CT: Praeger.

Japan Council on Independent Living Centers (JIL). (n.d.) 'About JIL'. Available at www.j-il.jp/jil.files/english/aboutjil.html (accessed 19 September 2011).

Japan Down Syndrome Network (JDSN, Nihon Daunshô Netowâku) (1998) 'Botai Kessei Mâkâ Kensa ni Kansuru Q & A [Q & A about Maternal Blood Serum Testing].' Available at http://rg4.rg.med.kyoto-u.ac.jp/JDSN/data/Q-A.html (accessed 29 March 2011).

Japan Organization for Employment of the Elderly and Persons with Disabilities (JEED). (2010) 'JEED 2010 Edition'. Available at www.jeed.or.jp/english/download/pamphlet.pdf (accessed 4 January 2011).

Japan Times. (2007) 'Editorial: Dignity for Disabled People'. Available at http://search.japantimes.co.jp/cgi-bin/ed20070214a1.html (accessed 5 July 2010).

Japanese Society for the Rehabilitation of People with Disabilities (JSRPD). (2004) 'Outline and History'. Available at www.jsrpd.jp/static/english/out.html (accessed 11 May 2011).

———. (2007–9) 'DINF (Disability Information Resources): The 38 Selected Japanese Laws Related to Persons with Disabilities', online pamphlet, pp. 1–18. Available at www.dinf.ne.jp/doc/english/law/japan/selected38/index.html (accessed 11 May 2011).

Jiko TV. (2007) 'Hōsōkinshi Yōgo Shōgaisha Sabetsu Yōgo [Broadcast Taboo Terms – Discriminatory Terms [regarding] People with Disabilities]'. Available at www.jiko.tv/housoukinshi/sabetsu4.html (accessed 1 November 2011).

Johnson, C. (1982) *MITI and the Japanese Miracle: The Growth of Industrial Policy, 1922–1975*. Stanford, CA: Stanford University Press.

Johnston, W. (1995) *The Modern Epidemic: A History of Tuberculosis in Japan*. Harvard East Asian Monographs. Cambridge, MA: Harvard University Press.

K-Planning. (2011) 'Keipuranningu geinobu kodomo SP kurasu [The K-Planning Entertainment Section's Children's Sp(ecial) Class'. Available at www.9292.co.jp/sp.html (accessed 13 December 2011).

Kasnitz, D., and R. P. Shuttleworth. (2001) 'Engaging Anthropology in Disability Studies', in L. J. Rogers and B. B. Swadener (eds) *Semiotics and Dis/Ability: Interrogating Categories of Difference*. Albany: State University of New York Press, pp. 19–42.

Kato, M. (2009) 'Selective Abortion in Japan', *The Focus: Genomics in Asia – IIAS Newsletter*, 52: 20–1.

———. (2010) 'Cultural Notions of Disability in Japan: Their Influence on Prenatal Testing', in M. Sleeboom-Faulkner (ed.) *Frameworks of Choice: Predictive and Genetic Testing in Asia*. Amsterdam: University of Amsterdam Press, pp. 125–44.

Kersten, R. (1996) *Democracy in Postwar Japan: Maruyama Masao and the Search for Autonomy*. London: Routledge.

Kikuchi, I. (1997) 'Hansen's Disease in Japan: A Brief History', *International Journal of Dermatology*, 36(8): 629–33.

Kilpatrick, D. G. (2000) 'Definitions of Public Policy and the Law'. National Violence against Women Prevention Research Center. Available at www.musc.edu/vawprevention/policy/definition.shtml (accessed 12 July 2010).

Kinsella, S. (2000) 'An Interview with Ōe Kenzaburō', *Japan Forum*, 12(2): 233–41.

Bibliography

Kleinman, A. (2010) 'On Caregiving', *Harvard Magazine*, July–August: 25–9.
Kohn, T., and R. McKechnie. (1999) 'Introduction: Why Do We Care Who Cares?', in T. Kohn and R. McKechnie (eds) *Extending the Boundaries of Care: Medical Ethics and Caring Practices*. Oxford: Berg, pp. 1–15.
Kokuritsu Shōgaisha Rihabiritēshon Sentā (National Rehabilitation Center for Persons with Disabilities). (n.d.) Official website. Available at www.rehab.go.jp/index.html (accessed 23 April 2010).
Kōseijimu Jikan Tsūchi. (n.d.) Summary of the '*Ryōiku Techō Seido no Jishi ni Tsuite [Regarding the Actual Rehabilitation Handbook]*', published in 1973. Available at www. maroon.way-nifty.com/welfare/shougai_techou_kijun/08_ryouiku_techou.pdf (accessed 21 May 2012).
Kōseirōdōsho Shakai Enjokyoku (Social Support Office of the Ministry of Health, Labour and Welfare). (2008) 'Heisei 18nen Shintaishōgaiji/sha Jittai Chōsa Kekka [Results of a 2006 Survey of Children and Adults with a Physical Disability]'. Available at www. mhlw.go.jp/toukei/saikin/hw/shintai/06/dl/01_0001.pdf (accessed 4 January 2011).
Koyama, E. (2006) 'From "Intersex" to "DSD": Toward a Queer Disability Politics of Gender". Keynote address for the 'Translating Identity' conference, University of Vermont. Available at www.intersexinitiative.org/articles/intersextodsd.html (accessed 23 April 2010).
Kwok, J. K. F., R. K. H. Chan and W. T. Chan. (2002) *Self-Help Organizations of People with Disabilities in Asia*. Westport, CT: Auburn House.
Kyodo News. (2010) 'Discrimination Felt by 70% of Disabled: Report', *Japan Times*, 12 June. Available at www.japantimes.co.jp/text/nn20100612a3.html (accessed 15 June 2010).
Kyōgoku, T. (2005a) 'Nihon no Jinkō Dōkō ni Tsuite [About Movements in Japanese Demographics]', *Nōmaraizeeshon – Shōgaisha no Fukushi*, September. Available at www.dinf.ne.jp/doc/japanese/prdl/jsrd/norma/n290/n290018.html (accessed 5 July 2010).
———. (2005b). *Shōgaisha Jiritsu Shien Hō no Kaisetsu [An Analysis of the Services and Supports for Persons with Disability Act]*. Tokyo: Zengoku Shakai Fukushi Kyōgikai.
Law, J. M. (1998) 'The Awaji Tradition', in K. Brazell and J. T. Araki (eds) *Traditional Japanese Theatre: An Anthology of Plays*. New York: Columbia University Press, pp. 393–7.
Long, S. O. (2000) 'Introduction', in S. O. Long (ed.) *Caring for the Elderly in Japan and the US: Practices and Policies*. London: Routledge, pp. 1–16.
———. (2008) *Social Change and Caregiving of the Elderly: The Demographic Challenge: A Handbook about Japan*. Leiden: Brill.
Mackie, V. (2002) 'Embodiment, Citizenship and Social Policy in Contemporary Japan', in R. Goodman (ed.) *Family and Social Policy in Japan: Anthropological Approaches*. Cambridge: Cambridge University Press, pp. 200–39.
———. (2003) *Feminism in Modern Japan*. Cambridge: Cambridge University Press.
MacLachlan, L. (2001) 'Turning Seeing into Believing: Producing Credibility in the Television News Coverage of the Kobe Earthquake', in B. Moeran (ed.) *Asian Media Productions*. London: Curzon, pp. 108–25.
McLelland, M. J. (2009) 'The Role of the "Tōjisha" in Current Debates about Sexual Minority Rights in Japan', *Japanese Studies*, 29(2): 193–207.
Marks, D. (1999) *Disability: Controversial Debates and Psychosocial Perspectives*. London and New York: Routledge.
Matsuda, I., and K. Suzumori. (2000) 'Prenatal Genetic Testing in Japan', *Public Health Genomics*, 3(1): 12–16.

Matsui, R. (1998) 'An Overview of the Impact of Employment Quota System in Japan', *Asia Pacific Disability Rehabilitation Journal*, 9(1). Available at www.dinf.ne.jp/doc/english/asia/resource/apdrj/z13jo0100/z13jo0106.html (accessed 5 July 2010).

Matsumoto, Y. (ed.) (2011) *Faces of Aging: The Lived Experience of the Elderly in Japan*. Stanford, CA: Stanford University Press.

Mauldin, L. (2008) 'Cultural Commentary: Trig or Treat? The 2008 Election, Sarah Palin, and Teaching Disability', *Disability Studies Quarterly* 28(4). Available at www.dsq-sds.org/article/view/133/133 (accessed 10 May 2010).

Medical News Today. (2003) 'New Test Opens Prenatal Genetic Diagnosis to All'. Available at www.medicalnewstoday.com/articles/3918.php (accessed 23 September 2011).

Miles, M. (2000) 'Disability on a Different Model: Glimpses of an Asian Heritage', *Disability and Society*, 15(4): 603–18.

Miller, L. (2006) *Beauty Up: Exploring Contemporary Japanese Body Aesthetics*. Berkeley: University of California Press.

Ministry of Education, Culture, Sports, Science and Technology (MEXT). (2009) 'Tokubetsu Shien Kyōiku [Special Needs Education]'. Available at www.mext.go.jp/a_menu/shotou/tokubetu/main.htm (accessed 8 January 2012).

Ministry of Health and Welfare (MHW). (1995) *Shakai Hoshō Benri Jiten [Handy Social Security Encyclopedia]*. Tokyo: Hōken.

——. (1999). 'White Paper: Annual Report on Health and Welfare 1998–1999 Social Security and National Life'. Available at www1.mhlw.go.jp/english/wp_5/vol1/p2c5s3.html (accessed 23 April 2010).

Ministry of Health, Labour and Welfare (MHLW). (2002) 'Long Term Health Insurance in Japan'. Available at www.mhlw.go.jp/english/topics/elderly/care/index.html (accessed 22 February 2012).

——. (2009a) 'Longitudinal Survey of Middle and Elderly Persons'. Available at www.mhlw.go.jp/english/database/db-ls/ls.html (accessed 22 February 2012).

——. (2009b) 'Survey of Institutions and Establishments for Long-Term Care'. Available at www.mhlw.go.jp/english/database/db-hss/siel-index.html (accessed 22 February 2012).

——. (2009c) 'Vital Statistics in Japan (Trends to 2008)'. Available at www.mhlw.go.jp/english/database/db-hw/dl/*1–1b2.pdf (accessed 21 June 2010).

Ministry of Internal Affairs and Communication (MIAC). (2005a) 'Employment Status of Employed Persons and Industrial Composition'. Available at www.stat.go.jp/english/data/kokusei/2005/poj/pdf/2005ch05.pdf (accessed 27 April 2010).

——. (2005b) 'Households with Aged Persons'. Available at www.stat.go.jp/english/data/kokusei/2005/poj/mokuji.htm (accessed 21 May 2012).

——. (2005c) 'Labor Force Status'. Available at www.stat.go.jp/english/data/kokusei/2005/poj/mokuji.htm (accessed 27 April 2010).

——. (2005d) 'Population by Sex and Age'. Available at www.stat.go.jp/english/data/kokusei/2005/poj/mokuji.htm (accessed 27 April 2010).

Mori, M. (2003) 'Ancient and Classical Japan: The Dawn of Shinto', in N. Inoue, S. Itō, J. Endō and M. Mori (eds) *A Short History of Shinto*. Abingdon: RoutledgeCurzon, pp. 12–62.

Mori Biru Kabushikigaisha. (2006) 'Omotesandō Hiruzu Purojekto [The Omotesandō Hills Project]'. Available at www.mori.co.jp/projects/omotesando/index.html (accessed 12 January 2007).

Mullins, M. R. (2011) 'Religion in Contemporary Japanese Lives', in V. Lyon Bestor, T. C. Bestor and A. Yamagata (eds) *The Routledge Handbook of Japanese Society and Culture*. New York: Routledge, pp. 63–74.

176 Bibliography

Muncey, T. (2005) 'Doing Autoethnography', *International Journal of Qualitative Methods*, 4(3): 1–12.

Murata, M. (1994, 2000) *Kurumaisu Kara Mita Machi* [*The City as Seen from a Wheelchair*]. Tokyo: Iwanami Shoten.

Murphy, R. (1987) *The Body Silent*. New York: H. Holt.

Nagase, O. (2008) 'Development of Disability Studies in Japan: A Brief Outline', *Disability Studies Quarterly*, 28(3). Available at www.dsq-sds.org/article/view/116/116 (accessed 10 May 2010).

Naikakufu. (2003) 'Heisei 15nenban Shōgaisha Hakusho [A White Paper on People with Disabilities 2003]'. Available at www8.cao.go.jp/shougai/whitepaper/h15zenbun/html/zuhyo/fig02_01_01_01.html (accessed 21 May 2012).

———. (2006) 'Heisei 18nenban Shōgaisha Hakusho [A White Paper on People with Disabilities 2006]'. Available at www8.cao.go.jp/shougai/whitepaper/h18hakusho/zenbun/honpen/zu_02_01_01.html (accessed 21 May 2012).

———. (2009) 'Shōgaisha Hakusho Heisei 21nenban [A White Paper on People with Disabilities 2009]'. Available at www8.cao.go.jp/shougai/whitepaper/h21hakusho/zenbun/pdf/index.html (accessed 21 May 2012).

———. (2010a) 'Heisei 22nendo Kōrei Shakai Hakusho [A White Paper on the Ageing Society]'. Available at www8.cao.go.jp/kourei/whitepaper/w–2010/zenbun/22index.html (accessed 21 May 2012).

———. (2010b) 'Shōgaisha Hakusho Heisei 22nenban [A White Paper on People with Disabilities 2010]', Available at www8.cao.go.jp/shougai/whitepaper/h22hakusho/zenbun/pdf/index.html (accessed 23 June 2010).

Nakamura, K. (2002) 'Resistance and Co-optation: The Japanese Federation of the Deaf and its Relations with State Power', *Social Science Japan Journal*, 5(1): 17–35.

———. (2005) 'Severe Disabilities, Liberalism and Social Welfare Policy in Japan and the US', *Anthropology News*, 46(9): 58.

———. (2006) *Deaf in Japan: Signing and the Politics of Identity*. Ithaca: Cornell University Press.

———. (2009) 'Disability, Destitution, and Disaster: Surviving the 1995 Great Hanshin Earthquake in Japan', *Human Organization*, 68(1): 82–8.

———. (forthcoming) *A Disability of the Soul: An Ethnography of Schizophrenia and Mental Illness in Contemporary Japan*. Ithaca, NY: Cornell University Press.

National Institute of Special Education. (2004) 'Special Education in Japan'. Online report. Available at www.nise.go.jp/en/Special_Education_in_Japan.pdf (accessed 8 January 2012).

Nelson, A. N. (1985) *The Modern Reader's Japanese–English Character Dictionary*. Rutland, VT and Tokyo: Charles Tuttle.

NHK Hōsō Bunka Kenkyūjo (NHK Broadcasting Culture Research Institute). (2009) 'Hōsō Genba no Gimon Shichōsa no Gimon [Doubts of the Broadcaster – Doubts of the Audience]'. Available at www.nhk.or.jp/bunken/kotoba/gimon/index.html (accessed 31 October 2011).

———. (2011) 'Kotoba (Hōsōyōgo) [Language (Broadcasting Terms)]'. Available at www.nhk.or.jp/bunken/kotoba/index.html (accessed 31 October 2011).

Nihon Shōgaisha Rihabiritēshon Kyōkai (Japanese Society of People with Disabilities for Rehabilitation) (JSRPD). (2006–11) 'Tōkai ni Tsuite Goaisatsu (About the Association – Greetings)'. Available at www.jsrpd.jp/static/about/gree/index.html (accessed 13 September 2011).

Niji Zaitaku Kanwa Kea Sentā (Rainbow Home Palliative Care Centre). (2003) 'Shōgai no Koshō - Hyōki wa Itsu Kara? [When Did the Naming/Declarations of Disability Start?].' Available at http:::/cen.web.infoseek.co.jp/baltuku/syougaihyouki.pdf (accessed 9 June 2010).

Nippon Hōsō Kyōkai (NHK). (2006) 'NHK Sutorecchiman2 Zengakunen Yōgo – NHK Dejitaru Kyōzai [For All Levels of Special Education NHK's Stretchman 2 – NHK's Digital Teaching Materials]'. Available at www.nhk.or.jp/sman/ja/frame.html (accessed 14 January 2007).

———. (2012). 'Seido no Tanima: Nanbyōkanja Shien no Kadai [A Chasm in the System: The Challenge of Supporting People with Chronic Illness]'. Available at www.nhk.or.jp/seikatsu-blog/ (accessed 27 March 2012).

Nishi Nihon Shimbun. (2008) 'Senshokutai Ijō no Chōonpakensa no Sonzai – Ishi, Oshieru Gimu Nashi – Sankaidantai ga Hatsushishin [Doctors Have No Obligation to Inform of Chromosomal Abnormalities Discovered by Ultrasound – The Obstetric Association Makes a New Guideline]'. Available at www.nishinippon.co.jp/nnp/national/science/20080331/20080331_003.shtml (accessed 23 September 2011).

Nishida, H. (1993) 'Outcome of Infants Born Preterm, with Special Emphasis on Extremely Low Birthweight Infants', *Bailliere's Clinical Obstetrics and Gynaecology*, 7(3): 611–31.

Nishida, K. (2011a) 'Defining Intellectual Disability', email communication, 9 May.

———. (2011b) 'Shōgaisha Jiritsu Shien Hō [Supports and Services for People with Disabilities Act]', interview at the Asia Institute, University of Melbourne, 22 March.

Norgren, T. (1998) 'Abortion before Birth Control: The Interest Group Politics behind Postwar Japanese Reproduction Policy', *Journal of Japanese Studies*, 24: 59–94.

Nozomisono (National Center for Persons with Severe Intellectual Disabilities). (2000–10) Official website. Available at www.nozomi.go.jp/ (accessed 19 May 2010).

Oda, H. (2009) *Japanese Law*, 3rd edition. Oxford: Oxford University Press.

Oda, H., and S. Stickings. (1997) *Basic Japanese Laws*. Oxford and New York: Oxford University Press.

Ōdikku (ODIK). (2011) 'Mizukoshi Keiko - Purofiru [Mizukoshi Keiko's Profile]'. Available at www.odik.co.jp/artist/musician/mizukoshi_keiko.html (accessed 13 January 2012).

Ōe, K. (1964) *Kojinteki na Jiken [A Personal Matter]*. Tokyo: Shinchōsha.

———. (1967, 1974) *The Silent Cry*. Tokyo: Kodansha.

———. (1977) *Teach us to Outgrow our Madness*. New York: Grove Press.

———. (1996) *A Healing Family*. Tokyo: Kodansha.

———. (2002) *Rouse Up O Young Men of the New Age!* New York: Grove Press.

———. (2003) *Somersault*. London: Atlantic Books.

Office for Planning of International Pension Affairs, General Affairs Division, Pension Bureau (OPIPA). (2004) 'Outline of the Japanese Pension System', pamphlet: 1–40.

Ogawa, K. (ed.) (1999) *Shashin Kaiga Shūsei Nihon no Fukushi [A Photographic and Pictorial History of Japanese Welfare] – Daisanmaki: Kanōsei o Maneku [Volume 3: Beckoning Possibility]*. Tokyo: Nihon Tosho Sentā.

Ohnishi, K., Y. Hayama and S. Kosugi. (2008) 'An Analysis of Patient Rights Violations in Psychiatric Hospitals in Japan after the Enactment of the Mental Health Act of 1987', *Issues in Mental Health Nursing*, 29: 1290–303.

Okamoto, G. (2012). 'Katawa Shojou Released'. Available at www.kotaku.jp/2012/01/katawa_shoujo_released.html (accessed 6 July 2012).

Okita, Y., W. D. Pfau and G. T. Long. (2011) 'A Stochastic Forecast Model for Japan's Population', *The Japanese Economy*, 38(2): 19–44.

Okuno, E. (1998) 'Disability Statistics in Japan', *Asia and Pacific Journal on Disability*. Available at www.dinf.ne.jp/doc/english/asia/resource/z00ap/003/z00ap00309.html (accessed 5 July 2010).

Oliver, M. (1990a) 'The Individual and Social Models of Disability', a presentation at the Joint Workshop of the Living Options Group and the Research Unit of the Royal College of Physicians, 23 July. Available at www.leeds.ac.uk/disability-studies/archiveuk/Oliver/in%20soc%20dis.pdf (accessed 21 May 2012).

———. (1990b) *The Politics of Disablement*. London: Macmillan.

———. (1996) *Understanding Disability: From Theory to Practice*. Basingstoke: Macmillan.

O'Neill, P. G. (1986) *Essential Kanji: 2,000 Basic Characters Systematically Arranged for Learning and Reference*. New York and Tokyo: John Weatherhill.

Otake, T. (2006) 'Disability in Japan: Is "Disability" Still a Dirty Word in Japan?', *Japan Times*. Available at http://search.japantimes.co.jp/cgi-bin/fl20060827x1.html (accessed 7 September 2006).

Ototake, H. (2001, 2004) *Gotaifumanzoku* [*Nobody's Perfect*]. 2nd edition. Tokyo: Kodanshabunkô.

Ozawa, Y. (ed.) (1999) *Shashin Kaiga Shūsei Nihon no Fukushi* [*A Photographic and Pictorial History of Japanese Welfare*] – *Daiyonmaki: Kyōsei o Mezasu* [*Volume 4: Aiming for Co-existence*]. Tokyo: Nihon Tosho Sentā.

Panitch, M. (2008) *Disability, Mothers and Organization: Accidental Activists*. New York and London: Routledge.

Paxton, M. (2000) 'Why Members of the Disability Community Oppose Prenatal Testing and Selective Abortion', pp. 147–50. Available at http://repository.library.georgetown.edu/handle/10822/517910 (accessed 23 September 2010).

Piotrowski, K. (2005) 'Keeping Pace with the Progress of the World: Article 9 of the Japanese Constitution', *Washington University Law Quarterly*, 83: 1653.

Plath, D. (1980) *Long Engagements: Maturity in Modern Japan*. Stanford, CA: Stanford University Press.

Porter, G. (2010) 'Genetic Tests and Insurance in Japan', in M. Sleeboom-Faulkner (ed.) *Frameworks of Choice: Predictive and Genetic Testing in Asia*. Amsterdam: University of Amsterdam Press, pp. 145–66.

Priestly, M. (1998) 'Constructions and Creations: Idealism, Materialism and Disability Theory', *Disability and Society*, 13(1): 75–94.

———. (2001) 'Introduction: The Global Context of Disability', in M. Priestly (ed.) *Disability and the Life Course: Global Perspectives*. Cambridge: Cambridge University Press, pp. 3–14.

Quataert, J. H. (2009) *Advocating Dignity: Human Rights Mobilizations in Global Politics*. Philadelphia: University of Pennsylvania Press.

Quinn, P. (1998) *Understanding Disability: A Lifespan Approach*. Thousand Oaks, CA and London: Sage.

Ralston, D. C., and J. Ho. (2007) 'Disability, Humanity, and Personhood: A Survey of Moral Concepts', *Journal of Medicine and Philosophy*, 32: 619–33.

Reader, I., and G. J. Tanabe Jr. (1998) *Practically Religious: Worldly Benefits and the Common Religion of Japan*. Honolulu: University of Hawaii Press.

Reproductive Genetics Institute (RGI). (2010) 'Chromosome Translocations', RGI, WHO Collaborating Center for Prevention of Genetic Disorders. Available at www.reproductivegenetics.com/translocations.html (accessed 21 May 2010).

Robertson, J. (2002) 'Blood Talks: Eugenic Modernity and the Creation of New Japanese', *History and Anthropology*, 13(3): 191–216.

Rosenblatt, R. (2011) 'What Disabled Children Teach Us', *New York Times*, 8 May. Available at www.nytimes.com/2011/05/08/books/review/book-review-the-boy-in-the-moon-by-ian-brown.html?pagewanted=all (accessed 8 May 2011).
Safilios-Rothschild, C. (1970) *The Sociology and Social Psychology of Disability and Rehabilitation*. New York: Random House.
Saitō, T. (2011) 'Chiteki Shōgai no Kora 200nin, Hinansen Tenten Shokuin "Mō Genkai" [200 Children with Intellectual Disabilities Moved from Evacuation Centre, Place to Place; Carers say "That's Enough"]', *Asahi Shimbun* (Tokyo). Available at www.asahi.com/special/10005/TKY201103280096.html (accessed 21 May 2012).
Sakai, R. (2005) 'Shōgaisha ni Saigai Jōhō wa Todoita ka – Chūetsujishinn Hisai no Shikaku Shōgaisha/chōkaku Shōgaisha Kiktori Chōsa Kara [Did Emergency Information Reach People with Disabilities? From a Survey of People with Visual and Hearing Disabilities in the Niigata-Chuetsu Earthquake]', *Hōsōkenkyū to Chōsa (Gekkyu)*, September: 16–25.
———. (2006) 'Shōgaisha to "Jōhō no yunibaasarudezain" – dejitaru hōsō jidai no kadai to kanōsei [People with Disabilities and the Universal Design of Information: Topics and Possibilities in the Digital Broadcasting Age]', *Hōsōkenkyū to Chōsa (Gekkyu)*, January: 30–41.
Sakamoto, Y. (2006) *Yoku wakaru Shōgaisha Jiritsu Shien Hō [Understanding the Support and Services for People with Disabilities Law]*. Tokyo: Chūō Hōgen.
Sato, K. (2005) 'The Employment of High School Graduates in Miyazaki Prefecture', *Social Science Japan* (Newsletter of the Institute of Social Science, University of Tokyo), 32: 12–14.
Saxton, M. (2000) 'Why Members of the Disability Community Oppose Prenatal Diagnosis and Selective Abortion', in E. Parens and A. Asch (eds) *Prenatal Testing and Disability Rights*, Washington, DC: Georgetown University Press, pp. 147–64.
Schoeni, R. F., J. Liang, J. Bennett, H. Sugisawa, T. Fukaya and E. Kobayashi. (2006) 'Trends in Old-Age Functioning and Disability in Japan, 1993–2002', *Population Studies*, 60(1): 39–53.
Schriver, T. (2010) 'The Bigotry behind the Word "Retard"', *Washington Post*. Available at www.washingtonpost.com/wp-dyn/content/article/2010/02/14/AR2010021402893.html (accessed 7 April 2010).
Sedler, R. A. (2011) 'Symposium on Censorship and the Media: Self-Censorship and the First Amendment', *Notre Dame Journal of Law, Ethics and Public Policy*, 25: 13–46.
Seishin Shōgaisha Fukushi Hō [Law for the Welfare of People with Psychiatric Disabilities]. (1950; last revised 2010). Available at http://law.e-gov.go.jp/htmldata/S25/S25HO123.html (accessed 21 May 2012).
Seligman, M., and R. B. Darling. (2007) *Ordinary Families, Special Children: A Systems Approach to Childhood Disability*, 3rd edition. New York: The Guildford Press.
Shakespeare, T. (1999), 'Losing the Plot? Medical and Activist Discourses of Contemporary Genetics and Disability', *Sociology of Health and Illness*, 21(5): 669–88.
———. (2000) 'Arguing about Genetics and Disability', *Interaction*, 13(3): 11–14.
———. (2005) 'The Social Context of Individual Choice', in D. T. Wasserman, R. S. Wachbroit and J. E. Bickenbach (eds) *Quality of Life and Human Difference: Genetic Testing, Health Care and Disability*. Cambridge: Cambridge University Press, pp. 217–36.
———. (2006) *Disability Rights and Wrongs*. Abingdon: Routledge.
Shakespeare, T., A. Leeder, D. Leeder, W. McEvoy, J. Whiting and D. Sayer. (2003–6) 'AnSWeR (Antenatal Screening Web Resource)'. Available at www.antenataltesting.info/default.html (accessed 23 June 2010).

180 Bibliography

Shintai Shōgaisha Fukushi Hō [Law for the Welfare of People with Physical Disabilities]. (1949). Available at http://law.e-gov.go.jp/htmldata/S24/S24HO283.html (accessed 21 May 2012).

Shishido, T., and K. Tanno (eds). (1999) *Shashin Kaiga Shūsei Nihon no Fukushi* [*A Photographic and Pictorial History of Japanese Welfare*] – *Dainimaki: Jiritsu e no Michi* [*Volume 2: The Road to Independence*]. Tokyo: Nihon Tosho Sentâ.

Shokugyō Antei Hō [Employment Security Law]. (1947; last revision 2007). Available at http://law.e-gov.go.jp/cgi-bin/strsearch.cgi (accessed 30 April 2010).

Shono, J., and N. Doi (directors). (2000) *Beautiful Life: The Days We Spent Together* (television series of eleven 60-minute episodes, 18 January–26 March 2000). Japan: Tokyo Broadcasting Systems.

Shōgaigakkai [Japan Society for Disability Studies]. (2010) Official website. Available at www.jsds.org/ (accessed 16 April 2010).

Shōgaisha Jiritsu Shien Hō [Services and Supports for Persons with a Disability Act]. (2005). Available at http://law.e-gov.go.jp/cgi-bin/strsearch.cgi (accessed 23 September 2011).

Shōgaisha Kihon Hō [Basic Act for Persons with Disabilities]. (1971; last revision 2004). Available at http://law.e-gov.go.jp/htmldata/S45/S45HO084.html (accessed 21 May 2012).

Shōgaisha no Koyō no Shokushin nado ni Kansuru Hōritsu [Law for the Promotion of Employing People with a Disability]. (1960; last amended 1992). Online; translation by the Japan Association for Employment of the Disabled. Available at http://wallis.kezenfogva.iif.hu/eu_konyvtar/projektek/vocational_rehabilitiation/japan/jap_rap/leg_3.htm (accessed 11 May 2010).

Sleeboom-Faulkner, M. (2010) 'Frameworks of Choice: The Ramification of Predictive and Genetic Testing in Asia', in M. Sleeboom-Faulkner (ed.) *Frameworks of Choice: Predictive and Genetic Testing in Asia*. Amsterdam: University of Amsterdam Press, pp. 11–26.

Snyder, S. L., and D. T. Mitchell. (2006) *Cultural Locations of Disability*. Chicago: University of Chicago Press.

Sotnik, P., and M. A. Jezewski. (2005) 'Culture and the Disability Services', in J. H. Stone (ed.) *Culture and Disability: Providing Culturally Competent Services*. Thousand Oaks, CA: Sage, pp. 15–30.

Sparkes, A. C. (2002) 'Autoethnography: Self-indulgence or Something More?', in A. P. Bochner and C. Ellis (eds) *Ethnographically Speaking: Autoethnography, Literature and Aesthetic*. Walnut Creek, CA: AltaMira Press, pp. 209–32.

Stangl, R. (2010) 'Selective Terminations and Respect for the Disabled', *Journal of Medicine and Philosophy*, 35: 32–45.

Statistics and Information Department – Minister's Secretariat. (2009) 'Outline of Health, Labour and Welfare Statistics', Ministry of Health, Labour and Welfare. Available at www.mhlw.go.jp/english/database/db-oh/index.html (accessed 23 April 2010).

Steele, S. L., and G. Ueno. (2010) 'Interview: The Structure of the Japanese Legal System Pertaining to Disability', 5 July, Melbourne Law School.

Stevens, C. (1997) *On the Margins of Japanese Society: Volunteers and the Welfare of the Urban Underclass*. London: Routledge.

———. (2007) 'Living with Disability in Urban Japan', *Japanese Studies*, 27(3): 263–78.

Stibbe, A. (2004) 'Disability, Gender and Power in Japanese Television Drama', *Japan Forum*, 16: 21–36.

Stockall, N. (2001) 'A Mother's Reconstruction of the Semiotic Self', in L. J. Rogers and B. B. Swadener (eds) *Semiotics and Dis/Ability: Interrogating Categories of Difference*. Albany: State University of New York Press, pp. 117–33.

Stone, E. (2001) 'A Complicated Struggle: Disability, Survival and Social Change in the Majority World', in M. Priestly (ed.) *Disability and the Life Course: Global Perspectives*. Cambridge: Cambridge University Press, pp. 50–63.

Sugeno, K. (2002) *Japanese Employment and Labor Law*. Durham, NC: Carolina Academic Press.

Sugimoto, Y. (1997) *An Introduction to Japanese Society*, 1st edition. Cambridge: Cambridge University Press.

Suzuki, M. (2008) 'Disability Studies in Japan: An Introduction', *Disability Studies Quarterly*, 28(3). Available at www.dsq-sds.org/article/view/115/115 (accessed 10 May 2010).

Suzuki, T. (2009) 'Disability Evaluation in Japan', *Korean Academy of Medical Sciences*, 24: 227–31.

Swain, J., and S. French. (2000) 'Towards an Affirmation Model of Disability', *Disability and Society*, 15(4): 569–82.

Tada, M. (1988) 'Osakan Popular Culture: A Down-to-Earth Appraisal', in G. McCormack and Y. Sugimoto (eds) *The Japanese Trajectory: Modernization and Beyond*. New York: Cambridge University Press, pp. 33–53.

Takagi, M. (1999) *Sabetsu Yōgo no Kisō Chishiki [Fundamental Knowledge of Discriminatory Language]*. Tokyo: Doyōbijutsu Shuppan.

Takahashi, M., K. Tanaka and H. Miyaoka. (2005) 'Depression and Associated Factors of Informal Caregivers versus Professional Caregivers of Demented Patients', *Psychiatry and Clinical Neurosciences*, 59: 473–80.

Takeda, H. (2005) *The Political Economy of Reproduction in Japan: Between Nation-state and Everyday Life*. Abingdon: RoutledgeCurzon.

Tateiwa, S. (1997) *Shiteki Shoyu Ron [On Private Property]*. Tokyo: Keiso Shobo.

———. (2004) *ALS Fudō no shintai to iki suru kikai [ALS: Immovable Body and Breathing Machine]*. Tokyo: Igakushoin.

———. (2006) 'Shōgai/Shōgaigaku [Disability/Disability Studies]', in K. Ōniwa (ed.) *Gendai Ronrigaku Jiten [Dictionary of Contemporary Ethics]*. Tokyo: Kōbundō.

———. (2009) *Tada no Sei [Sole Life]*. Tokyo: Chikuma Shobo.

———. (2010) 'Shōgaisha Undō/Gaku o Nihon 9 Onnatachi [Disability Movement/ Studies in Japan no. 9: Women]'. Available at www.arsvi.com/ts2000/20100099.htm (accessed 28 May 2010).

Taylor, N., and R. Kassai. (1998) 'The Healer and the Healed: Works and Life of Kenzaburo Oe', *The Lancet*, 352(9128): 642–4.

Thang, L. L. (2001) *Generations in Touch: Linking the Old and Young in a Tokyo Neighborhood*. Ithaca: Cornell University Press.

———. (2002) 'Promoting Interaction between Generations', in R. Goodman (ed.) *Family and Social Policy in Japan: Anthropological Approaches*. Cambridge: Cambridge University Press, pp. 156–76.

———. (2011) 'Aging and Social Welfare in Japan', in V. L. Bestor, T. C. Bestor and A. Yamagata (eds) *Routledge Handbook of Japanese Society and Culture*. London and New York: Routledge, pp. 172–86.

Thomson, R. G. (1997) *Extraordinary Bodies: Figuring Physical Disability in American Culture and Literature*. New York: Columbia University Press.

Titchkosky, T. (2003) *Disability, Self and Society*. Toronto: University of Toronto Press.

182 *Bibliography*

Tōkyō Shimbun. (2010) 'Editorial: Shōgai' Hyōki Yobareru Kawa no Tachiba Kara [A Declaration of Disability: From the Perspective of Being Called (Disabled)]'. Available at www.tokyo-np.co.jp/article/column/editorial/CK2010032202000082.html (accessed 7 April 2010).

Traphagan, J. W. (2000) *Taming Oblivion: Aging Bodies and the Fear of Senility in Japan*. Albany: State University of New York Press.

———. (2004) *The Practice of Concern: Ritual, Well-Being, and Aging in Rural Japan*. Durham, NC: Carolina Academic Press.

Traphagan, J. W., and J. Knight. (2003) *Demographic Change and the Family in Japan's Aging Society*. Albany: State University of New York Press.

Tsuge, A. (2010) 'How Japanese Women Describe their Experiences of Prenatal Testing', in M. Sleeboom-Faulkner (ed.) *Frameworks of Choice: Predictive and Genetic Testing in Asia*. Amsterdam: University of Amsterdam Press, pp. 109–24.

Tsunoda, R., W. de Bary and D. Keene. (1958) *Sources of Japanese Tradition, Volume I*. New York: Columbia University Press.

Tsutsumi, A. (1996) 'Kazoku – Koseki – Shōgaisha [Family – Family Registration System – People with Disabilities]', in Koseki to Tennōsei Kenkyūkai [The Association for Research on the Family Registration and Imperial Systems] (eds) *Koseki Kaitai Kōza [A Course in Dismantling the Family Registration System]*. Tokyo: Shakaihyōronsha, pp. 141–73.

Uikipedia [Wikipedia]. (2010) '*Yunikuro* [UNIQLO]'. Available at http://ja.wikipedia.org/wiki/ユニクロ (accessed 4 May 2010).

UNIQLO. (2009) *Fuku no Chikara*, vol. 1: *Shōgaisha to Hataraku to iu Koto [The Power of Clothing, vol. 1: Working with People with Disabilities]*. Online pamphlet. Available at www.fastretailing.com/jp/csr/clothes_p/ebook1/#page=1 (accessed 2 June 2009).

UNIQLO Customer Centre. (2009) e-mail communication: 12 June and 9 July.

United Nations. (2003–4) 'The United Nations and Disabled Persons –The First Fifty Years', United Nations, Department of Economic and Social Affairs, Division for Social Policy and Development. Available at www.un.org/esa/socdev/enable/dis50y00.htm (accessed 20 April 2010).

Valentine, J. (1990) 'On the Borderlines: The Significance of Marginality in Japanese Society', in E. Ben-Ari, B. Moeran and J. Valentine (eds) *Unwrapping Japan: Society and Culture in Anthropological Perspective*. Honolulu: University of Hawaii Press, pp. 36–57.

———. (2002) 'Naming and Narrating Disability in Japan', in M. Corker and T. Shakeaspeare (eds) *Disability/Postmodernity: Embodying Disability Theory*. London: Continuum, pp. 213–27.

Wall, S. (2006) 'An Autoethnography on Learning about Ethnography', *International Journal of Qualitative Methods*, 5(2): 146–60.

Wapner, R. J. (2009) 'Nuchal Fold and Nasal Bone: How Should we Use them in Down Syndrome Screening?', *American Journal of Obstetrics and Gynecology*, 199(3): 213–14.

Webb, P. (2002) 'Time to Share the Burden: Long Term Care Insurance and the Japanese Family', *Japanese Studies*, 22(2): 113–30.

Weisman, K. L. (2000) 'Creating the Universally Designed City: Prospects for the New Century', *Architectural Theory Review*, 5(2): 156–73.

Wendell, S. (1997) 'Toward a Feminist Theory of Disability', in L. Davis (ed.) *The Disability Studies Reader*. New York: Routledge, pp. 260–78.

White, M. (2002) *Perfectly Japanese: Making Families in an Era of Upheaval*. Berkeley: University of California Press.

World Health Organization and World Bank. (2011) *World Report on Disability*. Geneva: WHO and The World Bank. Available at http://whqlibdoc.who.int/publications/2011/ 9789240685215_eng.pdf (accessed 10 May 2010).

Wright, M. (1999) 'Who Governs Japan? Politicians and Bureaucrats in the Policy-Making Processes', *Political Studies*, 47: 939–54.

Yōda, H. (1999) *Shōgaisha Sabetsu no Shakaigaku: Jendā, Kazoku Kokka* [*The Sociology of Discrimination against People with Disabilities: Gender, Family and State*]. Tokyo: Iwanami Shoten.

———. (2002) 'New Views on Disabilities and the Challenge to Social Welfare in Japan', *Social Science Japan Journal*, 5(1): 1–15.

Yōgo to Sabetsu o Kangaeru Shimpojium Jikkkōiinkai [The Executive Committee for the Symposium on Terminology and Discrimination]. (1976) *Yutaka na Nihongo o Mezashite: Sabetsu Yōgo* [*Aiming for a Rich Japanese Language: Discriminatory Language*]. Tokyo: Choubunsha.

Yomiuri Shimbun. (2007) 'Yunikuro, Shōgaisha Kiyō Ichii [UNIQLO is the Number One Employer of People with Disabilities]', 27 April. Available at http://job.yomiuri.co.jp/ hunt/saizensen/sa_07042701.htm (accessed 11 May 2010).

Yoshida, K. (2006) 'Religion in the Classical Period', in P. L. Swanson and C. Chilson (eds) *Nanzan Guide to Japanese Religions*. Honolulu: University of Hawaii Press, pp. 144–62.

Yuasa, T. (1994) *'Kotobagari' to Shuppan no Jiyū* [*'Word Hunting' and Freedom of the Press*]. Tokyo: Akaishi Shoten.

Yue, S. (2008) 'Challenging *Gairaigo*: Original vs. Current Borrowed Meanings', *Gengo Bunkaron Kyū* [*Studies in Languages and Cultures*], 23: 27–41.

Yūsei Hogo Hō [Eugenics Protection Law]. (1948). Available at http://archive.hp.infoseek. co.jp/law/1948L156-old.html (accessed 5 May 2010).

Zenkoku Jiritsu Seikatsu Sentā Kyōgikai [Japan Council on Independent Living Centers, JIL]. (2001) 'New Approach to Promote Employment for the Disabled', *Public Policy*, 40. Available at www.jil.go.jp/jil/bulletin/year/2001/vol40-08/04.htm (accessed 21 May 2012).

———. (n.d.a) 'About JIL'. Official website. Available at www.j-il.jp/jil.files/english/ aboutjil.html (accessed 22 May 2012).

———. (n.d.b) 'Jiritsu no Rinen [the Concept of Independence]'. Available at www.j-il.jp/ about/rinen.html#content (accessed 28 April 2011).

Index

accessibility 8, 19, 39, 57, 138–54; as an aspect of citizenship 150–1; definition of 139–40; impediments to 142–9; in the Independent Living Movement 64, 91; *see also* barrier free, universal design
activism 33–5; activism in Japan 15, 33–42, 37–40, 42–3, 64, 91, 93, 125, 159, 161; disability activism and eugenics 98, 102–3; dynamics within groups 40–2; linguistic activism 44–5, 48, 53–4; versus passing 35–6
ADL (activities of daily life) 70–1, 116, 123
aging 18–19, 54, 112, 116–18, 119, 160, 163n9; and caregiving 31, 126, 129, 131–4, 135; and welfare 63, 69, 76
anthropology 1–2; autoethnography 2–3, 155; fieldwork 21; of Japan 125; reflexive anthropology 21
Aoi Shiba no Kai (Association of Green Grass; disability activist group) 37–9, 41, 91, 93, 125
ADA (American with Disabilities Act) 86, 141
amniocentesis 97, 99, 102

barrier free 19, 48, 89, 90–1, 138–42, 144–50, 153–4
Basic Act for Persons with Disabilities (Shōgaisha Kihon Hō) 63, 68, 78, 82–4, 87, 92–3; compared with the ADA 86

caregiving 16, 119, 121–37, 161; as affective labour 125; as a burden 121–2, 136–7; as described by Ōe Kenzaburō 128–31; and the family 124–7, 134–6; as gendered 125–8; versus needs 123
Chinese Characters in Japanese (*kanji*) 48, 50, 57, 65, 164n1

chronic illness 1, 7, 9, 32, 35, 39, 67, 75, 86, 118
censorship 17, 47, 56–8, 164n4

Davis, L. J. 9, 13, 49, 58, 86, 102, 161
disability, definition of 3–6, 17, 117, 155–6; according to disability studies in English 6–14; according to disability studies in Japan 14–15; legal definitions in Japan 28–31, 83; United Nations' definition 4–5, 156
disability policy in Japan 31, 42, 45, 54, 61–2, 64–8, 82, 88–94, 119, 127–8, 132–3, 159–60; compared with US 86
disability studies 6–17; in English 6–14; in Japanese 14; in Scandinavia 9–10; in the UK 8–9; in the US 9
disability welfare laws 69–88; *see also* The Basic Act for Persons with a Disability; The Law for the Promotion of Employing People with a Disability; The Six Laws of Welfare; The Services and Supports for Persons with Disabilities Act
Down Syndrome 27, 41–2, 63, 96, 104, 111, 131

Ebisu 24–5, 27, 38, 152–3
education, special 6, 31, 55, 63, 66, 81, 93–4, 96, 104, 106, 110–12, 139
employment of people with disabilities in Japan 26–7, 63, 78–82, 89, 112–13, 153, 160, 166n14; barriers to employment 139–40
eugenics 37, 97–8, 100–3, 118, 166n4, 166n5
The Eugenics Protection Law 37, 97–8, 101–2
euphemism 45, 59–60, 98, 126

Index   185

family (*ie*) 26, 66, 100, 111, 113–14, 122–3, 125–6, 134; as caregiver and provider 67, 76, 93, 122–3, 132–3, 136, 151
Family Registration Law (Koseki Hō) 63, 114–16, 128
feminism 3, 5, 8, 22, 33, 163n6, 164n10; in Japan 15, 41–3

gender 5, 6, 9, 12, 33–5, 37, 41, 43, 93, 114, 116, 123–4, 126–7, 130–1

handicap 22, 52, 139, 155; United Nations' definition of 4

iiekaeshū (saying in other words) 57; *see also* censorship
impairment 6, 7–15, 17, 20, 23, 25–6, 28, 34–43, 41, 70, 74, 96–7, 116–18, 122–3, 139, 155–6; United Nations' definition of 4–5
impairment literacy 159
independent living 25, 39–40, 64–5, 67, 85, 91–3, 96, 122, 127, 135, 161, 165n12
individual model of disability: *see* medical model of disability
intellectual disability 7, 9, 13–15, 25, 27, 28–31, 42, 46, 53–4, 66, 70, 77–82, 88, 90, 93–4, 106, 110, 113, 135, 139, 149, 152, 160, 165n6, 165n10, 166n1, 166n9; definition of 30; *see also* Law for the Welfare of People with Intellectual Disabilities; Tables 2.1, 5.2, 5.3, 5.4
in-nen (fate, destiny, karma) 25, 38

Japanese Civil Code 114–15, 125, 128, 165n2
Japanese Constitution 17, 62–3, 67–8, 82, 86, 88, 90–1, 93, 150, 162, 165n2, 165n3; compared with US Constitution 46

kotobagari (word-hunting) 46, 56–7, 59; *see also* censorship

language (about disability) 17, 44–60, 156, 164n1, 164n2
The Law for Promoting the Employment of People with a Disability (Shōgaisha no Koyō no Hōritsu) 63, 78–82, 89, 112, 160
learning disability 6, 32, 48, 110–11, 140
Long Term Care Insurance Program (*Kaigo Hoken Seido*) 19, 124, 127, 131–4, 136, 161

medical model of disability 6–8, 10–17, 39, 66, 77, 94–5, 155–6, 158, 160, 163n4
medicalization of disability 7, 10, 13–14, 65, 94, 163n4
marriage 113–15, 120, 128, 166n5
mass media 17, 44–6, 52–4, 57–9, 131, 164ch2n5, 164ch3n4
Maternal Body Protection Law (Botai Hogo Hō) 37, 41, 63, 97–8
Mental Hygiene Law (Seishin Eisei Hō) 77, 89

neoliberalism 21, 64–5, 87, 89–92, 132–3, 160
normalization 9–10, 48, 64–5, 87, 89–92, 136, 149, 160

Ōe, K. 18, 128–31, 135–6, 151
Oliver, M. 4–8, 10–12, 14–15, 21, 34, 94, 96, 112, 117, 138, 154, 156, 163n4, 163n5, 163n6

physical disability 7–9, 13–14, 24–5, 28–31, 39, 41–2, 53, 66, 69–71, 74–6, 78–9, 81–5, 88, 90, 93–4, 95; *see also* The Law for the Welfare of People with Physical Disabilities
population (as related to disability) 14, 18–19, 28–32, 42, 62, 96, 99, 116–19, 121, 126, 163n6
prenatal screening/testing 41–2, 95–7, 99–103, 118, 164n11, 166n2, 166n3, 166n7
productivity 1, 18, 31, 62, 65–7, 75–6, 78, 93, 96, 111, 115, 127–8, 136
psychiatric disability 14, 28–9, 31, 39, 42, 53, 63, 77–8, 80–2, 84–5, 88, 93–4, 135, 160; *see also* The Mental Hygiene Law; The Law for the Welfare of People with Psychiatric Disabilities

race 6, 8–9, 12, 22, 33–4, 43, 93, 114
rehabilitation 7, 14, 30–1, 39, 42, 61–2, 65, 67, 74, 89, 96, 127–9, 156
religion 23–7, 35, 103, 128, 151; Shinto 23–6, 128; Buddhism 23–6, 128, 134

segregation 5–6, 64, 80
The Senior Citizen Welfare Law (Rōjin Fukushi Hō; general welfare for the elderly) 63, 69, 76, 117–18, 126, 132
The Six Laws of Welfare (Fukushi Roppō) 63, 69–78, 87, 89, 93, 126, 161, 165n2

Shakespeare, T. 5, 8–10, 13–14, 20–1, 34, 64, 85, 99–100, 102–3, 122, 126, 153, 156, 163n1, 163n5, 163n7, 164n10, 166n7
social model of disability 8–17, 35, 45, 64, 77, 94, 95, 155–8, 160, 163n5, 164n4, 164n6
stigma 5–6, 28, 36, 58, 60, 132
The Supports and Services for People with Disabilities Act (Shōgaisha Jiritsu Shien Hō) 17–18, 30, 63–4, 71, 77–8, 83–9, 91–4, 132, 159–60, 164n3

Thomson, Rosemary Garland 4–6, 9, 20, 61–2, 89–90, 94, 150–1
television 27–8, 52–4, 57–8, 164ch2n2

universal design 19, 48, 139, 142–4, 150–1, 166n4; *see also* accessibility

The Welfare Law for People with Intellectual Disabilities (Chiteki Shōgaisha Fukushi Hō) 30, 63, 54, 69, 73–6, 84–5, 87, 108
The Welfare Law for People with Physical Disabilities (Shintai Shōgaisha Fukushi Hō) 63, 69–72, 75–7, 82–5, 87, 164ch2n3
The Welfare Law for People with Psychiatric Disabilities (Seishin Shōgaisha Fukushi Hō) 63, 77–8, 84–5, 87
wheelchair, as a symbol of disability 19, 157; *see also* accessibility

Taylor & Francis
eBooks
FOR LIBRARIES

ORDER YOUR FREE 30 DAY INSTITUTIONAL TRIAL TODAY!

Over 23,000 eBook titles in the Humanities, Social Sciences, STM and Law from some of the world's leading imprints.

Choose from a range of subject packages or create your own!

Benefits for you
- ▶ Free MARC records
- ▶ COUNTER-compliant usage statistics
- ▶ Flexible purchase and pricing options

Benefits for your user
- ▶ Off-site, anytime access via Athens or referring URL
- ▶ Print or copy pages or chapters
- ▶ Full content search
- ▶ Bookmark, highlight and annotate text
- ▶ Access to thousands of pages of quality research at the click of a button

For more information, pricing enquiries or to order a free trial, contact your local online sales team.

UK and Rest of World: online.sales@tandf.co.uk

US, Canada and Latin America: e-reference@taylorandfrancis.com

www.ebooksubscriptions.com

A flexible and dynamic resource for teaching, learning and research.

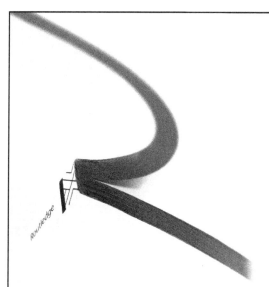

Routledge Paperbacks Direct

Bringing you the cream of our hardback publishing at paperback prices

This exciting new initiative makes the best of our hardback publishing available in paperback format for authors and individual customers.

Routledge Paperbacks Direct is an ever-evolving programme with new titles being added regularly.

To take a look at the titles available, visit our website.

www.routledgepaperbacksdirect.com

CPSIA information can be obtained
at www.ICGtesting.com
Printed in the USA
BVHW04s2016230918
528318BV00002B/18/P